GREEN AND CHASTE AND FOOLISH

Irish Literary
and
Theatrical Anecdotes

GREEN AND CHASTE AND FOOLISH

IRISH LITERARY
AND
THEATRICAL ANECDOTES

★ ★ ★ ★ ★

Padraic O'Farrell

GILL & MACMILLAN

To the memory of Peig

Published in Ireland by
Gill & Macmillan Ltd
Goldenbridge
Dublin 8
with associated companies throughout the world
© Padraic O'Farrell 1994
0 7171 2106 2

Design & print origination by
O'K Graphic Design, Dublin

Printed by
ColourBooks Ltd, Dublin

A catalogue record for this book is available from the British Library.

1 3 5 4 2

I returned to Ireland. Ireland green and chaste and foolish. And when I wandered over my own hills and talked again to my own people I looked into the heart of this life and I saw that it was good.

Patrick Kavanagh,
The Green Fool

CONTENTS

ACKNOWLEDGMENTS

I wish to acknowledge the following authors, their publishers and/or estates who have given permission to be quoted in this anthology. Mr J.P. Donleavy for extracts from *J.P. Donleavy's Ireland* (Michael Joseph, 1986); The Estate of the late Micheál macLiammóir for extracts from *All for Hecuba*; Simon Callow and Penguin Books for extracts from *Being An Actor* by Simon Callow (Penguin, 1985); Hugh Leonard and the *Sunday Independent*; Peters Fraser and Dunlop for extracts from *Leinster, Munster, Connaught* (Robert Hale) and *My Father's Son* (Gill and Macmillan, 1968), both by Frank O'Connor; The Estate of the late Tyrone Guthrie. If any copyright is inadvertently infringed, I apologise and will welcome notification of the omission.

I thank those whose names are mentioned in my introduction for their material and hospitality. My agent, Jonathan Williams, and editor, Fergal Tobin, offered advice and encouragement, and my wife, Maureen, willingly assumed the task of proof-reading. Niamh and Aisling assisted with word processing. The National Library of Ireland, Westmeath County Library, Trinity College Library, The Irish Theatre Archives and Roscommon County Library were extremely helpful in supplying or obtaining books, periodicals and manuscripts.

To all: '*Won't you come into the garden? I would like my roses to see you.*' (Richard Brinsley Sheridan)

INTRODUCTION

Defining an Irish literary anecdote is as simple as explaining the idiosyncrasies of the race from which they emerge. Dictionaries offer some guidance. An anecdote, they suggest, is a narrative of amusing or interesting incident, a brief account of an occurrence, biographical or otherwise. The adjective 'literary' may induce an expectation of elegant excerpts in prose or verse from a famous author, a story about a person of letters or an event in his life. Originality is demanded by some taskmasters. Lead with the word 'Irish', however, and conventional interpretations become blurred by a heady vapour of wit, fun, sarcasm, cynicism or downright 'divilment'. A form of transubstantiation takes place with every telling, for the most modern Irish storyteller follows the tradition of the *seanchaí* of yesteryear. He may now lean from a chrome and plastic bar seat instead of a creepy-stool and may handle a glass instead of rosary beads, but his skills are similar. Like the traditional musician, he embellishes, adorns, edits and presents his product to suit the occasion and the company. He has scant regard for fame — less for grandiosity. The local bard is as much entitled to a tale in his memory as Joyce or Yeats, so at once we perceive a conflict with those who hold that literature is valued for its form and content.

A persistent prober of persiflage may discover an occasional prime pretzel, only to be informed that, however adorable the alliteration, some published account proves his prize inaccurate in many respects. He must not feel daunted! Let him parry with, 'An aunt of mine was there on the very day' — even if the occurrence took place in his great-grandparents' time. This collection of Irish literary anecdotes, therefore, is proffered with certain qualifications. Its aim is to entertain rather than to educate. In most cases excerpts from

xi

published works are credited to authors only; their titles may be traced through the bibliography. Sources include expensive bound volumes, works and correspondence of authors or their biographers, but many of the anecdotes have been collected from conversations with those aunts who were there on the very day or uncles who were not but heard lies from authors' colleagues. They are now contained in a ragged bundle of papers tossed together over many years by a hungry predator of literary and theatrical folklore.

The late Alan Simpson, Eamonn Andrews and Hilton Edwards told me some of them. Benedict Kiely, Micheál Ó hAodha, Hugh Leonard, Seán Mac Réamoinn, John B. Keane, Phyllis Ryan, Carolyn Swift, Niall Toibin, J.P. Donleavy, Alpho O'Reilly and Patrick Henchy contributed too. A few of these tales may have stemmed from published sources but have been so vastly changed, perhaps improved, through recycling that they bear little resemblance to the original. If this is so, blessed be the hand that held the pen and may it forgive the discrepancies.

Selection posed particular problems. Should I concentrate on the more esteemed names in Irish literature? Would shorter entries from or about a larger number be more acceptable? How much licence should I demand from real or imagined restrictions imposed by the book's sub-title? In the end I called on Phaenon for guidance, for was not that beautiful youth created by the Titian Prometheus from clay? Of course, Prometheus was in the habit of submitting his creations to Zeus for approval, but Phaenon was so handsome that the check was waived.

The message I received was to choose and allot space for anecdotal worth rather than status; to quote from writers and narrate my stories just as I had heard them, with more concern for interest and brightness than accuracy or even authenticity. In other words, anything told orally or in written form qualified.

These Irish literary anecdotes are about authors of fact and fiction; about actors and theatres; about the Irish penchant for wit, drollery, understatement and for life lived to the full. May the reader's life be enriched by the good, great or dubious deeds of those who bestowed upon us a literary heritage of which to be proud, or enlivened by laughing at their mishaps, misdemeanours or miscalculations.

THE
ABBEY
THEATRE

The first theatre on the Abbey's site was the Theatre Royal Opera House (1820). A fashionable rendezvous, it was gutted by fire after a few years and replaced by a Mechanics' Institute, which was also a Temperance Hall. Thus the mechanics did not overuse the establishment and it became a venue for political meetings. William Smith O'Brien, John Mitchel and Thomas Francis Meagher spoke there. The body of Young Irelander and Fenian John O'Mahony (1816–77) lay in state there when the Pro-Cathedral authorities refused to accept it.

The building became a theatre again; first the Princess and later the People's Music Hall under comedian Patrick Langan. Boxing tournaments were held there too. Then, in 1901, J.B. Carrickford and Madam Grafton took over and called it the National Theatre. They staged one-man shows, vaudeville and music-hall, but Corporation fire precautions brought about its closure. In 1904 Annie Horniman bought the Penny Bank nearby, formerly the city morgue, and its addition to the site made it possible to comply with Corporation demands. Meanwhile, at a meeting of the National Literary Society in 1899, W.B. Yeats, Lady Gregory and Edward Martyn had founded the Irish Literary Theatre. This led to the Irish National Theatre Society, to which Miss Horniman offered free use of her Lower Abbey Street theatre. It opened there with On Baile's Strand (Yeats) and Spreading the News (Gregory).

The rest is history. The company operated there until the building burned down in 1951. After an exile in the Queen's, the National Theatre was installed in the new Abbey Theatre in 1966. Newspaper journalists often conjure up the ghosts of the past when they disapprove of an Abbey production, referring to mechanics, burlesque, music-hall, boxing matches and corpses. When lighting or design are inadequate, they harken back to J.B. Carrickford's fit-ups.

★ ★ ★ ★ ★

1

On 6 May 1910, King Edward VII died. Padraic Colum's *Thomas Muskerry*, directed by Lennox Robinson, was running at the Abbey. All Dublin theatres cancelled their Saturday matinée next day, except the Abbey. Robinson had wired Lady Gregory for instructions but her reply, calling for cancellation, did not reach the theatre, so Robinson went ahead with the performance. However, when he did not cancel the evening show either, Miss Horniman was furious that the theatre was being used once again for 'wicked politics'. A reticent notice of regret was published in the daily newspapers but she did not regard it as adequate and demanded the dismissal of Robinson and the theatre manager. Yeats refused but the manager, Norreys Connell, resigned. Horniman threatened to withhold £400 of her subsidy, then due, but the Abbey directors, in turn, would not pay the money due for the purchase of the theatre. An arbitrator was called in and after a year he found in favour of the directors. Miss Horniman thereupon broke off her connections with the theatre.

✶ ✶ ✶ ✶ ✶

Sir Neville Macready was Commander-in-Chief of the British Forces in Ireland from 1919 to 1921. One of their most wanted men was the revolutionary Michael Collins.

One evening at the Abbey Theatre, Dr J.F. Larchet, director of music, saw from the orchestra pit that Collins was sitting behind Macready and breathing on his head whenever he laughed. On Collins's own head at the time, allegedly, was a price of £10,000 — offered by Sir Neville for his capture.

✶ ✶ ✶ ✶ ✶

On Saturday, 26 January 1907, the first performance of Synge's The Playboy of the Western World *took place. The word 'shift' (chemise) provoked some hissing in the second act. Press reports were exaggerated and police were called in for the next performance on Monday. There was uproar during this. On Tuesday, applicants for tickets for* The Playboy *received a printed note:*

2

Dear Sir,

In response to your application, we enclose Voucher to be exchanged at booking Office at Theatre . . .

Should it be impossible to hear the play the night you select we will send you another Voucher on receiving your application.

Yours faithfully,

A. Henderson (Secretary)

★ ★ ★ ★ ★

There were disturbances during Sean O'Casey's *The Plough and the Stars* in 1926 too. Many who were there declared them less serious than subsequent press reports suggested. Gabriel Fallon, later theatre director but then an actor, remarked, 'I have been reminded of the Duke of Wellington's reaction to another's description of Waterloo: "My God, was I there at all?"'

★ ★ ★ ★ ★

W.B. Yeats gave a celebrated oration during a serious disturbance on 11 February. There have been persistent claims that he handed the speech into the *Irish Times* office before going to deliver it to the Abbey audience.

★ ★ ★ ★ ★

Performances of The Plough and the Stars *were planned for 2.30 p.m. and 8 p.m. on Saturday, 13 February 1926. There had been veiled threats that members of the cast would be kidnapped and so they were advised not to leave the theatre between shows. Food was served in the green-room and a pianist named Rummel, who had been giving a recital at the Royal Dublin Society, rushed over to entertain the beleaguered players before they faced what they were certain would be another disturbing evening. The party was later joined by a friend who had dashed from Lansdowne Road to give an account of the international rugby match there.*

Playwright Denis Johnston regretted not having been in the gathering, and in a Thomas Davis Lecture series on Radio Telefís Éireann many years later made the following wry comment:

3

I wonder what other city in the world could provide so many attractions and counter-attractions all at the same time: a public disturbance in the national theatre over the first production of Sean O'Casey's greatest play; a magnificent commentary by the poet Yeats; coffee and arguments with the author in the vestibule; a lively description of the best rugby international that had been seen for years, to the music of a celebrated international pianist, for the benefit of a cast under siege in its own theatre. And, finally, an evening performance to a packed house of paying public that had come notwithstanding a warning that the theatre was to be blown up.

★ ★ ★ ★ ★

World theatre columnists gleefully headlined the 1945 decision by the Abbey Theatre to stage a pantomime. The sell-out innovation attracted to its audience people like Anna Neagle and her husband, Herbert Wilcox. *Muireann agus an Prionnsa* (The Tomboy and the Prince) was scripted in Irish, but members of the cast often fell for the temptation to ad-lib a line or word in English. One evening Sean McClory, who played a lovable giant, mentioned a brand of soap. For this indiscretion, Ernest Blythe imposed a fine of ten shillings — a fifth of a week's pay at the time. However, McClory pleaded that 'Lux' was Latin for 'Light' and the harsh verdict was revoked on a technicality.

★ ★ ★ ★ ★

That was not McClory's first brush with Blythe. The Abbey boss once instructed the actor to buy a new suit of clothes for a part he was playing. McClory said he could not afford one, so Blythe gave him an advance of ten shillings, the money to be refunded at five shillings a week. Before the debt was cleared, McClory left the Abbey to make his name in Hollywood. Some years later he received a letter from Ernest Blythe. It contained a sharp reprimand about the outstanding sum of money.

It was after a performance of *The Plough and the Stars* on 18 July 1951 that the Abbey was burned to the ground. O'Casey said, 'The Abbey really died with that fire it had. It was as if God struck a match and set the whole thing alight.' Ironically, the play ends with British soldiers singing 'Keep the Home Fires Burning'. The company transferred the production to the Peacock without missing a performance. The tiny orchestra's chosen overture was Beethoven's *Prometheus* — Prometheus stole fire from Olympus and was sentenced by the gods to be bound to a rock.

✫ ✫ ✫ ✫ ✫

Hugh Leonard tells of his experience with the Abbey Company:

Abbey Theatre actors have the reputation of being spoiled. Late in rehearsals of my play *Time Was*, I noticed a misprint in the text: the word 'bugger' had been typed instead of 'beggar'. I drew it to the attention of the actor in question, who stared at me and said: 'Are you asking me to change it?' I said yes, seeing that it was a matter of a single vowel. He stared at me in a most put-upon manner and, before flouncing off, said: 'Well, I wish you'd said so three weeks ago!'

✫ ✫ ✫ ✫ ✫

In 1976 the National Theatre Company (Abbey) brought *The Plough and the Stars* to the United States. Micheál Ó hAodha organised the laying of a wreath at the grave of the great Irish melodramatist, Dion Boucicault, in Mount Hope cemetery, New York.

When the players and invited guests had gathered for the simple ceremony, the wreath could not be found. A member of the company, with a little unscrupulousness but considerable presence of mind, borrowed a wreath from another grave.

✫ ✫ ✫ ✫ ✫

From 18 to 23 March 1974, Chekhov's *Three Sisters* was playing at the Abbey, while downstairs in the Peacock

Eamonn Morrissey was giving his one-man show of Myles na Gopaleen's writings, *The Brother*. A lady rang the box office — which serves both theatres — to book seats and was asked if the seats were for *Three Sisters* or *The Brother*. She replied, 'What are you talking about? They're for myself and my cousin.'

★ ★ ★ ★ ★

The actor, Simon Callow writes:

The Speakers [from Heathcote Williams book] is a free-form piece, moving from public scenes in Hyde Park, to private scenes in the speakers' homes, or Rowton House, or wherever. The audience perambulates, being invited to heckle the speakers. It was a huge success wherever we went in Europe: Belgrade, Zagreb (where a Yugoslav policeman interrupted a character who was about to light up a cigarette, to be told, in character of course, to fuck off, at which the audience applauded) and Hamburg (where the ending, in which two London bobbies clear the audience out of the hall, was fiercely resented). It all held together, however, until Dublin. In Dublin, everything changed.

We were booked for a midnight spot at the Abbey, as part of the Dublin Festival. That means that most of the audience had been drinking since 11 a.m., just for a start. We, however, were caught up in the cross-currents of something much bigger. We had decided to do the show with the iron safety curtain down and the audience on stage with us, our great scaffolding lighting tower slap in the centre. So at ten past twelve, we started. Immediately we were heckled as we had never been heckled before: filibustering was more like it. Eventually, when it was impossible to continue or engage the hecklers in any kind of dialogue, I said to one of them, as my lower-middle-class Socialist Party of Great Britain speaker, 'OK, mate, you seem to have a lot to say for yourself, why don't you come up 'ere and tell us all about it.' He clambered up on to the box, opened his mouth, was unable to orate, so said, 'Oh fuck off the lot of youse, you're all a loud of cunts.'

Ironic applause, and I was able to continue. The speaker to my left had hit on the same ploy. His heckler, however, similarly silenced by standing on the box, unzipped his fly and started to urinate on the stage. Mild cries of 'shame' and much mirth. Suddenly, there was an irruption on the other side of the audience. 'That's the bastard that killed Frank Stagg!'[Stagg was an IRA hunger-striker who died in Wakefield prison in 1976.] A tiny white-haired gentleman was suddenly surrounded by a posse of tough-looking men, all from the audience. It was Mr Ó Dálaigh, the President of the Republic, on an incognito visit, and the posse were his bodyguard. Swiftly, he was removed from the theatre. His accusers, who seemed to be connected with our filibusterers, were jostled by remnants of the bodyguard, to cries of 'Shame, let them alone you pigs,' and so on.

Theatre in Dublin has to put up with a lot of stiff competition from life.

★

That was not all. Callow continues:

We speakers were valiantly droning on through all this. At last the moment came for the switch from public to private scenes. The lights change, and the focus is on Van Dijm, the tattooed speaker, and his thirteen-year-old helpmate. These scenes, which had commanded rapt attention all over Europe, the audience climbing over each other to be closer to the actors, peering over our shoulders and looking into our nostrils, were actually *heckled* by the Dublin audience, or that element of it clearly bent on disrupting the performance. We ploughed on. Then they hit on a new ploy. In the dark portion of the stage, three men climbed up on to the lighting tower and started swaying it back and forward. If it collapsed, which it was in grave danger of doing, it could easily kill people, not to mention the conflagration that would immediately ensue. The theatre manager was popping about, looking desperately anxious. He beckoned to me. I was the Equity deputy. 'What do you think we should do?' I wasn't sure. I thought that if we could contain the situation we should continue. I hadn't been able to speak to all the actors. I knew that some of them, like me, were frightened by the ugliness of the mood in the audience, but others were angry and defiant. The men had been dragged off the tower, which was now stable, but the uproar, which showed no signs of abating, was impossible to act through. One could hear bottles being broken, and the snarls of angry men. I leapt on to a box and screamed for silence which, unaccountably, fell. 'We are workers,' I said, improbably. 'Like any other workers' — I suppose I thought the disrupters were the Red Brigade or some Irish equivalent — 'we must have proper working conditions. We're not getting them. If you want us to continue, you must give us a fair hearing. It's up to you.' Total silence. I stepped down. The moment my shoe touched the ground, all hell broke loose. We left the stage. The manager came to see us in the dressing room. 'Of course, there's no question of the show carrying on. But some of the audience are asking if you'll talk to them, and explain your decision.' We did, and there followed a most extraordinary discussion. On the way to the stage, I said to the Abbey's Artistic Director, the enchanting Tomás Mac Anna, 'Sorry about all this.' 'Oh don't worry,' he exclaimed, 'this is the Abbey. We're used to riots here.'

One of Hugh Leonard's many stories about critics concerned an Abbey production:

A critic of one of the national newspapers had looked upon the Jameson when it was golden and was in a mellow condition when he attended the first night of a play called *The Great Hunger*. He dozed intermittently, coming awake to molest his neighbour and barrack the actors with cries of 'Load of rubbish!', 'Balls!' and the like. Afterwards, the story of his behaviour spread like wildfire, but one fellow critic denounced it as vile slander. 'I was sitting behind him,' he said stoutly, 'and I never heard him utter a word.' This was true: the other critic was sound asleep from first to last.

Did the poet F.R. Higgins supervise a production of The Playboy of the Western World *during his period as Abbey manager? Frank O'Connor claimed this although Abbey records do not corroborate. O'Connor wrote:*

The play opens after dark in a country pub, but when the curtain went up every blessed light on the stage was on — all amber — reducing the stage to an apparent depth of eighteen inches, and removing every trace of colour from furniture and dresses. Men came on with a lantern. The lights did not change. Pegeen lit the lamp, then lit a candle and turned out the lamp, and finally Christy blew out the last conceivable source of illumination while the stage still continued to look like Edinburgh Castle by floodlight. I left after the first act, but Yeats thought it a splendid production, and, Synge's shade appeased, Mount Jerome Cemetery had a quiet night.

✶ ✶ ✶ ✶ ✶

A large party of American tourists had booked for Chekhov's *The Cherry Orchard* at the Abbey. The day before their visit, the USSR pulled out of the Olympic Games in Los Angeles. Rising up in retribution, the American party cancelled its reservation!

✶ ✶ ✶ ✶ ✶

One of the Abbey paintings, by Louis le Brocquy, was unveiled by Cyril Cusack, who commented at great length about its sanctity of form, its piety of colour, its godliness of image. Hugh Leonard was standing nearby:

I heard him say, *sotto voce*, but not quite *sotto* enough: 'It looks like a sherry trifle.'

✶ ✶ ✶ ✶ ✶

ASSORTED ANECDOTES

A Little about a Number

A celebrated early (*c.* 561) copyright dispute began when St Finian of Clonard, Co. Meath accused St Columba of copying his psalter without permission. The High King, Diarmuid, was called upon to give judgment and pronounced, 'To every cow its calf and to every book its copy.' Columba refused to accept the ruling, went to war with the forces of the crown and won a mighty battle at Cúl Dreimhne, Co. Sligo. When he saw 3,000 dead on the battlefield, however, he went into exile at Iona and conducted missionary work in Scotland and the north of England.

✯ ✯ ✯ ✯ ✯

St Malachy (1094–1148), the Archbishop of Armagh, wrote a number of prophecies about the papacy, which were published by a Benedictine historian, Arnold Wion, in *Lignum Vitae* (1559). Believers in their authenticity point to similarities with actual events. For example, Pope John XXIII was Patriarch of Venice, famous for its waterways, before his election to the papacy in 1958. Malachy's prophecy was 'Pastor et Nauta' or 'Pastor and Mariner'. Before the 1958 conclave, some Vatican commentators reported that New York's Cardinal Spellman, a known devotee of the prophecies, had hired a boat in Rome, loaded it with sheep and sailed up and down the Tiber.

✯ ✯ ✯ ✯ ✯

George Petrie excelled in art, music and literature. At thirteen years of age he was in his father's studio when a lady called. Petrie's biographer Dr W. Stokes tells:

Petrie, then a little boy, was sitting in a corner of the room, when he saw a lady, thickly veiled, enter and walk straight to the easel on which the work rested. She did not notice the child and thought herself alone with the picture of her buried love. She lifted her veil, stood long and in unbroken stillness gazing at the face, then suddenly turning, she moved with unsteady step to another corner of the room and bending forward, pressed her forehead against the wall heaving deep sobs, her whole frame shaken with a storm of passionate grief. How long this agony lasted the boy could not tell, but it appeared to him to be an hour, and then with a sudden effort she controlled herself, pulled down her veil and as quickly and silently left the room as she had come into it. She was unaware of his presence, unconscious of the depths of silent sympathy she had awakened in the heart of the child whose sensitive and delicate nature kept him from obtruding on her grief.

The portrait was of the patriot Robert Emmet. The lady was his sweetheart, Sarah Curran.

★ ★ ★ ★ ★

The pioneer of Celtic studies, John O'Donovan, wrote a letter to Jeremiah O'Donovan Rossa the Fenian, during the Famine, which displays a remarkable resignation to tragedy:

I have buried my youngest, Morgan Kavanagh O'Connell O'Donovan, who died on the 11 February 1860 at the age of one year and forty-nine days, so that I calculate he went off the stage of this world without any stain from ancient or modern sin. I have no reason to be sorry for his departure from this wicked world. But his mother is so sorry after him that she refused to take food for two days, which has brought her to the brink of insanity.

Although born in Switzerland, John Pentland Mahaffy, Provost of Trinity College and teacher of Wilde, was a giant on the Irish literary scene. While he was a keen sportsman his aim was suspect. Sir Shane Leslie writes of him:

There were of course days when Mahaffy was missing birds and his eye had to be politely wiped by the nearest gun. When two or more had fired, the Professor could be heard crying to the keepers — 'my bird, I think, my bird!' and it was etiquette that he should not be contradicted.'

★ ★ ★ ★ ★

W.B. Stanford and R.B. McDowell, biographers of Mahaffy tell:

In 1891 the Dublin University made [Mahaffy] an honorary doctor in music. The robes of the degree — white flowered silk faced with rose satin — were his favourite academic dress among the many that he was entitled to wear. He liked to recall how once, when he was wearing this elegant and impressive robe in an academic procession at Louvain, mothers among the bystanders held up their infants for him to bless, thinking that he must be some very exalted prelate — and he blessed them.

★ ★ ★ ★ ★

Another anecdote, if authentic, implies a rather puerile flippancy. When Mahaffy saw an undergraduate coming without an academic gown to a college ceremony at which gowns were required, he called him over with, we are told, 'an imperious beckoning finger': 'Come here, boy! Who's your tutor? Don't you know that you are imperilling your immortal soul by being without a gown?' And then after a slight pause: 'And what is worse, the fine is five shillings.'

★ ★ ★ ★ ★

The Trinity College Gaelic society had been founded in 1907 with the aim of promoting the study of the language, the literature, the archaeology, art and economics of Ireland. The society decided to begin the academic year 1914/15 by holding, on 17 November, a meeting to commemorate the birth of Thomas Davis, a Trinity graduate who had made an outstanding contribution to the Irish nationalist tradition. The meeting was to be addressed by W.B. Yeats, Francis Bigger, an Ulster antiquarian and enthusiastic nationalist, and Patrick Pearse, the founder and headmaster of Saint Enda's, a school inspired by Irish nationalist ideals. Pearse was one of the leaders of the section of the Irish Volunteers which had repudiated Redmond's policy of participation in the Great War.

On 10 November Mahaffy wrote to the society saying he had been informed that 'a man called Pearse' who 'was a supporter of the anti-recruiting agitation' was to be one of the society's speakers, and could not permit him to address a meeting in college. 'Why,' he asked, 'do you place me in this unpleasant necessity?' A brisk interchange of letters followed. Mahaffy insisted that he would not allow Pearse, 'a speaker with these to me traitorous views', to address a meeting in college, unless Pearse assured him through the society that 'he said nothing against enlisting in the imperial army'. The committee of the society pointed out that Pearse had been secured as a speaker some time back, that it was prepared to relieve Mahaffy 'of any embarrassment, by not pressing on you their invitation to take the chair'. It also emphasised that the speakers would not make any references irrelevant to the subject under discussion, so that 'the matter of the present European war could not be introduced'. When Mahaffy proved obdurate, the committee expressed its regret that 'the teaching of Thomas Davis which at least represented the gospel of free speech and liberty of conscience should have borne no fruit in Trinity college'.

★ ★ ★ ★ ★

In his autobiographical Children of the Dead End, *Patrick MacGill tells:*

Once I had got bitten by a dog. The animal snapped a piece of flesh from my leg and ate it when he got out of the way. When I came into my own house my father and mother were awfully frightened. If three hairs of the dog that bit me were not placed against the sore I would go mad before seven moons had faded. Oiney Dinchy, who owned the dog, would not give me three hairs because I was unfortunate enough to be stealing apples when the dog rushed at me. For all that it mattered to Oiney, I might go as mad as a March hare. The priest, when informed of the trouble, blessed salt which he told my father to place on the wound. My father did so, but the salt pained me so much that I rushed screaming from the house. The next door neighbours ran into their homes and closed their doors when they heard me scream. Two little girls were coming to our house for the loan of a half-bottle of holy water for a sick cow, and when they saw me rush out they fled hurriedly, shrieking that I was already mad from the bite of Oiney Dinchy's dog. When Oiney heard this he got frightened and he gave my father three hairs of the dog with a civil hand. I placed them on my sore, the dog was hung by a rope from the branch of a tree, and the madness was kept away from me.

The poet Austin Clarke was drinking in Galway's Nighttown after curfew with the writer Pádraic Ó Conaire. It was during the 1920 Black and Tan terror. He described the evening to poet and broadcaster W.R. Rodgers:

Suddenly, a young lady who had probably had too much Guinness started a wild dance; quicker, quicker she whirled to the tune of what is known as 'gob music', and suddenly, as her skirts flew up, we saw with astonishment the flag of the Irish Republic; for that ingenious and patriotic daring young lady had chosen for her petticoat, knickers and so on, the colours of the forbidden flag, the green, the white and the yellow [*sic*].

★ ★ ★ ★ ★

Athlone-born author, journalist and politician Thomas Power O'Connor enlivened the House of Commons with witty speeches. At one sitting, he was passionately deploring the system whereby absentee landlords left tenants at the whim of greedy agents who impoverished them. In reply to an accusation of treason from across the floor, he delivered a delicious pun: 'Treason becomes reason because of an absent "T"!'

★ ★ ★ ★ ★

Jasper Tully, author of the wartime army book *Proudly the Note*, was more celebrated as editor of the *Roscommon Herald*. He wore a bowler-hat, a cravat and diamond pin. A Parnellite in his youth, he was imprisoned in an attempt to quash his newspaper. During the War of Independence, he routed British Auxiliaries from his premises. His most violent attack, however, was upon an official of the Typographical Union who had come to unionise his workforce. Hiding behind a door, he beat the visitor over the head with a metal em rule until he was almost unconscious. In that condition he forced his workers to carry the dazed official to the railway station and plant him on the Dublin train.

★ ★ ★ ★ ★

M.J. MacManus, author and journalist, dedicated his book A Jackdaw in Dublin *to Susan Mitchell, 'who, by damning my early attempts at serious verse with faint praises, spared Dublin the affliction of another minor poet'. He parodied Miss Mitchell's own style thus:*

There was a day, a far off day, a day we'll see no more
When in our witty city there were playboys by the score,
And my coruscating *jeux d'esprit* kept Dublin in a roar . . .

AE was not so weighty then, a fire was in his eyes,
Poor Synge was making Abbey Street resound with faction
        cries,
And W.B. had never dreamed of any Nobel Prize.

Those were the days when wickedly I fashioned rhymes
        sardonic
To help George Moore when he complained of troubles
        gastronomic,
And found for him (and others too) a never-failing tonic.

15

My classic joke is still recalled of Moore's divine grey
   mullet,
The only fish that would not stick in his fastidious gullet;
But now he shakes a leg elsewhere — and so I cannot
   pull it.

His books are now respectable — we thought them
   naughty then —
For stars with far more lurid flames have sailed into our
   ken,
And even George would jib at things from Mister
   Joyce's pen.

The playboys are all gone from us, the years are closing
   in,
The jokes ('though not their subjects) are growing
   somewhat thin;
The comic days are over — let the sad years now begin!

★ ★ ★ ★ ★

*The architectural historian Maurice Craig admits that it is mostly
not their fault that his publishers are his enemies:*

They are the middlemen who control the logistics of my
profession. They embody the constraints and limita-
tions, technical, financial and commercial, within which I
have to work if I am to have any effect at all. It is only to be
expected that they will want me to do things which I do not
want to do, and hinder me from doing what I should, ideally,
like to. They furnish my *matériel de guerre*. Like the
Admiralty, they are there to help me: but I would not be
human if I did not sometimes think the contrary.

★ ★ ★ ★ ★

André Bernard includes in Rotten Rejections *an early reaction to
J.P. Donleavy's* The Ginger Man:

[Its] publication . . . would not be a practical proposition in
this country [France]. So much of the text would have to be
excised that it would almost destroy the story, and even a

certain amount of rewriting would not overcome the problem.
. . . I do not think you will find another publisher who would
be willing to undertake the publication under present circumstances.

★ ★ ★ ★ ★

The Belfast poet and Presbyterian minister W.R. (Bertie) Rodgers,
once described as 'a gentle genius', made broadcasting for the BBC
his career. The publisher Dan Davin writes of him:

Anecdote was the staple of his conversation. . . . He mistrusted
the abstractness of pure argument . . . .Thus he would
tell a cherished tale of a parishioner rebuked for some trans-
gression who had replied: 'Never mind, your reverence, the
devil'll never light a whin-bush at your backside for my mistakes.' And he would smile and pull on his pipe and leave you
to draw the moral and to infer also, if you liked, that the
parishioner knew, or Bertie thought he knew, that the shep-
herd was one of his own black sheep. . . . Or, to illustrate the
love–hate between North and South, he would recall the man
challenged at the Border. 'Friend or foe?' No reply and your
man comes on, boots loud in the dark. 'Friend or foe? Answer
or I fire.' 'Foe.' 'Pass, foe.'

But in the end the soliloquy of that blackthorn mind would
pass to reverie. His low, withdrawn mumble would be less
and less audible, or comprehensible, the monologue totally
interior. But if his host, thinking of bed, pressed him too hard
for his meaning, the sharp reprimand could still flash from
the crepuscular, 'If you were as drunk as I am you'd know
what I was talking about.'

★ ★ ★ ★ ★

After a night's drinking in London with Dylan Thomas,
W.R. Rodgers and Dan Davin, Louis MacNeice was
stopped by a policeman, who wanted to know what he had in
his rucksack. Thomas retired early in Davin's house and arose
at lunchtime the next day, when MacNeice told him about his
interrogation. 'But didn't you tell him, Louis,' said Thomas,
'that you never travelled with anything but a change of verse
and a clean pair of rhymes?'

Abbey actor Harry Brogan once told Dan Davin that 'We don't want order. And we don't want disorder. What we want is orderly disorder.' Davin quotes Brogan talking to Seumas Kavanagh:

'My mother was a corpse-washer in Dublin, and once she took me with her to help turn over a big woman of twenty-two stone. I was a very impressionable age, Seumas, I was only eight at the time, and things like that could turn you against things. But thanks be to God, Seumas, I'm married and have a very nice family.'

★ ★ ★ ★ ★

Maurice Walsh's *Blackcock's Feather* (1932) received a fine window display at Dan Flavin's bookshop in Listowel, near the author's native Ballydonoghue. The author was back visiting and met Bryan MacMahon, who noticed a blackcock's feather in his hat and suggested that it should become the emblem of the local Gaelic football team. So touched was Walsh that he had a set of jerseys made bearing the feather on the breast and sent them to Listowel.

★ ★ ★ ★ ★

Writing of Walsh's final years, Steve Matheson recalls:

His son, Ian, who had married again, came home from the war with his wife, Patricia. He had decided to stay in the RAMC [Royal Army Medical Corps] so the visit was in the nature of a leave, but a joyous one. Maurice had taken to Patricia right away and gave her a copy of his book *Green Rushes* inscribed 'To Patricia, who once was green, the cratur'. (Patricia's maiden name had been Greene.) On that trip Patricia had brought some of the first nylon underthings that were then coming on the market. She had washed them and hung them out to dry when it started to rain. Thomasheen James brought them in, all crushed up in one hand. Maurice looked at them and shook his head. 'Once upon a time,' he said, 'you didn't know what you were getting until you unwrapped it.'

★ ★ ★ ★ ★

Patrick Kavanagh was alleged to have smeared dung on his boots in order to exaggerate his bucolic image. The poet Seumas O'Sullivan (James Starkey) was on a Dublin footpath talking to an acquaintance when a lorry-load of farmyard manure passed by. Drolly he remarked, 'I see Paddy Kavanagh is moving. There go his furniture and effects.'

★ ★ ★ ★ ★

When Thomas Pakenham was writing his book about Ireland's 1798 rebellion, he met Maurice Craig on the steps of the London Library and both agreed to adjourn to a nearby pub for lunch. Craig continues the story:

As we walked along King Street I asked him how he was getting on with his book . . . . He had finished or nearly finished it, he said, and went on to tell me that the impression the whole business had left with him was that of the absurd frivolity of the leaders. There they were, he said, all set to overthrow the British empire or, more probably, be caught and hanged. And what did I suppose, he went on, warming to his subject, what did I suppose Lord Edward [Fitzgerald] was doing in that house in Thomas Street just before Major Sirr came rushing up the stairs to arrest him? Checking over stores of arms and disposition of forces? Not a bit of it. He was reclining on a *chaise longue*, reading some rubbishy novel called — oh, let me see — yes, called *Gil Blas*, by somebody called — what was it? — Lesage. I ask you . . . !

'But, my dear Thomas,' I said, 'every cultivated gentleman carries a copy of *Gil Blas* in his pocket to read at odd moments,' and I pulled it out of mine, having just borrowed it to reread, my own copy being in storage at home in Dublin. The effect was all I could have hoped for. He nearly fell flat on his back, and dined out on it for long afterwards. As did I.

★ ★ ★ ★ ★

Portraits from sources quoted by Anne Chambers (mainly Kathleen Joy Evans) underline the complex personality of diva Margaret Burke-Sheridan, even in retirement:

Her large bosomed (my 'balcone' as she called it) figure emerged daily down the steps of the Gresham [Hotel]. As the trams trundled to and fro from the Pillar, she sallied flamboyantly forth, wearing high Italian platform-soled shoes, dressed in pastel blue, with flowing chiffon scarves and draperies and a large brimmed hat with veil. Her cupid-bow lips were accentuated with a dash of lipstick . . . . One friend and admirer was Micheál macLiammóir. Their meetings in the street were straight from the stage. Playing to the gallery of passers-by and in a mixture of Italian and English, Margaret and Micheál loudly proclaimed their mutual joy at meeting: 'Caro Michele,' Margaret would cry, arms outstretched. 'Ah, Margherita bellissima,' Micheál would respond, embracing her continental style with kisses on both cheeks . . . . Hilton Edwards, however, had little time or tolerance for Margaret's insistence on 'acting when the curtain has come down'.

✴

Despite the continental mannerisms and outlook, [Margaret] was attuned to the more parochial elements of Irish society . . . . During the weekend of an all-Ireland Hurling Final, a robust bunch of Cork supporters came into the Gresham dining room. One burly fellow, on sitting down to the table, emitted a loud sneeze. There was a brief embarrassed hush, whereupon, from a corner seat across the room, came the voice of Margaret, aimed at the Corconian table, 'Germs and *foreign germs* at that' [the Gaelic Athletic Association had imposed a ban on foreign games].

✴

During the war years, when foreign companies were unable to travel to Ireland, opera was maintained at a high standard by local artists. During one such opera, a local soprano gave a memorable performance, receiving a standing ovation from the audience. In her box, Margaret rose also to acclaim the performance and momentarily the spotlight operator moved the light from the soprano on stage to the famous prima donna. The audience in turn applauded Margaret as she paid her tribute. At the curtain, Margaret went backstage to convey her congratulations in person to the soprano, only to be verbally attacked and accused of stealing her applause by the indignant singer . . . . But as ever, Margaret had the last word: as she turned in disdain from the outburst, she cuttingly remarked, 'My dear, you're just a Woolworths' soprano.'

★ ★ ★ ★ ★

When Eric Cross's The Tailor and Ansty *was banned as being 'in its general tendency indecent', Mr Buckley (the Tailor) and his wife, Anastasia, subjects of the work, suffered the wrath of neighbours around Gougane Barra in west Cork. When the Tailor died, they relented. Frank O'Connor wrote in an introduction to the 1964 edition of the book:*

The old neighbours decided to ignore the disgrace he had brought upon them all and Ansty made a sour comment on the way they drank up all her good tea. At the funeral next day she made ribald ones on the men who attended. That night the men sat round the fire as they used to in the old days and swapped stories about the Tailor. There was general agreement that the great tragedy of the whole business was that at the very time the Tailor died, Guard Hoare was gallantly cycling out all the way from Ballingeary with a bottle of whisky for him. The bottle of whisky he had not drunk had cast a gloom over the proceedings. Suddenly, Ansty, who as usual was fussing about by the door with her broom, rested her arms on it and said, 'There'll be great talk above tonight.' It had suddenly dawned on her that her own loss was Heaven's happiness.

★ ★ ★ ★ ★

It was during Writers' Week in Listowel. A local lounged against a pub wall as kegs of Guinness were being unloaded and passed down into the cellar. One keg rolled on to the road and burst, and the black liquid flowed past the loiterer. He looked at it and said, 'Ink for Writers' Week, bejaysus!'

★ ★ ★ ★ ★

Edward and Christine, the sixth Earl and Countess of Longford,
believed they had a mission to bring good theatre to the provinces.
Circumstances demanded cost-cutting. Christine ran the box office
and would 'count the house' each evening, just as Yeats had at the
Abbey years before. John Cowell writes:

Edward's activities might be no more involved than selling
programmes but, unwittingly, he could be good at that.
Once an American soldier asked Christine if it was true the
outfit was run by a lord. 'Yes,' she assured him. 'By a real lord
— you know, an earl?' 'Yes,' she said again, 'there he is,'
pointing to Edward, who was standing in the foyer with a
bundle of unsold programmes in his hand. 'Wha!' exclaimed
the GI, 'an earl selling theatre programmes?' 'Why not?' said
Christine. Moved with film-star adulation, the young man
went up [to Edward]. 'Gee, Earl, I'll buy the lot,' he said, and
he did.

★

Cowell recalls Lord Longford's bad temper:

A story still extant . . . concerns an incident in Galway in
the 1940s. In his generosity, Edward was the first theatrical manager to give his actors contracts (which of course
caused jealousy in other theatres). Margaret Lawlor's contract
was principally as Secretary to Longford Productions
(1940–45) and 'to act as required' — on the stage, that is.
Because of her administrative work, any parts she took were
necessarily small. For one such part, the *Connaught Tribune*
gave her a rave notice, ignoring the remainder of the cast —
clearly what Edward considered an imbalanced review. He
worked himself into one of his purple rages. Instant depres-
sion gripped the entire company. Fed up with his stupid
hysterics, half of them resigned on the instant.

Edward paced the floor, wailing disconsolately: 'The company's finished. What'll I do, Christine, the company's
finished?' In the midst of the turmoil, Dan Treston, the producer of the time, slipped a gramophone record on the
turntable. In a moment the public address system boomed

out *The Dead March from Saul*. Edward's wail changed to a fighting challenge: 'Who the hell's put on that record?' No reply, only the strains of the funeral march. 'Who the hell's put on that record?' he yelled above the din. Nonchalantly, Kay Casson stepped up and popped a fruit drop in his mouth. He liked anything sweet. Immediately he was silenced and everyone laughed, and that was that — the end of another storm in a teaspoon.

✦ ✦ ✦ ✦ ✦

On the art of short-story writing, Bryan MacMahon recalls:

I had developed and made my own a method derived from a comment made either by Sean O'Faolain or Frank O'Connor (I incline to O'Faolain, though neither of these great writers has mentioned this method in the book on the short story each has written). Meeting me by appointment in a tea-shop in Dublin, both had welcomed me to the pages of *The Bell*. Playing the part of the artless tiro up from Kerry, I asked, let us say O'Faolain, 'How do you write a short story?' He smiled and replied enigmatically, 'You get a male idea and a female idea. You couple them, and the children are short stories.'

✦ ✦ ✦ ✦ ✦

In a programme note for the play Mother of All the Behans, *Ulick O'Connor writes about the subject, Kathleen Behan:*

I remember once bringing an American ambassador to see her at Sybil Hill Home in Raheny. We adjourned, at Kathleen's suggestion, to the Old Shieling nearby for a few rossiners. I watched her carefully, as I was always fascinated by the method she used to warm up her company and get the crack going.

'Do you know the American national anthem?' she asked the ambassador. He said he did. 'But do you know the second verse?' He said he'd never heard of it. Like a flash she was off into the second verse of the American anthem. Where she got it from I don't know to this day. Then she asked the ambassador did he know the Chinese national anthem. He had to admit he didn't. She sang him 'Chin, Chin, Chinaman'.

O'Connor continues:

Soon the ambassador was singing himself, and his million-airess wife, from one of the oldest American colonial families, was joining in. On the way back to Sybil Hill Home, Kathleen was sitting up in the front of the Rolls, between the chauffeur and the ambassador, with her arms around His Excellency, while the two of them sang 'The Red Flag'.

★ ★ ★ ★ ★

In his biography of Brendan Behan, O'Connor also writes of the author's mother:

Kathleen did love the limelight. She recognised her powers of lifting people up. After the 'Russell Harty Show' on St Patrick's night four years ago, where I appeared with her, I slipped off from the Embankment [a public house] in Tallaght at 2 a.m. exhausted.

There was a tangled group of tin whistle players, concertina players and fiddlers sitting on the floor as I passed. A voice hailed me from the middle of them. It was Kathleen Behan, aged ninety-four. A year later, when a splendid record of her songs was launched in the same place, she asked me to accompany her to the microphone.

She used to hold my hand on such sessions as if she was drawing strength from me, although I am inclined to think it was the other way round. After she'd been singing for an hour, I got alarmed for her well-being. I slipped away for a second to find her son, Rory, and ask him to make her come down from the platform before she collapsed.

'Listen, old son,' Rory said, 'you got her up, you get her down. There's no one I know would stop her once she gets started.'

She did stop eventually — when they were closing the bar.

★ ★ ★ ★ ★

SIR JONAH BARRINGTON
1760–1834

In Personal Sketches of his own Time *and* The Rise and Fall of the Irish Nation *(1833), Barrington from Knapton, near Abbeyleix produced lively contemporary accounts of blades, bucks and duelling members of parliament. He described the revolution of 1798 as 'the most bungling, imperfect business that ever threw ridicule on a lofty epithet by answering it unworthily'. A graduate of Trinity College, he was called to the bar in 1788 and was later MP for Tuam, Clogher and Banagher. As a judge, he led an extravagant lifestyle and misappropriated court funds to pay his debts. He was dismissed and emigrated to Versailles, where he died.*

✭ ✭ ✭ ✭ ✭

Among Barrington's sketches is the following:

In those days the common people ideally separated the gentry of the country into three classes, and treated each class according to the relative degree of respect to which it was entitled. They generally divided them thus:

1. Half-mounted gentlemen.
2. Gentlemen every inch of them.
3. Gentlemen to the backbone.

✭ ✭ ✭ ✭ ✭

Barrington quotes a loyal Orange toast, part of which goes:

May we never want a Williamite to kick the **** of a Jacobite! and a **** for the Bishop of Cork! And that he won't drink this, whether he be priest, bishop, deacon, bellows-blower, grave-digger, or any other of the fraternity of *the clergy*; may a north wind blow him to the south, and a west

25

wind blow him to the east! May he have a dark night — a lee shore — a rank storm — and a leaky vessel, to carry him over the river Styx! May the dog Cerberus make a meal of his rump, and Pluto a snuff-box of his skull; and may the devil jump down his throat with a red-hot harrow, with every pin to tear a gut, and blow him with a *clean* carcass to hell! Amen!

✶

Sir Jonah considers the toast a mere 'excuse for getting loyally drunk as often as possible'. He adds a footnote:

Could his majesty, King William, learn in the other world that he has been the cause of more broken heads and drunken men, since his departure, than all his predecessors, he must be the proudest ghost and most conceited skeleton that ever entered the gardens of Elysium.

✶ ✶ ✶ ✶ ✶

Despite their poverty, Irish peasants are described by Barrington as 'the happiest in Europe'. Not, however, Ned at the Barrow water, who 'with the greatest felicity, g[o]t rid of, probably, the thickest and heaviest article belonging to him':

I think it was in or about the year 1796, a labourer dwelling near the town of Athy, County Kildare . . . was walking with his comrade up the banks of the Barrow to the farm of a Mr Richardson, on whose meadows they were employed to mow; each, in the usual Irish way, having his scythe loosely wagging over his shoulder. Lazily lounging close to the bank of the river, they espied a salmon partly hid under the bank. It is the nature of this fish that, when his head is concealed, he fancies no one can see his tail (there are many wise-acres in the world, besides the salmon, of the same way of thinking). On the present occasion the body of the fish was visible.

'Oh! Ned — Ned, dear!' said one of the mowers, 'look at that big fellow there: it is a pity we ha'nt no *spear*, now, isn't it?'

'Maybe,' said Ned, 'we could be after picking the *lad* with the scythe-handle.'

'True for you!' said Dennis: 'the spike of yeer handle is longer nor mine; give the fellow a *dig* with it at any rate.'

'Ay, will I,' returned the other: 'I'll give the lad a *prod* he'll never forget any how.'

The spike and their sport was all they thought of: but the *blade* of the scythe, which hung over Ned's shoulders, never came into the contemplation of either of them. Ned cautiously looked over the bank; the unconscious salmon lay snug, little imagining the conspiracy that had been formed against his tail.

'Now hit the lad smart!' said Dennis: 'there, now — there! rise your fist: now you have the boy! now, Ned — success! — success!'

Ned struck at the salmon with all his might and main, and that was not trifling. But whether 'the boy' was piked or not never appeared; for poor Ned, bending his neck as he struck at the salmon, placed the vertebrae in the most convenient position for unfurnishing his shoulders; and his head came tumbling splash into the Barrow, to the utter astonishment of his comrade, who could not conceive *how* it could *drop off* so suddenly. But the next minute he had the consolation of seeing the head attended by one of his own ears, which had been most dexterously sliced off by the same blow which beheaded his comrade.

The head and ear rolled down the river in company, and were picked up with extreme horror at a mill-dam, near Mr Richardson's, by one of the miller's men.

'Who the devil does this head belong to?' exclaimed the miller. 'Oh Christ — !'

'Whoever *owned it*,' said the man, 'had *three ears*, at any rate, though they don't match.'

★ ★ ★ ★ ★

Cork-born nationalist and lawyer John Philpot Curran was to be guest of honour at a dinner party hosted by Reverend Jack Reed, 'a three-bottle parson of Carlow'. Barrington and 'several other jolly neighbours' arrived on time but Curran, usually punctual, was absent:

Every guest of the reverend host having now decided on his chair, and turned down his plate, in order to be as near as possible to Counsellor Curran, proceeded to whet his knife against the edge of his neighbour's, to give it a due keenness for the most tempting side of luscious sirloin, which by anticipation frizzed upon its pewter dish. Veal, mutton, turkey, ham, duck, partridge, all 'piping hot,' were ready and willing to leap from their pots and spits into their respective dishes, and to take a warm bath each in its proper gravy. The cork-screw was busily employed . . . and the punch, jugged, and bubbling hot upon the hearth-stone, perfumed the whole room with its aromatic potsheen [sic] odour.

Barrington describes the waiting, the theories proffered for Curran's delay, the anxiety gradually giving way to alarm when 'day had departed, and twilight was rapidly following its example'. He continues:

As Curran was known every day to strip naked and wash himself all over with a sponge and cold water, I conjectured, as most rational, that he had, in lieu of his usual ablution, gone to the Barrow to bathe before dinner, and thus unfortunately perished. All agreed in my hypothesis, and hooks and draw-nets were sent for immediately . . . to scour the river for his body. The beef, mutton, and veal, as if in grief, had either turned into broth, or dropped piecemeal from the spit; the poultry fell from their strings, and were seen broiling in the dripping pan. The cook had forgotten her calling, and gone off to make enquiries.

So too did the remainder of the house staff and neighbours as a full-scale search was organised. It was thought that Diver, the rector's dog, would be useful in the search, but the animal could not be found. After an intensive search outside, a maid, Mary, was despatched to search the bedrooms. She returned to Barrington and the waiting guests in a state of great agitation:

'O, holy Virgin! holy Virgin! yes, gentlemen! the counsellor is dead, sure enough. And I'll die too, gentlemen! I'll never recover it!' and she crossed herself twenty times over in the way the priest had taught her . . . I saw his *ghost*, please your reverence . . . and a frightful ghost it was! just out of the river, and not even *decent* itself. I'm willing to take my affidavy that I saw his ghost, quite *indecent*, straight forenent me . . . in the double-bedded room next to your reverence's.'

All rushed upstairs, forgetting to bring candles. But a moon threw an eerie shaft into the room, presenting 'an exhibition far more ludicrous than terrific':

In a far corner of the room stood, erect and formal, and *stark naked* (as a *ghost* should be), John Philpot Curran, one of his majesty's counsel, learned in the law, — trembling as if in the ague, and scarce able to utter a syllable, through the combination of cold and terror. Three or four paces in his front lay Diver, from Newfoundland, stretching out his immense shaggy carcase, his long paws extended their full length, and his great head lying on them with his nose pointed toward the ghost, as true as the needle to the pole. His hind legs were gathered up like those of a wild beast ready to spring upon his prey. He took an angry notice of the first of us [but] the moment his master appeared [seemed to say], 'I have done my duty, now do you yours:' he looked, indeed, as if he only waited for the word of command, to seize the counsellor by the throttle.

A blanket was now considerately thrown over Curran by one of the company, and he was *put to bed* with half a dozen more blankets heaped upon him: a tumbler of hot potsheen punch was administered, and a second worked miracles . . . Related by *any* one [his story] would have been good; but as told by Curran . . . was superexcellent; — and we had to thank Diver, the water-dog, for the highest zest of the whole evening.

Barrington explains how Curran had arrived early and repaired to a bedroom to wash when Diver entered and, concluding he had 'no very honest intention', challenged:

Curran, unaccustomed to so strange a valet, retreated, while Diver advanced, and very significantly showed an intention to seize him by the naked throat; which operation, if performed by Diver, whose tusks were a full inch in length, would no doubt have admitted an inconvenient quantity of atmospheric air into his oesophagus. He therefore crept as close into the corner as he could, and had the equivocal satisfaction of seeing his adversary advance and turn the meditated assault into a complete blockade — stretching himself out, and 'maintaining his position' with scarcely the slightest motion . . . . Once or twice Curran raised his hand: but Diver, considering that as a sort of challenge, rose instantly, and with a low growl looked significantly at Curran's windpipe. Curran therefore stood like a model, if not much like a marble divinity. In truth, though somewhat less comely, his features were more expressive than those of the Apollo Belvidere [*sic*]. Had the circumstances occurred at Athens to Demosthenes, or in the days of Phidias, it is probable my friend Curran, and Diver, would have been at this moment exhibited in virgin marble at Florence or at the Vatican; — and I am quite sure the subject would have been better and more amusing than that of 'the dying gladiator'.

THERE CANNOT BE A JUSTER APHORISM THAN '*POETA NASCITUR, NON FIT*': THE PAUCITY OF THOSE LITERARY PRODUCTIONS WHICH DESERVE THE EPITHET OF POETRY, COMPARED WITH THE THOUSAND VOLUMES OF WHAT RHYMING AUTHORS CALL POEMS, FORMS A CONCLUSIVE ILLUSTRATION
Sir Jonah Barrington

SAMUEL BECKETT 1906–1989

Samuel Beckett was born in Foxrock, Co. Dublin. His father had a successful quantity surveying and construction business, and the family lived in an impressive house, 'Cooldrinagh'. Although shy, Beckett did the usual things that boys of his time enjoyed — bird-nesting, playing football and chasing dogs. Sometimes he liked to climb to the top of a tree and throw himself off it, arms and legs spreadeagled, hoping he could fly. But he was shrewd enough to drop into the spreading lower branches to break his fall.

Beckett was privately educated from the age of five by Miss Ida Elsner. He subsequently attended the same school as Oscar Wilde — Portora, Enniskillen, where he distinguished himself more in athletics than in literature. Then to Trinity College Dublin in October 1923, where he was received with some reservations because of his youth. He was to become a lecturer in French there. A cycling trip in France in 1926 initiated a lasting affection for that country. Trinity supported an exchange arrangement with the École Normale Supérieure and Beckett was lecteur there from 1928 to 1930. Under the terms of his contract, he was obliged to return to Trinity for a period but later he settled in Paris, where he did some research and translations for Joyce. Beckett's novels were initially accepted only by a small following, but his play Waiting for Godot *(1952) brought him to a wider audience.*

He considered English 'a good theatre language, because of its concreteness, its close relationship between thing and vocable'. Always aloof, he shunned publicity and gave interviews only on rare occasions. Many of the characters in Beckett's work have names beginning with the letter M, the thirteenth letter of the alphabet. A number of family events occurred on the 13th day of the month and its double, the 26th.

★ ★ ★ ★ ★

Of all the children in his piano class, Samuel was the most dedicated and diligent in practising, but he was also the most heavy-handed and mechanical player. Miss Beatrice Skipworth complained constantly throughout the lessons to the other children that Sam was 'all technique and no feeling', and she always reserved him for last, as if girding herself for the ordeal. As she complained, he sat stoically in her waiting-room, peering with near-sighted intensity at back copies of *Punch* dating from half a century earlier.

At Trinity College, Beckett was a member of a coterie that included Alfred Péron, École-exchange lecteur *Thomas Rudmose-Brown and others. Deirdre Bair tells of a hoax in which he involved them:*

He delivered a long, scholarly paper to the Modern Languages Society about a literary movement called 'Le Concentrisme', led by one Jean du Chas, which was supposedly revolutionizing Parisian intellectual circles with its Rabelaisian humour and bawdy writing. He persuaded several of his friends to support the paper by reading other 'examples' of 'Concentrismiste' writing. The body of the membership, all serious scholars, spent the remainder of the meeting diligently discussing the possible literary merit of this shocking new school of writing. However, 'Le Concentrisme', which existed only in Beckett's imagination, was never heard of again after that evening, except for Jean du Chas, who became, in abbreviated form, one of the characters in *More Pricks than Kicks*.

An infatuation with suicide as a subject began in Trinity. Richard Aldington thought Beckett was a 'splendidly mad Irishman [who] wanted to commit suicide, a fate he nearly imposed on half the faculty of École by playing the flute — an instrument of which he was far from being a master — every night in his room from midnight to dawn'.

* * * * *

A preference for male company while drinking was regarded as very Irish by Beckett's French friends. Irish acquaintances considered him almost misogynistic in his youth. He was conscious of this and when another professed 'man's man' spotted him escorting a prostitute along Westland Row one night, Beckett hopped behind a pillar to hide. The next time Beckett was lauding the advantages of male company, he was taunted about the Westland Row incident, but replied, 'This thing called love; there's none of it, you know. It's only fucking.'

★ ★ ★ ★ ★

A rejection of Beckett's Dream of Fair to Middling Women, *quoted by André Bernard, reads:*

I wouldn't touch this with a barge-pole. Beckett's probably a clever fellow, but here he has elaborated a slavish and rather incoherent imitation of Joyce, most eccentric in language and full of disgustingly affected passages — also indecent: the book is damned — and you wouldn't sell the book even on its title.

★

Molloy *and* Malone Dies *fare little better:*

I couldn't read either book — that is, my eye refused to sit on the page and absorb meanings, or whatever substitutes for meaning in this type of thing . . . . This doesn't make sense and it isn't funny . . . . I suspect that the real fault in these novels, if I cared to read them carefully, would be simply dullness. There's no sense considering them for publication here; the bad taste of the American public does not yet coincide with the bad taste of the French avant garde.

★ ★ ★ ★ ★

Deirdre Bair writes about Beckett and James Joyce's daughter, Lucia:

P assivity in many forms has been the distinguishing characteristic of all Beckett's relationships with women throughout his life, and he carried it to the extreme with Lucia. He decided to play a waiting game, to do nothing overt for as long as possible in the hope that her feeling for him would dissolve, just as her interest in other men had.

In May [1930], Lucia tried to force a resolution to the situation by inviting Beckett to lunch in a small Italian restaurant opposite the Luxembourg Gardens where they had dined previously with her parents. Lucia had taken great pains with her usually sloppy appearance: she had had her hair fixed especially for the occasion and was wearing makeup and a new dress.

Beckett did not want to be alone with her, and so he persuaded his friend Georges Pelorson to go along. The unwitting Pelorson knew nothing of the crisis Beckett anticipated, and accepted the invitation for a free lunch. They waited for Lucia outside the restaurant and watched as she came up the street smiling at Beckett. When she discovered that he had invited Pelorson to join them, her face fell and she began to quiver. She composed herself and allowed the two men to escort her into the restaurant, where Beckett carefully seated her on the banquette and sat opposite, on a chair next to Pelorson.

As the meal progressed, the silence thickened. Pelorson was appalled as he watched Lucia staring into space, haphazardly slinging an occasional bite of food into her mouth. Her lipstick grew smeared, her mascara blurred, the carefully done hair grew disarranged. She became a ghastly caricature, like a painted mannequin that had been left out in the rain. After barely touching her food, she stood up slowly as if in a trance, then ran out of the restaurant and down the street. By the time they settled the bill and ran after her, she had disappeared. Beckett and Pelorson parted in mutual embarrassment. For a long time after, they took pains not to discuss the luncheon, but Beckett typically offered no explanation or apology.

★ ★ ★ ★ ★

Brendan Behan frequently visited Beckett in Paris during 1952 — mostly in the early hours, drunk. He would hammer on the door until admitted.

One night, before an important rehearsal of *Waiting for Godot* [*En attendant Godot*], Beckett's sleep was fitful and so he was weary when he heard Behan singing and shouting outside. Still gentlemanly, he admitted him and endured the raucous discourse until rehearsal time was near. In order to get rid of Behan without giving offence, Beckett piloted him to the office of the editor of the literary quarterly *Merlin*, assuring Behan that the man was enthusiastic about his work and wished to interview him. Only one staff-member, the English poet Christopher Logue, was present. He was drowsily drinking coffee when Beckett dragged in his ward, aimed him at the nearest chair and departed hurriedly.

✷ ✷ ✷ ✷ ✷

Rehearsing *Endgame* in London, Jack MacGowran (a well-known exponent of Beckett's work) asked the author how he should deliver the line, 'If I knew the combination of the safe, I'd kill you.' Beckett's answer was logical, if a little unhelpful: 'Just think that if you knew the combination, you would kill him.'

✷ ✷ ✷ ✷ ✷

THAT PASSED THE TIME
Samuel Beckett

35

BRENDAN
BEHAN
1923–1964

A Dubliner through and through, Brendan Behan was taught by nuns and Christian Brothers before abandoning formal education at the age of fourteen. His family being involved in the national movement, he became a member of Fianna Éireann, a republican youth group, at the age of ten. An uncle, Peadar Kearney, wrote the song that became the Irish national anthem. Not surprisingly, therefore, Behan joined the IRA at fifteen years of age. He was sentenced to three years in a Borstal institute at sixteen for possessing explosives in Liverpool, and at eighteen, then a painter by trade, he was deported for shooting at a policeman.

A further prison sentence in Ireland helped to inspire his celebrated play The Quare Fellow. *Stories about the author's drinking sprees are matched only by his own recorded verbosity. But his wild antics assisted his writing; people looked forward to first nights of his work, hoping that the author would turn up and create a scene in or about the theatre. Live television interviews must have been nightmares for producers; Behan was apt to say anything that came into his head, the more controversial the better.*

Some critics claim that Behan's prose works are superior to his plays. His autobiographical Borstal Boy *was a bestseller, but his dramas required considerable work from directors, mainly Joan Littlewood and Alan Simpson, to make them suitable for production.*

Establishing authenticity for Behan anecdotes is difficult. Yarns about him can be heard in Dublin, New York or London, most often receiving their tenth or twentieth telling. All are typical of the boisterous, bawdy but likeable rogue compared by an anonymous commentator to a barrel of porter — full of goodness, heady, not to be taken in excess and containing sediment that should not be stirred up.

★ ★ ★ ★ ★

As a child, Brendan Behan was being walked out in his pram by his grandmother. A passer-by was heard to remark, 'Isn't it terrible to see such a lovely little boy deformed?' 'How dare you,' chided Brendan's grandmother. 'He's not deformed; he's just drunk.' And he was!

✶ ✶ ✶ ✶ ✶

Accused in Paris on one occasion of being a gentleman of Hellenic diversity, Behan, the former house-painter, replied: 'I must have caught it off Angelica Kauffmann in Dominick Street when I was scraping it down for an undercoat.'

✶ ✶ ✶ ✶ ✶

In Dead as Doornails, *Anthony Cronin tells about his escapades in France with Behan. The pair finished up without any money and, abetted by a man named O'Brien, attempted to stow away in the coal-hold of a ship bound for Dublin. Discovered, the black-faced pair were frogmarched off the craft:*

A small knot of workmen had gathered on the quayside and as we went down the gangway they also thought it proper to display amusement. Brendan told them in English to go and fuck themselves. The gangway was run in again. The engines had started and the ship began to move. O'Brien was leaning over the bulwarks at the stern.

'What'll I do with them bags?' he called.

'Leave them in McDaid's,' said Brendan fiercely. 'McDaid's of Harry Street. Have a drink on me.'

✶ ✶ ✶ ✶ ✶

Behan's first play was written in Mountjoy jail. *The Landlady* had a gruesome throat-cutting sequence and contained some foul language. At least, the prisoners thought so; during rehearsals they staged a riot, complaining that the drama was obscene and blasphemous, and refused to continue with the staging. From another jail, Arbour Hill, a year later, the author wrote to a friend pleading that the characters in *The Landlady* were 'as genuine as any of O'Casey's battalion', adding, 'Them that says they're not true to life are illiterate.'

The Quare Fellow and its assorted productions have gained as celebrated a reputation among raconteurs as among theatre buffs. When Behan was serving a sentence in Mountjoy jail, a condemned prisoner, Bernard Kirwan, provided inspiration for the play. A remand prisoner was the subject of an anecdote.

Thady Flynn was on trial for drowning his wife, Hannah, in a well. He was accused of placing a turkey in a bucket and lowering it into the water to make it appear that the victim had been trying to rescue it. The jury returned a verdict of 'Guilty but insane' against Flynn, who, among other things, alleged that while in Mountjoy he heard strange voices. Behan jokingly claimed, therefore, to have saved Flynn's life by driving him mad creeping up behind him singing:

Ding, dong, dell. Hannah's in the well.
Who put her in? Little Thady Flynn.

★ ★ ★ ★ ★

During rehearsals for the first performance of *The Quare Fellow* at Dublin's Pike Theatre, Behan often arrived drunk. Once he was accompanied by a similarly besotted friend. Childishly, he nudged his pal in the ribs every so often, saying 'I wrote that.' As opening night approached, the author drank more and more so that at the start of the final dress rehearsal, he collapsed in the auditorium. The play's director, Alan Simpson, had him laid along a back bench, 'splendidly comatose'. But in such a small theatre, the cast could not hear their cues over his loud snores. Novel duties were allotted to the assistant stage-manager that afternoon; he sat beside the playwright and shook him whenever the decibels of resonant slumber became intolerable.

★ ★ ★ ★ ★

Behan recalled for the BBC's Colin MacInnes an American broadcast in which he had been asked about the message contained in his work and had retorted, 'What message? I'm a playwright, not a bloody postman.'

He also told MacInnes:

I'm a daylight atheist. If I'm in daylight and the sun is shining, I couldn't . . . care less. I'm like the Swedes. But somebody said the Swedes have the highest suicide rate in the world; it's a lot of rubbish. The reason they have a high suicide rate is that they give the returns, whereas in England or Ireland or Scotland or Wales if somebody croaks themselves, they say, 'Oh, he didn't know the gun was loaded,' or 'He didn't know that seven million aspirins could knock you off.'

★ ★ ★ ★ ★

The Hostage is a translation of a play which Behan wrote in Irish (*An Giall*). It is a mixture of drama, music-hall and ballad. In July 1959 Behan was in a Dublin hospital when the play opened at Wyndham's Theatre in London's West End. A postcard from him was read from the stage, its reader adding that the author was with them in spirit — itself an ironic pun. Behan was with them in person the following evening. Discharging himself from hospital, he borrowed a dinner-jacket and flew to London. He had intended placing himself in the care of his sister-in-law, Celia Salkeld, who was acting in the play. She was not at home, so Behan made his way to a bar near the theatre.

A busker outside was not doing much business until Behan emerged, resplendent in dinner-jacket, requesting an Irish song. He was obliged with 'When Irish Eyes are Smiling', but by the time a heart had been stolen away a crowd had gathered, because Behan had donned the busker's hat and was singing a different song:

> Bold Robert Emmet, the guardian of Erin,
> Bold Robert Emmet will die with a smile.
> Farewell companions, both loyal and daring;
> I'll lay down my life for the Emerald Isle.

He passed around the hat then and the bemused gathering donated handsomely. Behan handed the collection to the delighted street-singer but chastised him, saying that 'When Irish Eyes are Smiling' was not an Irish song.

★ ★ ★ ★ ★

When *The Hostage* opened in New York, the theatre had the added entertainment of an inebriated author singing its songs, repeating its gags, heckling the players and being taunted by journalists; audience participation reached a bawdy zenith. The spree continued into the following day, when Behan was arrested on a charge of drunkenness. The magistrate could not quite decide whether the accused was being abusive or patronising, so he imposed a fine of five shillings. Behan returned to Ireland and to hospital, where he wrote about his experience for the *People* newspaper, opening, 'For a start, let me tell you that I am neither dead, drunk nor dotty.'

★ ★ ★ ★ ★

Both my uncle and my aunt were at the first-night party of *The Hostage* [wrote the author in *Brendan Behan's New York*] and we went to Downey's restaurant. Lauren Bacall was in the company, and Jason Robards Jr and Jackie Gleason.

'Come on,' Jackie said to me, 'let's talk Irish.'

'Where the hell did you learn Irish?' I asked him.

'Oh, I can count up to ten,' he said.

So I asked him in Irish, 'How are you, Jackie?'

'One, two, three, four,' he replied.

★ ★ ★ ★ ★

HARPO MARX: Once, when I was playing *A Night at the Opera* —

BEHAN: Stop! That's like Leonardo da Vinci saying, 'Once, when I was painting *The Last Supper*.

★ ★ ★ ★ ★

Of one appearance on an American television show, Behan's co-participant, Jackie Gleason, said he 'came over one hundred per cent proof. It was not an act of God, but an act of Guinness.'

★ ★ ★ ★ ★

On 'The Jack Parr Show' in 1959, talk turned to the Paddy Chayefsky play *The Tenth Man*, which is set in an Orthodox synagogue and had enjoyed a big Broadway success at a Jewish benefit evening. Behan said it was an unfair test, a bit like 'showing *National Velvet* to an audience of jockeys'.

★ ★ ★ ★ ★

On 'Open End', host David Susskind enquired if it were true that Behan hated policemen. Behan denied hating anybody, but the interviewer persisted, saying, 'You hate constabulary,' whereupon Behan conceded, 'I have never come across a situation so dismal that a policeman would not have made it worse.'

★ ★ ★ ★ ★

Tennessee Williams, Anthony Quinn and Tony Richardson were on a television programme with Behan. They deliberated on aspects of sex in drama, but Behan did not contribute anything until near the close of the discussion, when he made an unoriginal but startling interjection: 'In sex, I think anything is alright provided it is done in private and doesn't frighten the horses.'

★ ★ ★ ★ ★

'When I was growing up,' said Behan, 'getting drunk was not a social disgrace; getting enough to eat was considered an achievement but getting drunk was a victory.'

When his brother Brian produced a biographical collection, *With Chest Expanded*, Brendan remarked, 'The cat at number seventy will be writing next,' and when another brother Dominic's comedy *Posterity Be Damned* was staged in 1959, Brendan's comment was, 'Does he think that geniuses are born in litters?'

★ ★ ★ ★ ★

Ulick O'Connor tells how Behan called to the Wicklow home of J.P. Donleavy when the house was empty and refreshed himself with a strange concoction of flour, cornflakes, eggs, butter, raisins, sardines, sugar, cooking chocolate and porter. He also interfered with a manuscript upon which Donleavy was working at the time. O'Connor

41

claims that some suggestions noted by Behan on the folios were included in the final draft of The Ginger Man. *Interviewed in 1993, Donleavy admitted as much. He had found apparently insignificant suggestions about changing a comma or a colon to be quite effective. He regretted not taking a particular piece of advice offered:*

One fascinating thing which I did not follow concerned tuberculosis. Behan was sensitive about the disease and I was conscious of this, having been attending at post mortems; I was reading bacteriology at the time. So *Gingerman* had references made to it and I think the term 'White Death' comes to mind. Now that was a very sensitive issue to Behan, so he had suggested that I soften it somehow or not mention it. There had been [many cases of] tuberculosis in slums where he grew up and he had this deep-seated fear about it.

★ ★ ★ ★ ★

Years after the event, 'Mike' Donleavy, as Behan called him, was to write of such a Wicklow visit:

I returned to find the oil stove blackened along with every pot in the place. And was confronted by disarray on every side as if a robbery had been committed. Which it seemed it had for there was the mystery of all but one pair of my twenty pairs of shoes gone. It did not take long to find out who the culprit was who'd unlatched a window and climbed in. Stepping out to my studio, I found there on my makeshift desk, a manuscript lying next to my own manuscript copy of *The Ginger Man*. Picking up the crumpled, stained and wrinkled sheaf of pages and in just turning a few I could see from words such as peeler, nark and screw that the setting was that of a British correctional institution. And as I was holding in my hand the manuscript of *Borstal Boy*, I recalled that day outside Davy Byrne's, Behan's proffered hand and his words 'Sure I'm a writer and you're a writer too.

And fuck the
Ignorant bunch of them
Back in there.'

Through the window of his home one morning, Donleavy saw Behan petting a bull:

Rushing naked out of bed I grabbed a pitchfork kept nearby for such emergencies and ran out on the lawn just as the bull's pawing forelegs were scooping up sods and sending them flying into the sky. Behan thinking this the beast's invitation to play.

'Ah, don't harm the poor creature, Mike, he means no harm.'

The bull charged the pitchfork and with a hook of his horns into the prongs sent it flying out of my hands and as I jumped behind a wheelbarrow full of weeds it, too, promptly was the next to go skywards, the weeds raining down on Behan like confetti, upon whom the realization had also dawned that he had better run for his life. But as he always could at such dire times, he had ready a merry quip.

'Ah, Jasus, Mike, for the love of the Salvation Army would you keep the horns of that ton of bloody beast away from rooting me up the hole out of which all of me wisdom comes' . . . Behan skedaddling knees in the air, as he went shouting curses through a patch of stinging nettles and threw himself up on top of a hedge of briars. The roaring bull in close pursuit as Behan finally clambered up a young ash tree . . . . Behan, a devout proclaimed atheist in conversation, was on this occasion perched up in the ash tree, praying loudly to the Almighty for deliverance.

'Let me tell you, Mike, for a moment there, I did not think that my redeemer liveth.'

★

Donleavy gives a spirited account of Behan 'on the ran-tan':

I chauffeured Behan and as he demanded we stopped in pubs on the way, where he would sing and astonish the habitués with his quips and burlesque. Pouring pints over his head while reciting various statutes from British law. Finally we arrived in the rough, squalid streets of Dublin's Night Town.

Entering pubs there where Behan knew all the inmates as well as they knew him. In the corner snugs Behan urging me to hug all his old ancient lady acquaintances, grandmothers long retired from motherhood and its desperate struggle of survival. Behan whispering in my ear as he'd push me into a cackling old lady's arms.

'Mike, she was these forty years now as dedicated as any nun, selling her arse for a few bob down the quays, to buy a bit of bread and tea for the childer and she's deserving of a heartfelt squeeze now at the end of her long ordeal. Come on, give the old girl a decent and better kiss and embrace than that.'

✷ ✷ ✷ ✷ ✷

A master mimic, Behan regaled his friends by playing Toulouse-Lautrec, the painter, or Rupert Brooke, the romantic Georgian poet, going down a coalmine! As Mother Ireland spewing satirical barbs, he would toss his coat-tail over his head. As D.H. Lawrence bringing his mother to a football match, he had an easy win with his audience. Topics ranged from the Abbey Theatre's attitude to sex, through political patronage, religion, robbery and rebellion. But 'Give us the wheelchair, Brendan' was the call from discerning party-goers which produced an irreverent impression of the Canon in Paul Vincent Carroll's Shadow and Substance. *Ulick O'Connor recounts John Ryan's recollections of the performance:*

He would do all the movements of turning the wheels with his hands as he moved the chair across the room. He would then call on the housekeeper. The housekeeper would come in and Brendan would put his coat over his head to resemble a shawl. There would be a lot of stuff about 'hot toddy', 'not enough whiskey', and the housekeeper would grumble, 'You'll have to get out of the wheelchair to get it.' Then the young curate would enter, full of bright ideas, raffles and trips to the country. Brendan would be the young curate. Then he would mention a dance on Friday night and he would jump back into the Canon's part.

Canon: 'What are you torturing me about? Didn't I tell you you could have lemonade at the dance?'

Curate (nervously): 'But, Canon, I was wondering about the men and the women.'

The Canon would turn round irritatedly, using his hands to swing the wheels of the chair round all the time, and say:

'What about the men and women? Didn't I tell you you could have men and women at the dance?'

Curate (this time very nervous): 'Yes, Canon, but I was wondering if you would allow the men and the women to dance with each other.'

Canon: 'How dare you! I might as well have a Protestant for a curate as you.'

★ ★ ★ ★ ★

The Bohemian clientele of McDaid's public house and 'The Catacombs', a cellar refuge, demanded a certain slovenliness. Behan was displeased one day, therefore, when complimented by a friend on the new suit he was wearing. He found a filthy gutter, lay down in it and rolled about until the suit was in a fit state for artistic company.

★ ★ ★ ★ ★

An epic 'Pageant of Saint Patrick' was staged at Croke Park, Dublin in 1953. It culminated with a spectacular scene during which the Patron, played by Anew McMaster, called upon God to destroy Ireland's pagan idols. Papier mâché figures fell in all directions amid fireworks and simulated thunder. This was followed by one of those moments of silence as the audience decides whether applause is appropriate. The hush was broken by Behan's call from the rear of the audience: 'Good auld God!'

★ ★ ★ ★ ★

The English journalist Alan Brien once asked Behan if he ever thought about death. 'Think about death?' repeated Behan, 'Begod, I'd rather be dead than think about death.'

★ ★ ★ ★ ★

During the attempt to arrest the cast of *The Rose Tattoo* (see page 229), Behan found himself a soapbox and delivered a speech decrying the depopulation of the nation while all the government could do was apprehend a harmless group of actors. He sang a satirical ballad, 'The Peeler and the Goat', and, right on cue, the goat used in the play emerged from the stage door of the tiny Pike Theatre. Behan screamed, 'Never mind the goat; bring out the fucking peeler!'

Behan and the sculptor Desmond MacNamara decided to erect a bogus statue, to be called Monsieur Rabelais. It was to have Behan's features, as well as other imaginative touches like artificial bird droppings and mildew. They planned its overnight appearance in St Stephen's Green, Dublin, and laid bets that it would not be noticed. Work was progressing and the head was sculpted from some material which shall never be identified — because Behan was arrested and imprisoned yet again and the practical joke fell through. Some time later, however, MacNamara prevailed on Behan to pose for him in London. The author slept through the sitting — which included a preparatory shave by MacNamara. A completed clay model formed the basis of a papier mâché bust. The substance was compounded from an *Irish Times* serialisation of *The Scarperer*, which was eventually published as a novel, and cuttings of Behan's *Irish Press* humorous column. It was sold at Sotheby's of London in 1992 for £2,800.

When *Borstal Boy* was banned on obscenity grounds in Ireland, its author sang to the air of 'McNamara's Band':

Oh my name is Brendan Behan, I'm the latest of the banned,
Although we're small in number, we're the best banned in the land.
We're read at wakes and weddings and at every parish ball;
And under library counters, you'll have no trouble at all.

★ ★ ★ ★ ★

An extremely affected newspaper columnist passed Behan on Dublin's fashionable Grafton Street.

'Hey head! How is the old writin' goin'?' The columnist pretended not to hear and hurried on, whereupon Behan added, 'Sure that old column is only retailing. You'll make no money until you take up the writing wholesale like me.'

★ ★ ★ ★ ★

TOUCHER (having been refused by Behan): I remember the time when you hadn't a shaggin' farthing to your name.
BEHAN: You don't remember it half as well as I do.

★ ★ ★ ★ ★

Behan wrote, in Brendan Behan's New York:

In Ireland, of course, Saint Patrick's Day is observed as a religious festival, and up until about two years ago, the only place in Dublin where you could get a drink was at the Royal Dublin Society's Dog Show, which is held on that day. I was up there once with two painters, Sean O'Sullivan and Harry Kernoff, for to get a couple of drinks, and we paid our entrance money and mixed around with the Anglo-Irish and the imitation Irish and they'd put years on you with their awful tweedy hats. I think they make their hats from used kilts or something.

★ ★ ★ ★ ★

Behan recalls of the Latin quarter of Paris and its celebrated book-woman, Sylvia Beach:

[Joyce] sent a play of his, called *Exiles*, to the Théâtre de l'Oeuvre but it was returned to him. 'Mr Joyce,' the rejection slip read, 'we have just fought a World War and there are a lot of widows and orphans as a result. We think your play a bit too sad.'

'I suppose I should have given Richard a cork leg to jolly things up a bit,' Joyce remarked to Sylvia Beach, and he put the play aside and went on writing *Ulysses* which he had nearly finished.

Now I think that a bit of jollying-up does no harm, so I have decided to call my next play *Richard's Cork Leg*.

Writing about Micheál macLiammóir, Behan delivers an aside:

While I am on the subject of Michael macLiammoir, my mother was sent by my granny, one time, for a ninepenny pig's cheek. Such a thing at the price was not easily come by, even twenty-five years ago. But anyway, in the heels of the reels, Mr Hugh Melinn of Dorset Street, as then was, dug up a cheek which he was willing to part with at the price mentioned.

The poor cheek had been squeezed up against the side of the barrel, which twisted his jaw and gave his one eye a most alarming squint.

My mother looked at it for a moment and ventured to say to the shopman, 'Mr Hugh, that's a very peculiar looking cheek.'

'And what,' asks Mr Hugh, 'do you expect for ninepence — MeHail Mock Lallamore?'

★ ★ ★ ★ ★

Behan was approached by a Munster man who claimed to have been in the same IRA brigade as the author. Behan did not recognise him, however, and glowered at him before dismissing him with: 'The only brigade you would be fit for is the fire brigade.'

★ ★ ★ ★ ★

Visiting the public house of raconteur Kruger Kavanagh in Dunquin, Co. Kerry, Behan was shown the owner's collection of autographed photographs, mostly of Kruger shaking hands with some celebrity. In boastful tones, Kavanagh pointed out one signed 'To Kruger, from Mae West' and another 'To Kruger from Jack Dempsey', others 'To Kruger with love, Greta Garbo', 'To Kruger with affection, Myrna Loy', and so on.

Behan became bored, finished his drink and took his leave. As he neared the door, he took a pen from his pocket and scrawled across a picture of the Sacred Heart: 'To Kruger, from Jaysus'.

Behan liked to tell of an aunt who lived by the canal bank and invited friends to 'Drop in any time you're passing.'

★ ★ ★ ★ ★

The memory of Brendan Behan deserves another type of anecdote. Walking with a friend one day, he left him on the footpath saying he wished to visit somebody and would not be long. After a considerable wait, the friend made his way into the house that Behan had entered. There he was, weeping and singing softly to an old lady who was dying. When they left the house, Behan hammered on the wall with his fists and shouted, 'Why should a bollocks like me be left alive and a good woman like that die?'

★ ★ ★ ★ ★

Micheál macLiammóir told a strange story about Behan's demise:

We were never bosom friends, and that makes my behaviour on a certain night in Australia all the more inexplicable. From the moment of arrival at the airport in Sydney where my tour of 'The Importance of Being Oscar' and 'I Must be Talking to my Friends' began, I had been asked about [Behan] and once or twice had made some remark of a lightly snappish nature from the sheer monotony of hearing so many questions on the same subject. One evening, just before my opening performance, there was one of those radio or television interviews inseparable from an actor's life on tour, and for some reason unknown and unexplained I began to talk of Brendan as I had never done in my life. It was very curious. I heard my voice saying things that were perfectly sincere yet that came from a source of which I seemed to know nothing at all: it was as though I were listening to the voice and words of somebody else. When at last the interview was over my manager, Brian Tobin, said to me: 'I never realised before how much you liked and admired Brendan: anybody listening to you tonight would think he was your ideal writer as well as your dearest friend. What in God's name came over you?'

I could not tell him. I did not understand myself. I still do not understand. All I know was that on the following day the news of Brendan's death was in the newspapers and on every radio in the country. We made careful calculations in the differences of time between Dublin and Sydney. Brendan had died at the moment I was pouring out my panegyric to the air.

CRITICS ARE LIKE EUNUCHS IN A HAREM. THEY'RE THERE EVERY NIGHT, THEY SEE IT DONE EVERY NIGHT, THEY SEE HOW IT SHOULD BE DONE EVERY NIGHT, BUT THEY CAN'T DO IT THEMSELVES
Brendan Behan

★ ★ ★ ★ ★

PADRAIC COLUM 1881–1972

Padraic Colum was born in Longford, but was reared on his grandfather's farm in Cavan. He moved to Dublin when his father, a former Master of the Workhouse, became stationmaster at Sandycove. Setting out to educate himself, he was soon described by George Russell (AE) as 'a rough jewel . . . but a real one'. A play, Broken Soil, *was his first literary achievement of note. At about thirty years of age he wrote his popular lyrics 'She Moved Through the Fair' and 'A Cradle Song'. Somewhat too innocent for the Dublin literary circle, he appears to have been the butt of jokes among his contemporaries. He and his wife, Mary (née Maguire), moved to the USA in 1914, where they both lectured in comparative literature at Columbia University. His writing turned to Irish and Hawaiian folklore, but he still wrote poetry. Eamon de Valera urged him to remain in the United States, reasoning that the presence there of Irish writers was more important than visits from politicians.*

He visited Dublin frequently, however. Patricia Boylan described him as having many graces but no airs:

'If he knew that sex and snobbery are the most telling agents in advertising one's wares he gave no sign. He had no mistresses. He never sought the society of the rich and powerful as they sought his. There was a kind of incandescent innocence about him untouched by his intimacy with such sophisticates as Yeats, Lady Gregory, Joyce and many more. He was in Dublin in 1959 for the publication of his biography of Arthur Griffith, Ourselves Alone *[New York]. In 1987 a prominent member of the [United Arts] Club asked, "Who is Padraic Colum?" He was President of the Club from 1959 until he died in 1972, if anyone else should ask.'*

Colum died in Enfield, Connecticut and is buried in Sutton, Co. Dublin.

★ ★ ★ ★ ★

Micheál macLiammóir attended a theatre party at which a lady called Lulu was prominent. MacLiammóir thinks it may have been Colum's party. He was certainly there:

It was exactly like the rest. It might have stepped out of the pages of any writer from Apuleius to Victor Margueritte, and it was only perhaps a little more fantastic than any of the others because of Lulu.

Lulu had been for a long while what one can only describe as a grimly determined mascot to the theatre. She was a youthful female of uncertain height and colouring, she had large pale wandering eyes and she hailed originally from England, where . . . someone must have said to her: 'Now, Lulu, you are not particularly beautiful or particularly brilliant, are you? But, my dear, we can all be *something* in this sad old life. We can all do something to make others happy. Do you know what you can do? Why, just smile! Smile away, Lulu, and you will find that everywhere you go there'll be a smile for you too.'

This, or something similar, must at some time have been said to her. For Lulu smiled all the time. She never stopped smiling at all. Not even when Meriel [Moore, the actress] said, 'Oh, stop fawning on me, you silly bitch!' She just went on smiling. Nor was the smile the end of Lulu. No; Lulu had been told to be helpful too. And kind. And always cheerful. So whenever any one was tired or cross, there was Lulu with her wandering oyster-coloured eyes, her can-I-help-you look, and her smile; ready with a cup of tea, a cigarette, a cushion from the prop room. And her offerings were invariably accepted. As a natural consequence every one wanted to strangle Lulu.

'*Will* you get rid of her,' Coralie [Carmichael] or Meriel, supported by the entire cast, would beg, and Hilton would say, 'Look here, Lulu, you've been walking on for nearly a year now — isn't it?' (No one could remember when Lulu first appeared. My own opinion is that she never came at all, we gradually perceived that she was in the building.) 'Yes, for at least a year,' he would continue, 'and we don't pay you any money, do we? And it's really rather silly, isn't it, as there are no parts going! So as you're not even walking on in this play, don't you think . . . ahem . . . well, that you . . . you see what I mean.'

'You silly old thing,' Lulu would say in her high, dry little voice, 'you know you don't mean a word of all that,' and she would sidle rapidly away and presently another cup of tea, perhaps with an aspirin or two placed with hideous tact in the spoon, would appear from a shadowy doorway, and the parched, rattling voice would say cheerfully, 'There! That's what the Big Tired Man wants, isn't it?'

Lulu, on this night of the party, was getting drunk. This was a new departure for her: was she not for ever associated in our minds with cups of tea and maybe a biscuit in the saucer getting slowly sodden as the tea splashed over the inside in her eager journeyings to and fro? It was cruel to make her drink. Poor Lulu. There was Edward Longford with brandy in one hand and champagne in the other, while Lulu, having consumed a vast amount of stout and whisky in a corner, leapt smilingly up and down in front of him, holding out a thick tumbler and begging for more like a fox terrier.

'Oh, Edward, do be a sport,' she was rattling, 'do give me some more. I'm awfully funny when I'm tight — I am really! Not,' she continued, glancing back over her shoulder like a bedraggled Emma Hamilton, 'that any one could *make* me tight; no. My head's as clear as a bell. You ask any one. Oh, lovely!' as Edward yielded and the tumbler slopped over and she threw back her head and gulped and coughed and screwed up her eyes. 'Oo! Pardon! Of course I know nobody thinks much of me here, but some one awfully brainy told me once I was just like Nefertiti. You know, the Egyptian one with the long neck and the pot on her head; oh, Edward, do give me your carnation; well, I shall take it, so there; how does it look behind my ear? Do I look Spanish, Edward? Oo! Pardon! . . . '

'It's Lulu,' crowed Edward with immense enthusiasm as if it had been Baronova [Irina, dancer] at least, 'she's now completely out of her mind!' And he leaned his elbows on the stage — there is no orchestra pit at the Gate — and began to accompany her with his favourite song:

Keep them off: they're coming through the window!
Keep them off: they're coming through the door!
Keep them off: they're coming down the chimney!
Oh, my God! They're coming through the floor!

'Lovely party, Mr Colum,' Christine was murmuring to the poet. 'Lovely! No one has been sick at all yet. Mmm! That's so rare, isn't it?'

'When I was in Galway last summer,' Colum said, his eyes fixed on Lulu's corybantics under the changing lights, 'I heard a man say that all his friends and relations had died on him and he'd been put out of his house, and there was nothing left to him now but a young goat and the Son of God. Isn't that very nice, now? I was thinking the young lady there seemed to be much in the same plight.'

'And she hasn't even got a goat,' shouted Edward, now completely beside himself, and Coralie muttered, 'Never mind, she's got every one else's,' and then a pallid young man whose business was to control tickets at the top of the stairs was overcome with emotion and mixed liquor and had to be borne away by the scene-shifters to the nearest tap. Christine said, 'Oh dear, someone's going to be sick and it isn't Lulu; pity, mm!' And after that we all began to encourage Lulu's bacchic frenzy until she collapsed on the edge of the stage. She lay there, seemingly happy and reciting as she waved her arms:

Fairies skip hence!
I have foresworn his bed and company.

★

MacLiammóir is amusing in his assessment of Colum's reaction to the wild spree:

I remember agreeing with many hilarious and shadowy figures afterwards, all of us in that stage where reason and affection have merged life's difficulties into one blinding radiance, how terribly nice a man he must have been, how far above our own meanness and lowness, how unspotted by the world, to say, as he had continually said throughout the evening, 'A more charming lot of boys and girls I've never met in my life. Look at them! Not one rotten face among them. Congratulations, Hilton and Micheal. A more delightful set of people I never met. Never.'

In reality we were not at all charming or delightful at that party; but Colum, the poet of *Wild Earth*, had eyes perhaps that saw through or beyond all the wretched fabric of pretence and hysteria and futility that spreads itself inevitably over such evenings. They have been described in such good English by Aldous Huxley, Noel Langlye, Ivor Novello, M.J. Farrell, Beverley Nichols, Mary Manning, and a hundred more; these parties of overworked people where no one is really happy or really wise or even really young, and who gather together for no particular reason.

✹ ✹ ✹ ✹ ✹

The late Stan Gébler Davies, in his biography of Joyce, tells:

Joyce astonished Colum by coming to him with a project to start a new daily newspaper for Dublin, to be published, on the continental model, in the afternoon. He had precisely calculated not only the exact cost of the project (£2,000, a fantastic sum, it seemed to Colum. Indeed it was), but the format and the tone of the articles which would appear (in return for [Francis, later Sheehy] Skeffington's co-operation he had agreed to some Socialist and Feminist content). More, he had registered (or claimed to have registered) the name of the newspaper, not that anyone was likely to appropriate it. He wanted it called *The Goblin*.

Colum's part in the scheme was to put Joyce in touch with moneyed people. Alas, said Colum, he knew no one with money. Well then, said Joyce, who knew better, did he know any Jews? Jews had money. [Colum remarked how it was strange] 'that the creator of the most outstanding Jew in modern literature did not at that time know any of the Jewish community in Dublin'.

✳

Later on in his work, Gébler Davies writes:

Colum did know two Jews, brothers called Sinclair who had an antique shop in Nassau Street and were considered intellectuals. He took Joyce along to meet them. One was present. What he thought of this remarkable overture is not recorded but evidently he did not have £2,000 to spare, or, if he did, did not care to part with it. He must have been civil because he gets a favourable mention in *Ulysses*, when Bloom contemplates a visit to his co-religionist, 'a well-mannered fellow'.

Joyce was aware that Colum did have a patron, an American millionaire called Thomas Kelly, resident at Celbridge in County Kildare, who had undertaken to subsidize Colum's existence for three years while Colum, after the example of Synge, studied the aboriginals of the true Ireland and wrote about them. Kelly, in return for this generosity, was to have title to the American copyright of all masterpieces subsequently produced by Colum. Joyce having prised Kelly's address out of Colum made the fourteen-mile trek to Celbridge, unannounced, and was told to go away by Kelly's lodge-keeper. He trudged back through the December night to Cabra, turning up in rather a bad mood.

✳ ✳ ✳ ✳ ✳

On 7 January 1932, Joseph Holloway attended a performance of Mogu of the Desert *at the Gate Theatre. He writes in his diary:*

I was speaking to Padraic Colum in the interval between Acts 2 and 3. He imagines the transposition of Scenes 1 and 2 of Act 2 would make a better ending to the Act, and I agreed with him. He asked me if I heard the players well, and I said, 'For the most time, yes, but Edwards and Welles are inclined to mumble their words frequently. They should take Stephenson's crystal clear enunciation in speaking and singing as an example and guide . . . ' And Colum replied, 'But Stephenson has been taught by Frank Fay, and that accounts for his clearness of utterance . . . .'

I told him I had been reading his articles on Joyce's child-gibberish, later work, and also his article on Roger Casement which latter I thought very well done.

'I was pleased to write that,' he said. 'I wrote it for an American magazine and had it simultaneously printed here.'

I said, 'It is a waste of time for you to try to explain what Joyce is driving at. It is like the ravings of a mad man. Joyce . . . can write good English; why turn to such idle chatter of incomprehensible matter?'

Colum thought Joyce derived beauty in his description of the river. 'It is an experiment, but I fear few will worry to make it out.'

'Why should they?' I queried, 'when people have so much fine writing to read?'

TREAD SOFTLY, SOFTLY,
O! MEN COMING IN
Padraic Colum

★ ★ ★ ★ ★

MARIA
EDGEWORTH
1767–1849

Born and educated in England, Maria Edgeworth came to Longford at the age of fifteen. Her father, Richard Lovell Edgeworth, is said to have installed the first central-heating system in Ireland at Pakenham Hall, near Castlepollard, Co. Westmeath. Maria co-operated with him in a number of writing projects. A family manuscript, which became known as 'The Black Book of Edgeworthstown', was written mainly by her father, but Maria took over the work at an advanced stage. The book reflects on the life of Richard Lovell and his cousin Abbé Edgeworth, who was confessor to Madame Elizabeth of France. (The Abbé took the name deFirmont when he found that the French were unable to cope with the phonetics of Edgeworth!) The Black Book of Edgeworthstown and Other Edgeworth Memories 1587–1817 *was later published in London by Faber & Gwyer.*

In 1796 Edgeworth began her literary career with Letters to Literary Ladies. *The following year* The Parent's Assistant *appeared and in 1798 she and her father co-wrote* Practical Education, *which, according to her stepmother, 'was praised and abused enough to make the authors immediately famous'. Edgeworth defended women's rights to education and some of her work was burdened with moralising. She deplored absentee landlords and in later life, when managing her brother's estate, protected tenants from him and educated their children. Sir Walter Scott credited her with inspiring his historical novels.*

✯ ✯ ✯ ✯ ✯

In one section of The Black Book of Edgeworthstown, *Edgeworth gives an anecdotal account of a significant period in Irish history:*

The French, who landed at Killala, were on the march toward Longford. The touch of Ithuriel's spear could not have been more effectual than the arrival of this intelligence in showing people in their real forms. In some faces joy struggled for a moment with feigned sorrow and then, encouraged by sympathy, yielded to the natural expression. Still my father had no reason to distrust those in whom he had placed confidence; his tenants were steady; he saw no change in any of the men of his corps, though they were in the most perilous situation, having rendered themselves obnoxious to rebels by becoming yeomen, and yet standing without means of defence, their arms not having arrived.

The evening of the day when the news of [their] approach came to Edgeworthstown, all seemed quiet. But early the next morning, September 4, a report reached us that the rebels were up in arms within a mile of the village, pouring in from West Meath [*sic*], hundreds strong. We could not at first believe the report. An hour afterwards it was contradicted. An English servant, who was sent out to ascertain the truth, brought back word that he had ridden three miles from the village . . . and that he had seen only twenty or thirty men with green boughs in their hats and pikes in their hands, who said they were standing there to protect themselves against the Orangemen, who were coming down to cut them to pieces.

★

Edgeworth goes on to relate how her father got a despatch to the commanding officer of the garrison in Longford requesting help, and how an officer in charge of an ammunition escort arrived, offering protection if the family wished to evacuate to Longford. They declined — fortunately for them:

About a quarter of an hour after the officer and the escort had departed, we, who were all assembled in the portico of the house, heard a report like a loud clap of thunder. The doors and windows shook, and a few minutes afterwards the officer galloped into the yard and threw himself off his horse into my father's arms almost senseless. The ammunition cart had blown up, one of the officers had been severely wounded, and the horses and the man leading them killed; the wounded officer was at a farm-house on the Longford Road at about two miles distance. Mrs Edgeworth went immediately to give her assistance; she left her carriage for the use of the wounded gentleman, and rode back. At the entrance of the village she was stopped by a gentleman in great terror who, taking hold of the bridle of her horse, begged her not to attempt to go further, assuring her that the rebels were coming into town. But she answered that she must and would return to her family. She rode on and found us waiting anxiously for her. No assistance could be afforded from Longford; the rebels were reassembling and advancing towards the village, and there was no alternative but to leave our home as fast as possible. As we passed through the village, we heard nothing but the entreaties, lamentations and objurgations of those who could not procure the means of carrying off their goods or their families; most painful when we could give no assistance.

Richard Lovell Edgeworth was eccentric and, on being introduced to someone, invariably began conversation by offering a potted autobiography. Maria's embarrassment was acute on one occasion when he said to another, in her presence:

Now, Sir, you know the great Mister Edgeworth and you may possibly wish to know something of his birth, parentage and education. I shall first give you my reasons for being an Englishman, and I shall leave you your choice to call me which you please. I was born in England; I married two English wives; I have several children, who were born in England. Now for my reasons for being an Irishman: I married three Irish wives; I have a large estate in Ireland; I have a number of Irish children; my progenitors were Irish; and I have lived most of my life in Ireland. Sir, I am a man who despises vulgar prejudice; for two of my wives are alive and two, who are dead, were sisters.

✲

In The Black Book, *there is an account of how Maria was staying with her aunt, Mrs Ruxton, when she received the first copies of* Castle Rackrent *(1800). She tore out the title pages of one copy and gave the rest to her aunt:*

Her aunt read it without the least suspicion of who was the author and, excessively entertained and delighted, she insisted on Maria's listening to passage after passage as she went on. Maria affected to be deeply interested in some book she held in her hand, and when Mrs Ruxton exclaimed, 'Is not that admirably written?' Maria coldly replied, 'Admirably read, I think.' And then her aunt, as if she had said too much, added, 'It may not be so very good, but it shows just the sort of knowledge of high life which people have who live in this world.' Then again and again she called upon Maria for sympathy, till quite provoked by her faint acquiescence, she at last accused her of being envious and unable to endure the praises of a rival author.

★ ★ ★ ★ ★

Maria was well thought of by her father. Richard Lovell Edgeworth wrote a memorandum before his death which was never intended for publication. Early on 9 June 1817, he called Maria and her sisters Harriet and Fanny to his bedside and advised from it:

When I die, you, Maria, will be left in excellent circumstances. You will be rich. You have many brothers and sisters and friends, who may each in their turn have claims upon you. You will want to give away your fortune, first to one, then to another — you will give the same sum twice over and forget you have given it, and wonder you have it not still. One of your sisters is going to be married! to a captain of dragoons. He wants a thousand pounds to buy a commission. Oh! you'll give it. She is married — has children — is in distress — there's an end of your thousand — or a house is to be bought and like — it is to be sold again for half its value, and there's an end to your gift. Therefore I entreat that you will never, to oblige any human being, part with any of the principal of your fortune . . . on my dying bed I entreat you not to squander away your property on whoever at the moment you may think may want it. Always have a will and never have the meanness to give any of your relations the hope that you will leave them anything.

★ ★ ★ ★ ★

In these days of word processors, bytes and floppy disks, it is interesting to read how Maria Edgeworth went about her writing:

She wrote almost always in the library undisturbed by the noise of the large family around her, and for many years on a little desk her father had made for her. She afterwards used a writing-desk which had been her father's, placed on a little table of his construction, to which she had attached many ingenious contrivances — a bracket for her candle-stick, a fire-screen and places for her papers. She wrote on folio sheets of paper, which she sewed together in chapters. To facilitate the calculation of the MS. for printing, and to secure each page containing nearly the same amount of writing, she used to prick the margin of her paper at equal distances, and her father made a little machine set with points by which she could pierce several sheets at once. A full sketch of the story she was about to write was always required by her father when she began it, and though often much changed in its progress, the foundation and purpose remained as originally planned. She rose early and, after taking a cup of coffee and reading her letters, walked out till breakfast time, a meal she always enjoyed especially (though she ate scarcely anything); she delighted to read out and talk over her letters, and listened a little to the newspapers; but she was no politician . . . . She generally sat down at her desk soon after breakfast and wrote till luncheon-time, after which she did some needlework, often unwillingly when eager about her letters or MSS., but obediently as she had found writing directly after eating bad for her.

★ ★ ★ ★ ★

In Essay on Irish Bulls *(1802), Maria and her father describe the subject phenomenon as 'A laughable confusion of ideas'. They relate an example, 'Paddy Blake's Bull':*

When Paddy heard an English gentleman speaking of the fine echo at the lake of Killarney, which repeats the sound forty times, he very promptly observed — 'A Faith that's nothing at all to the echo in my father's garden, in the county of Galway; if you say to it — 'How do you do, Paddy Blake?' it will answer, 'Pretty well, I thank you sir.'

Thomas Babington Macaulay visited Killarney in 1849. He disliked riding, but found that access to the most scenic views was by pony and by boat. One of four oarsmen boasted about rowing Sir Walter Scott and Maria Edgeworth on the same day many years before. That was an honour, he said, even if he did miss a public hanging on its account.

✴ ✴ ✴ ✴ ✴

OUR IRISH BLUNDERS ARE NEVER BLUNDERS OF THE
HEART
Maria Edgeworth

✴ ✴ ✴ ✴ ✴

HILTON
EDWARDS
1903–1982

(See also 'Micheál macLiammóir' and 'The Gate Theatre'.)

★ ★ ★ ★ ★

Although London-born, Hilton Robert Edwards must be included in any book of Irish literary anecdotes. At seventeen years of age he toured Ireland with the Doran Shakespearian Company. Back in England, he acted with the Old Vic and sang with its Opera Company. He returned to Ireland in 1927 and never left. He and Micheál macLiammóir were both members of Anew McMaster's touring company. Their initial working partnership was in Galway, where Liam Ó Briain invited the pair to become involved in the new Taibhdhearc na Gaillimhe, the only permanent Irish-language theatre in the country. Ó Briain and others founded the theatre in 1928 and macLiammóir's drama Diarmuid agus Grainne *was its first production. Edwards directed, although he had no comprehension of the language.*

The two men decided upon a theatrical alliance and produced Peer Gynt *at the Peacock Theatre, Dublin a year after they had met. Two years later they moved to the Gate Theatre, where Edwards' directional and lighting techniques brought a new dynamism to the classics and invigoration to tired audiences. The partnership flourished and blossomed into an intimate personal relationship. The pair could be seen sitting inside the entrance to the Gate auditorium on first nights, chatting with members of the audience during the interval and after the show. Edwards also spent a period as Head of Drama in Radio Telefís Éireann.*

He told me once that his favourite role was Broadbent in John Bull's Other Island, *and his least that of Tranio in* The Taming of the Shrew, *a part for which he was selected by McMaster. He also disliked playing 'the man who exits, chased by a bear, in* The Winter's Tale' *(Antigonus).*

★ ★ ★ ★ ★

Micheál macLiammóir was painting in the Gate scene-dock one day when Edwards called him up to meet a young man who had arrived looking for work. Micheál came and saw waiting there a tall, stout youth who claimed to have acted with New York's Guild Theatre, written a play and toured as a sword-swallowing female impersonator. It was Orson Welles. He wanted to demonstrate his worth, so Edwards offered a copy of *Jew Süss*, a play by Ashley Dukes, based on a novel by Lion Feuchtwanger. It was scheduled to open at the Gate the following month.

The aspirant was told to read the part of the Duke. He begged to be allowed to read Naomi instead, but Edwards was adamant — the Duke or nothing!

MacLiammóir described what followed as one of the strangest sights he had ever witnessed. Welles hurled a chair across the stage, then a table and some of the stage décor; some books and cushions were flung about too, before he demanded more lighting (he had got none!). It was an astonishing performance, 'wrong from beginning to end but with all the qualities of fine acting tearing their way through a chaos of inexperience'.

Edwards called him down from the stage.

'Terrible, wasn't it?' Welles ventured.

'Yes, bloody awful, but you can have the part.'

Edwards offered advice, of course. He offered money too, but Welles said he merely wanted his tram fare. Edwards told him he was an extraordinary young man and Welles agreed but added that Ireland was an extraordinary country and playing the Duke in *Jew Süss* at the Gate was reward enough for him.

⋆ ⋆ ⋆ ⋆ ⋆

On their second Egyptian tour, Edwards and macLiammóir had a hashish-smoking adventure with Anew McMaster. The trio joined a group of students in a turquoise-lit den in Heliopolis, the ancient centre of sun-worship. They sat for a night eating fruit, drinking wine and chain-smoking the doped cigarettes. Nothing happened!

At one stage, macLiammóir leaned over to Edwards, told him he felt as if he were sinking through the sofa and wondered if that suggested anything. Edwards said it suggested that it was getting 'bloody late' and that they were all too well fed for the hashish to have any effect.

✵ ✵ ✵ ✵ ✵

The Edwards-macLiammóir Company enthused about their stay in Athens. They loved the Royal Theatre and its superb staff, equipment and design. They were charmed by the city's flower-sellers and by the hospitality of its citizens. Splendid parties were thrown in their honour at embassies; more were hosted by friends; each was marvellously enjoyable. Despite all this, one actor was continually complaining about his hotel room. Edwards responded acerbically, 'The poor fellow is not at all happy with his room. I don't wonder. Indeed, something will have to be done. Why, all he's got is the usual furniture and a view of the Acropolis! It's outrageous!'

✵ ✵ ✵ ✵ ✵

Informed that a certain theatre critic's wife had given birth, Hilton Edwards remarked, 'I don't believe it. All that fellow ever gave anybody was a bad notice.'

✵ ✵ ✵ ✵ ✵

NEEDLE-SHARP WIT THAT WOULD LAY A DRAGON LOW
Hilton Edwards

✵ ✵ ✵ ✵ ✵

WILLIAM PERCY FRENCH 1854–1920

'I was born a boy and remained one ever since,' said Percy French, a likeable rascal who lived his sentiment to the fullest. His place of birth was Clooneyquin, Co. Roscommon and he was educated at Windermere College and Foyle College before attending Trinity College Dublin. French wrote satirical sketches, prose and songs. His second love was painting and he combined this considerable talent with his stagecraft; he played the banjo and painted as he performed. Indeed, he had a singular facility whereby he would turn a completed picture about to give an altogether different impression. While still a student, he wrote the popular songs 'Abdulla Bulbul Ameer' and 'The Mountains of Mourne'.

Graduating in civil engineering, French got a surveyor's appointment in County Cavan. This was immortalised in his hilarious monologue 'William, Inspector of Drains'.

French married, but after just a year of bliss his young wife, whom he loved dearly, and her newborn infant died. He overcame the tragedy and embarked on a solo career, featuring his well-known numbers 'Phil the Fluter's Ball', 'Come Back, Paddy Reilly' and 'Slattery's Mounted Foot'.

A favourite sideshow at race meetings was his Christie Minstrel-type presentation. Included in this line-up was Charles Manseragh, a Tipperaryman who later married the singer Fanny Moody. Charles changed his name to Manners, and with Fanny founded the Moody-Manners Light Opera Company. Mozart, Verdi or Wagner had no place in the banjo-and-bones repertoire of French and Manners when they conceived their stage act and launched it in an unusual situation.

They commandeered a waiting-room at Kingsbridge (now Heuston) railway station, Dublin on a summer morning in 1881. There they blackened their faces with burnt cork, donned Christie Minstrel waistcoats and boaters and dashed out to board an excursion train bound for Punchestown Races. In retrospect, Charles Manners gave a good account of the day, but French claimed that their act was badly received on the train *because they did not include any music-hall numbers. Their reception at the racecourse was little better; they were told that their presentation was vulgar beyond words. Disillusioned, they retired behind the regulation fence and washed off their make-up, before returning to Naas to spend their day's takings — eightpence! French moved to London in 1890 and died in Lancashire.*

★ ★ ★ ★ ★

Happy, frivolous, lively — these are the adjectives which spring to mind whenever the name of Percy French is mentioned. But, given his philosophy of having been 'born a boy' and remaining one ever since, it is worth considering his behaviour on one occasion as a child when his father called him 'Fatty' in front of a house guest. The lad stamped out of the room, seized his wooden seaside shovel and disappeared into a laurel grove. He was planning the murder of his father!

Beneath a fine Portugal laurel he constructed a sort of bear-trap to capture and kill his name-calling parent. A sharpened stick rammed into its centre would impale the victim when he stepped into it. Mr French did not die by his son's hand — because nobody but a small boy could use the narrow route across which the trap was laid; and furthermore, the pit was only a few inches deep.

★ ★ ★ ★ ★

One French song with a refrain, 'Are you right there, Michael?', ridiculed the narrow-gauge West Clare Railway and led to a libel action. When he arrived late for the hearing, French is alleged to have apologised by saying, 'I travelled by the West Clare, Your Lordship!'

★ ★ ★ ★ ★

Once, when burning old pictures from his painting act in the yard of Armagh's City Hall, French was helped by a boy who had seen his show. 'How much did you pay?' asked French. The boy told him he had paid a shilling, but there were seats at two and three shillings also. 'Robbery,' said French, 'for listening to and watching an old man amusing himself.'

★ ★ ★ ★ ★

French wrote about a 'boots' (shoeshine) called Finnegan:

When an artist goes to the West of Ireland, there is often trouble in getting a suitable place to stay in. There are lodgings that advertise bed and board for five shillings, but you can't tell very often which is the bed and which is the board.

Generally, I put in a night at Peter Finnegan's Hotel. Peter is an important man in the locality, and a great friend of mine, and though his four-poster bed is really a tripod, and wants the least taste of the window sill to make it a permanent structure, and though by long usage the hens have established a right of way through the coffee room, these little drawbacks count for nothing; for Peter to me is a permanent joy.

'Did you ever remark,' he said to me one day, 'that the three best drinks are in one syllable? Well, it's a fact — port, clar't, and sp'rits.'

We were looking out of the window at a new house being built, when Peter commented:

'Twould be a great addition to that house, if that gable was taken away.'

He certainly has a quaint way of putting things.

Finnegan runs the hotel on lines of his own. The bells generally don't work; if you want to attract attention you have to go out and throw your hat at them. An English visitor, having at last secured a reply, asked for some water.

'There is no carafe in my room,' he said, 'no water bottle.'

'Well now,' commented Finnegan, 'and I always thought a giraffe was a bird.'

The same visitor had trouble the next morning with the boots.

'Look at my shoes,' he said. 'I put them out last night, and nobody has touched them.'

'That's the sort of hotel we keep,' was the answer. 'Ye might put yer gold watch outside, and nobody would touch it!'

French played for and met with royalty, but took it all in his stride. He said that since their remarks consisted of 'Thank you . . . we have enjoyed ourselves . . . oh really, Mr French, that last sketch was just too, too clever' and the like, he didn't think such polite platitudes worth recording.

'But these great people', said French, 'do not consult me about the balance of power or the choice of a career, so I devote my writing to the people I have met and really conversed with.'

THERE'S GANGS OF THEM DIGGING FOR GOLD IN THE
STREET
Percy French

THE
GATE
THEATRE

Dublin's chief maternity hospital, the Rotunda, is one of the oldest lying-in hospitals in the world (1757). It was founded by Dr Bartholomew Mosse, its first master, who carried out improvements to its grounds. There he organised concerts, recitals and other entertainments that helped to swell the almoner's coffers. Other buildings were added over the years and were put to various uses. In the 1950s there was the Ballerina Ballroom, one of the many in Ireland where the devil was said to have appeared! Then the Ambassador Cinema arrived.

By 1930 the part of the complex known as the Assembly Rooms had become the Dublin Gate Theatre, but the main portion of the building is still a maternity hospital.

★ ★ ★ ★ ★

John Cowell tells of a Gate tour:

A Shakespeare play was included, [and] a matinée was held for the children of Limerick, and Christine [Lady Longford] allowed herself to be goaded into one of her rashly defensive actions on behalf of dear Edward. A mob of impatient children was banging on a side door waiting for admittance to the cheap seats. Eventually, their patience exhausted, they took to shouting through the chinks: 'Fuck off, Lord Longford, you can fuck off, Lord Longford.' From inside Christine heard the insults and her blood boiled. Flinging the door wide open, she shouted as she pursued the fleeing youngsters, 'And you fuck off too.' At a safe distance they stopped, rooted to the ground as they watched her retreat into the hall. Never had they heard *that word* spoken so beautifully.

Theatre critic John Finegan recalls a wartime incident:

The date was November 1940 when the Nazi armies were in control of much of Western Europe and Hitler's dream of world domination seemed almost a possibility. [Lennox] Robinson, a master of theatre-craft, had taken his plot from a short story by the French novelist, Guy de Maupassant, called 'Boule de Suif', which can be translated as 'Ball of Fat', or 'Roly Poly'.

The French writer set his scene at the time of the Franco-Prussian war of 1870 and his story involved a group of French people endeavouring to get from German-occupied Rouen to French-occupied Dieppe. On the journey the coach ran into a German contingent, with a young officer in charge. The officer took an immediate fancy to one of the passengers in the coach, a girl who happened to be a well-known prostitute in Rouen. It was made plain to the passengers that the coach would be allowed to continue on its journey only if the girl agreed to spend the night with the officer. At first quite unwilling, the girl, for the sake and safety of her fellow travellers, agreed to the officer's request. Next morning, however, as the coach was waved on by the Germans, the girl was hypocritically shunned by her fellow passengers.

With great daring Robinson set his play in 1940, in June of that year, when the Nazis overran France. Robinson had his French folk going by bus from Rouen to Bordeaux on route to England when they were halted by a German unit at Tours. The play thus had a blazing topicality, coming as it did less than five months after the events it set out to portray.

The first night was Tuesday November 19. It was, as I recall, one of the most exciting premieres in the Irish Theatre. Hilton Edwards directed a notable cast, with Shelah Richards as the prostitute, Tom St John Barry as the German officer, and with Christopher Casson, Coralie Carmichael, Meriel Moore, Liam Gaffney, Robert Hennessy and Roy Irving and Hilton himself as the French travellers.

The Gate was packed to the doors and the audience, thrilled to the marrow, gave the play a rapturous reception.

Next day in the *Evening Herald* I said I thought *Roly Poly* was one of the best plays by Robinson, and that Shelah Richards's portrayal was gripping. My fellow critics at the time, including Brinsley MacNamara, agreed with me.

Roly Poly seemed set for a long and prosperous run. However, when the German and German-controlled Vichy French diplomatic mission in Dublin read the reviews, they were not at all pleased. Quite the contrary. Representatives from both legations (as they then were) hurried to the Gate for the second performance to assess the play. Less than an hour after the fall of the curtain, strong protests were lodged with the Government of de Valera maintaining that Robinson and his play had violated Irish neutrality. The following day, Thursday, the Government ordered *Roly Poly* to be withdrawn, so, as was stated, to protect Irish neutrality during a highly critical phase of the war.

That night the audience had already assembled for the third performance when the banning order arrived in the theatre. An official from the Ministry for Justice went backstage and warned the author, director and cast that the play must not go on. Detectives were on hand to ensure that the order was obeyed.

Hilton Edwards came before the curtain, saying he regretted it would not be possible to stage *Roly Poly* that evening. He was followed by Micheál macLiammóir, who told the dumbfounded audience that all the money paid would be refunded. The theatre quivered with excitement. However, Lennox Robinson, ever resourceful, was not to be defeated. After a heavy pause he advanced to the centre of the stage to declare that the performance would go on that night. 'Keep your seats!' he proclaimed. 'I have bought out the house. You are all my guests for this evening. *Roly Poly* goes on.'

And it did, twenty minutes later than advertised, and to even greater applause than was heard on the first night. The performance was, in effect, free and private, and the detectives — and the protesting legations — were rendered powerless for that one night.

The character Robert Emmet is wounded in the opening act of Denis Johnston's *The Old Lady Says 'No!'*. Whenever Hilton Edwards was in the cast, usually as Major Sirr, he would move forward to the apron and ask if there was a doctor in the house to deal with the accident.

The directional ploy was suspected in another 1944 Gate play, *Death Takes a Holiday*, when Micheál macLiammóir collapsed as a result of a burst blood-vessel which followed a tooth extraction earlier in the day. Playing the part of Death, with black cloak and mask, he was telling Duke Lamberto of his plan to take a holiday in order to cogitate on why he was so hated by people. Liam Gaffney, as the duke, was amazed when he noticed the great actor was unsure of his lines and flabbergasted when macLiammóir collapsed at his feet. Gaffney called for the curtain. A few minutes later, Hilton Edwards faced the audience and assured them that this was not another gimmick. He begged their pardon while he himself read his partner's lines for the remainder of the performance. Despite the name, 'Death' is a romantic role and Edwards never played such parts. At the end, he jokingly told the audience: 'Wait till you see my Romeo!'

★ ★ ★ ★ ★

On the opening night of a Gate Theatre production of *Lady Windermere's Fan* on 20 March 1973, Patrick Bedford, as Lord Darlington, was being served tea by Susan Fitzgerald, playing Lady Windermere. First-night nerves caused a slight shake in Bedford's hand. This made the cup rattle on its saucer. It seemed noisier to the actors on stage than it did to the audience, of course, but nevertheless Fitzgerald had some trouble aiming the tea at precisely the right spot! On the second night, when Lady Windermere invited, 'Tea, Lord Darlington?' she got the unrehearsed but not unwise answer, 'No, thank you'!

★ ★ ★ ★ ★

If Patrick Bedford's hand was suspect, his head certainly was not. One evening during the run of the same play, an errant candelabrum dropped flaming candle-grease and caused a slight fire just as Lord Darlington was serving drinks. Quick as a flash, he seized the soda-siphon and expertly extinguished the flames.

Groome's Hotel, opposite the Gate Theatre, was a popular watering-hole for patrons. Hugh Leonard tells the tale of a raid at a late hour after a performance. The proprietor, Joe Groome, had been warned of the intrusion and had got everyone to sign the hotel register (legally, residents could drink till a later hour):

The guards duly arrived and seemed rather nonplussed on learning that we were all 'residents'. The youngest of them was, however, of an academic turn of mind and proceeded to examine the register. I can still remember the pole-axed look on his face when he murmured, 'Jaysus, there's an average of fifty-seven people staying in every room.'

★ ★ ★ ★ ★

The Gate Company brought O'Casey's *Juno and the Paycock* to the 1986 Jerusalem Festival. Donal McCann played Captain Boyle, who, during Act One, says, 'Chiselurs [children] don't care a damn now about their parents . . . .' Translation into Hebrew offered this as 'Monumental sculptors don't care a damn now about their parents . . . .'

★ ★ ★ ★ ★

OLIVER ST JOHN GOGARTY
1878–1957

Oliver St John Gogarty was the prototype for 'Stately, plump Buck Mulligan', who appears in the opening episode of Joyce's Ulysses. *Dublin-born, he was once likened to a Renaissance prince reigning over the city. He was educated in Clongowes Wood College in County Kildare, where Joyce also studied, and at Trinity College Dublin. He epitomised the libertine Dublin medical student, but was so devoted to the classics that he was befriended by historian and philosopher John Pentland Mahaffy. He spent two terms at Oxford, allegedly attempting to win the Newdigate Prize for English poetry, as Oscar Wilde had done. After graduating in medicine, Gogarty quickly established a reputation in Dublin as a nose and throat surgeon and as a wit and conversationalist. He wrote parodies and poems.*

In the Bailey bar and restaurant he entertained people like Sir William Orpen, James Joyce and Arthur Griffith. In the cold Irish Sea he swam with the poet Seumas O'Sullivan. Far from the city's bustle, he roamed mountain paths with Padraic Colum, saying poems in a resonant voice. All this and more qualified him as a 'character' — a special type of Irish eccentric. In addition, he was a senator, playwright and athlete. With Yeats, he dabbled in the occult. He lived for short periods in London and New York.

Research into sinus infection and lucrative medical and surgical practices made 'the laughing lesionaire' extremely rich. His serious side included a detestation of Eamon de Valera, of whom he said, 'He can certainly be called Hibernian since he resembles something uncoiled from the Book of Kells.' Gogarty was an ardent admirer of Arthur Griffith and Michael Collins. He embalmed the body of Collins and wrote a poem about him a week later.

Gogarty bought a large house in Renvyle, Connemara, to which he loved to escape from the city. He expressed a wish to be buried there.

★ ★ ★ ★ ★

Gogarty and some fellow students needed money for drinking. They noticed a better-financed friend who was very drunk, put him in a sack and brought him to the Royal College of Surgeons, where they sold him as a corpse for medical experimentation. The victim of the prank eventually sobered up, tore his way out of the sack and escaped from the room of bagged bodies. He chastised Gogarty, saying, 'That's the last time I'll die to pay for your drink.'

✳ ✳ ✳ ✳ ✳

In Ireland, it is considered unlucky to meet a red-haired woman when going to fish or to engage in any other work. Gogarty took the superstition further. As students gathered outside an examination centre in Trinity College, they heard the loud noise of a horse-drawn cab speeding across the cobblestones. Its blinds were drawn. When it halted, Gogarty alighted, his face hooded, and called upon the cabby to lead him into the building. He explained that seeing a red-haired student would mean failure in his examination.

✳ ✳ ✳ ✳ ✳

Gogarty tells how, during his brief interlude at Oxford:

I drank the sconce . . . a silver tankard that holds more than five pints. It is called for as a punishment on those who transgress at meals by making a pun or quoting from the classics . . . . It was the resentment of the abominable Bamburger who sat next to me at table that was to blame for my being sconced. He knew that I was supposed to be reading medicine and because I forebore to answer his endless questions as to what was good for training in the way of food he hated me. He was to represent Oxford as a lightweight in the annual inter-varsity boxing competition, hence his question about what he should eat.

Bamburger called for the sconce.

'Now, Bamburger,' I said, 'you know the rules: if I drink the sconce without taking it from my lips, I am privileged to sconce every man at this table. I will sconce you. I will sconce only you and that won't do you and your training much good.'

77

He called to the butler, 'Bring in the sconce.'

Again I protested: 'Look here, Bamburger, you don't know what you're up against. I am not referring to the Cambridge lightweight but to myself. I can drink as many pints as my pals put up. I was weaned on pints.'

It was unavailing.

There was silence in the hall when the butler with due ceremony bore in the sconce on a salver. It was full to the lid with cold ale. I felt 'mortified' as they say in Dublin. All eyes were on our table; and at the high table, where the dons were, conversation ceased . . . .

I planted my elbows firmly on the table and raised the silver tankard to my mouth. I took a deep breath. I began to drink. The first two pints went down pleasantly enough. It would have been enjoyable if there had not been so much depending on the draught. You would never guess what affected me most. Not a feeling of repleteness. No . . . . It was the awful cold that hurt me on both sides of the throat and went up into my ears. Don't believe them when you hear that the English don't know how to cool their ale. They keep it in the wood in a cellar and that does not conduce to conduction (A pun! Enough to sconce any man). I held on, conscious still . . . . I suppose it took two or three full minutes, and two minutes are enough to die in . . . . At last I reached the bottom and I put my head back to drain the thing so that it would not drip when I held it upside down. Cheers broke out all over the hall; even the imperturbable butler permitted a gleam of admiration to enliven his countenance. The dons at the upper table looked down at our table. I tried to get the conversation going again and off myself.

'Bamburger, I warned you. Now you can take on.' There was little sign of approval for that because all the table was afraid of the pugilist. Next day he was knocked out in the first round by an accidental blow of the blond Cambridge man's head.

★ ★ ★ ★ ★

As a surgeon, Gogarty refused to take a fee for treatment from Gabriel Fallon. The ill-paid actor asked how he was going to live, since most of his patients were impoverished. Gogarty explained that he was expecting a duchess from England and would 'settle her snout for a century'.

★ ★ ★ ★ ★

Subsequently more celebrated as an architect, Michael Scott was an actor when Gogarty operated on him. Due to an ineffective anaesthetic, the patient regained consciousness too soon and attempted to draw his surgeon's attention to this. Gogarty called to a nurse and said, 'Kindly put your hand over that man's mouth; we are not interested in the actor's subconscious.'

★ ★ ★ ★ ★

To a junior who panicked during an operation and shouted, 'O Jesus Christ!' Gogarty replied, 'Cease calling on your unqualified assistant!'

★ ★ ★ ★ ★

A surgeon colleague's sexual indiscretion led to a divorce action which absorbed all his wealth. Gogarty referred to him as 'the only man I ever knew who made a fortune with his knife and lost it with his fork'.

★ ★ ★ ★ ★

Lady Gregory was noted for the scant financial rewards she offered Abbey playwrights. Wishing to expose this in public, Gogarty donated a royalty cheque of £2.10s (£2.50) to the *Evening Herald* Boot Fund, a popular charity which always published details of subscriptions received.

★ ★ ★ ★ ★

Written under the pseudonym Gideon Ousley, Gogarty's play *A Serious Thing* was enjoying a revival at the Abbey Theatre in August 1919 when the author was arrested by the Black and Tans. During a brief detention he recommended the work to his captors. Peeping into the auditorium that evening, Gogarty was pleased to see that they had taken his advice and were sitting in the front stalls laughing loudly at the action on stage. They did not realise that, under the guise of portraying Roman occupation of the Holy Land, the play was a satire on British rule in Ireland.

A supporter of the 1921 Treaty, Gogarty was captured by anti-Treaty activists during the ensuing Civil War. He escaped by swimming the river Liffey and expressed his gratitude to the river by promising to bestow a pair of swans upon it. At London's Savile Club, W.B. Yeats was astounded when he received a telephone call from Gogarty seeking compatible cygnets. Similarly, the writer Shane Leslie read a letter with awe:

> The swans Colonel Crighton was to give me were to be given by the King; this I could not accept as I intended them for political purposes, so I am at a loss for birds to present to the Liffey.

The incident that was to inspire the title of Gogarty's 1924 collection of poems, *An Offering of Swans*, and also a poem, 'To the Liffey with Swans', began with a champagne lunch in the Shelbourne Hotel on 24 March 1924. Birds had been imported from Sussex and were quarantined in the Zoological Gardens. During the lunch, they were transferred to Trinity College Boat Club's premises near Islandbridge, where the President of Ireland, W.T. Cosgrave, later arrived and was joined by Yeats, Lennox Robinson and members of Gogarty's family.

Solemnly, Yeats began quoting poetry. The crate in which the birds had been brought was opened — but they refused to emerge. Gogarty tried to coax them out as the President laughed, causing Yeats to adopt a grave mien. Frustrated at his unsuccessful cajolings, Gogarty gave the box a kick and the two swans blanketed wings and scurried into the river. A vow had been fulfilled and Dubliners tell how there were no such birds on river or canal in Dublin before and how, ever after, when Gogarty walked near the city's waters, swans came out to greet him.

✶ ✶ ✶ ✶ ✶

Gogarty's one-liners about his contemporaries and society are legendary.

When Parnell's opponent, Tim Healy, in 1922 became Ireland's first Governor General and occupied the Viceregal Lodge, Gogarty called it 'Uncle Tim's Cabin'.

☆

He remarked that the Abbey Theatre sent out an SOS for geniuses and that everybody applied.

☆

Gogarty suspected a solicitor of depriving him of his inheritance. Reading in a newspaper that this man had been hit by a Rolls-Royce, Gogarty said, 'At last! Struck off the Rolls!'

☆ ☆ ☆ ☆ ☆

Gogarty was a keen amateur airman. *The Times* caused a stir by reporting his killing of a sheep when landing a plane. Gogarty wrote to Lady Londonderry, 'I hit an unsaleable sheep. I said "The Government's policy is right". Then I knew I had concussion of the brain.' (He disliked the new de Valera government intensely.)

☆ ☆ ☆ ☆ ☆

When Gogarty's successful *As I Was Going Down Sackville Street* was published, antique dealer Henry Morris Sinclair successfully sued for defamation of character. It hurt Gogarty that Samuel Beckett gave evidence against him, but it was the exchanges between rival counsels that caused most furore. A *Daily Express* journalist commented, 'Only *The Pickwick Papers* rewritten by James Joyce could capture the atmosphere . . . .'

☆ ☆ ☆ ☆ ☆

Richard Ellmann recalls an investigatory raid by Gogarty and Joyce on the premises of George Russell's Hermetic Society, a group of middle-class mystics, in Dawson Chambers. The quotations are Gogarty's:

The members had not yet arrived for their meeting, so the two men surveyed the 'yogibogeybox', with its occult

reference books such as Madame Blavatsky's *Isis Unveiled*, and
the bench where Russell throned, 'filled with his god', 'the
faithful hermetists . . . ringroundabout him'. In a corner was a
suitcase belonging to [publisher] George Roberts, who
combined wandering in the astral envelope with travelling for
ladies' underwear. Gogarty took a pair of women's drawers
from the suitcase, strung them up, placed a broomstick in the
middle, and attached a note signed John Eglinton, at the time
an ostentatious celibate, with the rubric, 'I never did it.'

★ ★ ★ ★ ★

*Interviewed by W.R. Rodgers, Shelagh O'Mahoney, journalist and
broadcaster, recalled an operation which Gogarty had arranged to
perform on the commander-in-chief of the British forces in Ireland
during the War of Independence. That morning, the surgeon-poet
was awakened by gunfire and loud knocking on his door:*

As he opened the door a tall figure of a woman in a shawl
lurched breathlessly past him into the passage. Gogarty
cautiously put on the light, saw this figure tear off the shawl
and discard a very palpable female wig. Then the figure
suddenly seemed, like something out of *Alice in Wonderland*,
to shoot up, and a brawny, root-like arm was cast
affectionately on Oliver Gogarty's shoulder and a buttery
West Cork voice said, 'Begob, Oliver, they nearly had me that
time, boy.' Who was it but Michael Collins, Gogarty's friend,
the rebel leader, who was once again on the run from the
Crown Forces. Meanwhile, up at the Castle, Sir Neville
[Macready], who was a very punctual man, was just setting
out for Gogarty's house for the operation, and at nine o'clock
precisely he arrived complete with armoured cars and
bristling with all sorts of panoply of war. The maid opened
the door and the bodyguard of about six or seven officers, all
trench-coated and hands on holsters, swept past the poor
maid and followed the receptionist and Sir Neville right into
the improvised operating theatre. Here they were met by
Gogarty who was calm, but very affable, and in the corner of
the operating theatre was the rather burly figure of a dark

young man with a white overall and a surgical mask. Very calmly and suavely Gogarty said, 'Excuse me, gentlemen, I haven't introduced you to my new anaesthetist, Dr Collins.'

★ ★ ★ ★ ★

The poet Austin Clarke remembered Gogarty driving him home from a party:

It was about half-past one in the morning, and he drove — as he always did — at a terrific speed, all the more so as the streets at that time were completely deserted. Suddenly he said 'Let's go down to Monto,' that being the local name for the brothel district, at one time notorious as one of the worst [of] all European cities, perhaps Eastern ones too, and of course known from that lugubrious Victorian chapter in *Ulysses* known as 'Nighttown'. I must hasten to add that Nighttown was no longer there. So we came to that strange, silent district in the moonlight and drove slowly past empty slum houses with boarded-up windows and my senior talked to me of those days he'd known long ago, evoking memories of almost legendary figures — a veritable dream of fair but frail women; May Oblong, Mrs Mack the Bawd, Fresh Nelly, Liverpool Kate, Piano Mary and that well-known shebeen keeper, the incomparable Mrs Becky Cooper.

★ ★ ★ ★ ★

Brian Aherne, Abbey actor and later film star, described the scene in a New York bar where Gogarty was telling his stories and receiving the utmost attention. Just as he was coming to the punch-line of one, a youth placed a coin in the jukebox:

All hell broke loose. The expression on Gogarty's face changed; he became very sad, a combination of sadness and anger, and he said, 'Oh dear God in Heaven, that I should find myself thousands of miles from home, an old man at the mercy of every retarded son of a bitch who has a nickel to drop in that bloody illuminated coal-scuttle.'

★ ★ ★ ★ ★

Padraic Colum writes:

There are other things to be said in Gogarty's favour. I remember an instance of his impulsive generosity. At the time of his friendship with Joyce I was working in a railway office in Kildare Street. As I was paid monthly, I could around payday lend a student friend a half-crown or even a half-sovereign, as I sometimes lent Joyce. One day, wearing a resplendent waistcoat, Gogarty came to the office and asked me for the loan of a half-sovereign. I told him I was just then in need of a half-sovereign myself. 'Is that so?' Gogarty exclaimed, leaping away down the steps. In twenty minutes he was back, his coat buttoned up. He pressed a goldpiece into my hand. He had pawned the waistcoat and brought me the amount of the pledge.

★ ★ ★ ★ ★

Gogarty died in New York and his body was flown home. A moving BBC conversation between Professor Liam Ó Briain and Monsignor Patrick Browne (published in Irish Literary Portraits, *edited by W.R. Rodgers) described his funeral in Renvyle, the country choir in the simple church, then the burial:*

Ó BRIAIN: When we came outside, it was fine, but cold, and there was a journey of seven or eight miles to the graveyard . . . . We had a long drive along a narrow winding road, along the side of a mountain which sloped down to the sea, and formed below there a sort of very small fjord.

MGR BROWNE: The cemetery is sloping, a rather steep slope, and Gogarty's grave was at the very lowest corner of it beside the lake. Over his grave there was a willow tree that grew from one end and was bent down and reached to earth again on the other side. Then, when the grave was filled, Father Hanrahan, the parish priest, the celebrant of the mass, came and poured the Holy Water on Gogarty's grave.

Ó BRIAIN: And here, I really had to chortle. Because the bottle which contained the Holy Water was a whiskey bottle. And I said to myself, how Oliver would enjoy this. I seemed to feel a shake in the coffin which had gone down. Just as the ceremonies were begun by the priest, a swan appeared below in the water — in this little fjord. And this swan turned round and looked up, and all through the funeral that swan stayed there without a stir, looking at us the whole time.

MGR BROWNE: Oh, it was a wonderful sight, that was. The swan came out from among the reeds, drew himself up beside the bank and was still for two or three minutes, and then, like the swan at the end of *Lohengrin*, as if he were bearing the soul and not the body of Oliver with him, turned, and went out in the lake between another set of reeds, and was lost. And we felt then that the spirit of Gogarty had gone away.

★ ★ ★ ★ ★

OUR FRIENDS GO WITH US AS WE GO
DOWN THE LONG PATH WHERE BEAUTY WENDS
Oliver St John Gogarty

OLIVER
GOLDSMITH
1728–1774

Longford and Roscommon both claim Oliver Goldsmith as theirs; the former's case is stronger. Even his famous poem The Deserted Village, *written in 1770, is controversial. Some believe it celebrates a Wiltshire hamlet, but most commentators agree that it is set in Ireland. Having been educated locally and at Trinity College Dublin (from which he ran away), Goldsmith was rejected by the Church in which his father was a parson. After trying to earn a living, he settled on writing as a career but never managed to be other than penniless. He complained that education and wit fell on infertile ground at home while his Irish birth seemed an impediment to obtaining employment in England. His writings could be delicately sentimental or sharply satirical. His biographer, F. Frankfort Moore, dubbed him 'the best loved of English writers . . . the Benjamin of the large family of eighteenth-century poets, of whom Dryden was the Jacob and Pope the Judah'. 'We venerate Dryden,' he said, 'we admire Pope, we esteem Young, we quote Gray, we neglect Thomson, we ignore Johnson, we tolerate Cowper, but we love Goldsmith.' Up to comparatively recently, almost every primary school-leaver could recite at least two full pages of* The Deserted Village, *though often in the wrong order.*

★ ★ ★ ★ ★

Goldsmith's medical degree has been described as dubious but an 1836 publication, Anecdotes of Books and Authors, *gives him due title:*

Doctor Goldsmith, though one of the first characters in literature, was a great novice in the common occurrences of life. Sitting one evening at the tavern where he was accustomed to take his supper, he called for a mutton chop, which was no sooner placed on the table, than a gentleman near him, with whom he was intimately acquainted, showed great tokens of uneasiness and wondered how the Doctor could suffer the waiter to place such a stinking chop before him. 'Stinking!' said Goldsmith, 'In good truth, I do not smell it.' 'I never smelled anything so unpleasant in my life,' answered the gentleman, 'the fellow deserves a caning for bringing you meat unfit to eat.' 'In good troth,' said the poet, relying on his judgement, 'I think so too; but I will be less severe in my punishment.' He instantly called the waiter, and insisted that he should eat the chop as punishment. The waiter resisted, but the Doctor threatened to knock him down with his cane if he did not immediately comply. When he had eaten half the chop, the Doctor gave him a glass of wine, thinking that it would make the remainder of the sentence less painful to him. When the waiter had finished his repast, Goldsmith's friend burst into a loud laugh. 'What ails you now?' asked the poet. 'Indeed, my good friend,' said the other, 'I could never think that any man whose knowledge of letters is so intensive as yours, could be so great a dupe to a stroke of humour; the chop was as fine a one as ever I saw in my life.'

'Was it?' said Doctor Goldsmith, 'then I will never give credit to what you say again; and so, in good truth, I think I am even with you.'

★ ★ ★ ★ ★

Goldsmith's sister, Catherine Hodson, told a historic story:

Upon the occasion of his leaving home for his last term at [Reverend Patrick Hughes's] school, some friend had given him a guinea, and on his way to [the school at] Edgeworthstown which was about twenty miles away from his father's house [then at Elphin], he had diverted himself the whole day by viewing the gentlemen's seats on the road, until, at the fall of night, he found himself in a small town named Ardagh. Here he inquired for the best house in the place, meaning an inn, but his bumptious simplicity being taken advantage of by a local humorist, he was directed to the house of a private gentleman, where, calling for somebody to take his horse and lead him to the stable, he alighted and was shown into the parlour, being supposed to be a guest come to visit the master, whom he found sitting by a good fire. This gentleman immediately discovered Oliver's mistake, and being a man of humour and also learning from him the name of his father, who happened to be among his acquaintance, he encouraged the deception. Oliver accordingly called about him, ordered a good supper, and generously invited the master, his wife, and daughters to partake of it; treated them with a bottle or two of wine, and when going to bed ordered a hot cake to be prepared for his breakfast; nor was it till, at his departure, when he called for the bill, that he found he had been entertained in a private family.

A fortunate practical joke — the incident inspired Goldsmith's play She Stoops to Conquer *(1773).*

★ ★ ★ ★ ★

There was inadequate preparation or rehearsal for Goldsmith's play. George Colman, Covent Garden manager, had treated it and its author badly — indeed, only on the morning of the opening was the name She Stoops to Conquer *decided upon. That evening, Goldsmith was guest at a dinner party given in his honour. F. Frankfort Moore writes:*

It is easy to picture this particular function. The truth was that Colman's behaviour had broken the spirit, not only of the author, but of the majority of his friends as well. They would all make an effort to cheer up poor Goldsmith; but every one knows how cheerless a function is that which is organised with such a cheerful intention. It is not necessary that one should have been in a court of law watching the face of the prisoner in the dock when the jury have retired to consider their verdict, in order to appreciate the feelings of Goldsmith when his friends made their attempt to cheer him up. The last straw added on to the dreariness of the banquet was surely to be found in the accident that every one wore black! The King of Sardinia had died a short time before, and the Court had ordered mourning to be worn for some weeks in memory of the potentate.

After the depressing dinner, Goldsmith went missing. He was found wandering aimlessly in St James's Park and was inveigled to go to the theatre only on the pretence that alterations to the finale might be required. The play was in its fifth act when he arrived at the stage door. A hiss startled Goldsmith and he asked what it was. Colman sneeringly replied, 'Pshaw sir, do not be afraid of a squib when we have been sitting these two hours on a barrel of gunpowder.'

★ ★ ★ ★ ★

A man called Adam Drummond was often invited to performances by theatre managers, because his hearty and infectious laugh stirred audiences into an appreciative frame of mind. Colman was pessimistic about *She Stoops to Conquer* and only under pressure (and having checked on Drummond's availability?) did he agree to stage it. He realised, however, that Goldsmith's comedy might be above Drummond's head, so he placed the fellow of infinite jest in a box where he could observe Dr Samuel Johnson. Drummond's instructions were to laugh whenever Johnson smiled.

At first all went well and the laughs from the box came on cue. But they were of such a nature that they drew more attention than the actors' words. Drummond was warned at the interval that he was overdoing things a bit; but it was to no avail. The man was seeing fun in everything; even the serious parts of the dialogue competed with his guffaws. He disregarded Dr Johnson, especially when the audience began to applaud him [Drummond] instead of the players. In desperation, an emissary from the manager arrived in the box, turned Drummond's back to the stage and sat between him and the audience. But he still laughed!

That evening, there were four jolly pigeons instead of three in *She Stoops to Conquer*. And after it all, Goldsmith remarked: 'The neighing of a horse would have been a whisper to it.'

★ ★ ★ ★ ★

James Boswell was fond of Goldsmith and demurred when Samuel Johnson condemned his ostentatious manner, saying, 'For my part I like very well to hear honest Goldsmith talk away carelessly.' 'Why, yes, sir,' said Johnson, 'but he should not like to hear himself.' Goldsmith did not always reciprocate this charity. When Boswell praised Johnson on one occasion, Goldsmith accused him of 'making a monarchy out of what should be a republic'.

✯ ✯ ✯ ✯ ✯

Moore quotes from a letter which Goldsmith wrote to his cousin Jane Lawder, from Temple Exchange Coffee House, near Temple Bar, London on 15 August 1758. He apologises at length for previous begging letters, before stating:

I have given my landlady orders for an entire reform in the state of my finances. I declaim against hot suppers, drink less sugar in my tea, and check my grate with brick-bats. Instead of hanging my room with pictures I intend to adorn it with maxims of frugality. These will make pretty furniture enough, and won't be a bit too expensive; for I shall draw them out with my own hands, and my landlady's daughter shall frame them with the parings of my black waistcoat. Each maxim is to be inscribed on a sheet of clear paper, and wrote with my best pen; of which the following will serve as a specimen. *Look sharp. Mind the main chance. Money is money now. If you have a thousand pound, you can put your hands by your sides and say you are worth a thousand pound every day of the year. Take a farthing from an hundred pound and it will be an hundred pound no longer.*

Thus, which way soever I turn my eyes, they are sure to meet one of those friendly Monitors; and as we are told of an Actor who hung his room round with looking-glasses to correct the defects of his person, my apartment shall be furnished in a peculiar manner to correct the errors of my mind.

✯

After more beating about the bush, Goldsmith grasps the nettle:

But I must come to business; for business, as one of my maxims tells me, must be minded or lost. I am going to publish in London a book entitled *The Present State of Taste and Literature in Europe.* The Booksellers in Ireland republish every performance there without making the author any consideration. I would in this respect disappoint their avarice, and have all the profits of my labours to myself. I must therefore request [your husband] Mr Lawder to circulate among his friends and acquaintances an hundred of my Proposals, which I have given the bookseller, Mr Bradley in Dame Street, directions to send him. If, in pursuance to such circulation, he should receive any subscriptions, I entreat when collected they may be sent to Mr Bradley's as aforesaid, who will give a receipt and be accountable for the work, or a return of the subscription. If this request (which, so far complied with, will in some measure be an encouragement to a man of learning) should be disagreeable or troublesome, I would not press it; for I would be the last man on earth to have my labours go a-begging; but if I know Mr Lawder, and sure I ought to know him, he will accept the employment with pleasure. All I can say — if he writes a book I will get him two hundred subscribers, and those of the best wits in Europe.

John Wilson Croker, parliamentarian and author, chronicled a story of a certain Colonel O'Moore's which F. Frankfort Moore includes in his biography:

O'Moore said he was going with [Edmund] Burke to dine with Reynolds when they passed through a crowd who were about a hotel where some foreign ladies were displaying themselves rather conspicuously. Goldsmith was a short way behind Burke, also on his way to Sir Joshua's; and on arriving at the house, Burke, who was always ready for a practical joke, gravely taxed Goldsmith with having said out loud in the middle of the crush, 'What stupid beasts these people are for staring with such admiration at those painted Jezebels, while a man of my talents passed by un-noticed!' 'Surely, surely, my dear friend,' cried Goldsmith, 'I did not say so.' 'But if you had not said so, how could I have known it?' said Burke. 'True,' said Goldsmith. 'Well, I am very sorry. It was very foolish. I do recollect that something of the kind passed through my mind, but I did not think I had uttered it.'

★ ★ ★ ★ ★

Goldsmith writes in The Vicar of Wakefield:

It was within about four days of [my daughter's] intended nuptials, that my little family at night were gathered around a charming fire, telling stories of the past and laying schemes for the future; busied in forming a thousand projects, and laughing at whatever folly came uppermost.

'Well, Moses,' cried I, 'we shall soon, my boy, have a wedding in the family; what is your opinion of matters and things in general?'

'My opinion, father, is that all things go on very well; I was just now thinking, that when sister Livy is married to Farmer Williams, we shall then have the loan of his cider-press and brewing tubs for nothing.'

★ ★ ★ ★ ★

Vain, socially ambitious, lady-killing actor-manager David Garrick was summed up in a few pithy words by Goldsmith. 'On stage, he was natural, simple, affecting. 'Twas only when he was off that he was acting.'

★ ★ ★ ★ ★

Goldsmith never married, but he had an ardent admirer and true friend in Mary Horneck, whom he named his Jessamy Bride. Moore tells how:

When the last duty had been discharged and the face of the dead was already hidden, his Jessamy Bride came into the darkened room with her sister, and what had been done had to be undone for the moment. The black lid was removed; she was allowed to see once more the plain face of the man she had valued above all men, and she took from his head a lock of hair to remain with her while she lived. The story of a man's death, however full of gloom it may seem, cannot be thought utterly forlorn when it is associated with such an incident as this. The last hand that touched his cold forehead was the hand of the girl who understood what manner of man he was, the girl who had done more than all the rest of his friends to brighten the last years of his life.

Mary Horneck kept the memento of him until the day of her death. Sixty years after she was laid in the vault by the side of the Princess who had been her friend [I] was invited by a descendant of the lady to whom she had bequeathed her jewels, to see these interesting souvenirs; and among them, enclosed in a small gold locket, was the memento she had so treasured. This thin coil of faded brown hair lay under the glass, and on the rim of gold was engraved the name of Oliver Goldsmith.

ILL FARES THE LAND, TO HAST'NING ILLS A PREY,
WHERE WEALTH ACCUMULATES, AND MEN DECAY
Oliver Goldsmith

TYRONE GUTHRIE 1900–1971

At Annaghmakerrig, Newbliss, Co. Monaghan, there is a lasting memorial to the distinguished director, actor and producer Sir William Tyrone Guthrie, who was administrator of the Old Vic and Sadler's Wells theatres during World War II and was knighted for his services to theatre. The artists' retreat there has soundproof rooms, studios and other amenities, and is financed jointly by the Arts Councils of the Republic of Ireland and of Northern Ireland. Guthrie's will stipulated the use to which the family home should be put. The gesture perpetuates a long family tradition, for his great-grandfather was the nineteenth-century actor Tyrone Power. The film star of the same name was his great-grandson. Although English-born, Guthrie is well entitled to inclusion here.

★ ★ ★ ★ ★

Guthrie's mammoth productions at the Edinburgh Festival often called for the use of amateur actors in crowd scenes. At a rehearsal for *A Satire of the Three Estates* (1552), the Scottish morality play by Sir David Lyndsay, he was on the look-out for common amateur faults like wearing bright costume jewellery, or digital watches with assorted cinquefoils.

He spotted an enthusiastic youth who had allowed his imagination to run riot as he made up. Guthrie exclaimed, 'Oh, here's a young chap made up as a flag!'

★ ★ ★ ★ ★

Scene: Morning. The Old Vic Theatre. Stage crew awaits arrival of director, Tyrone Guthrie, for a technical rehearsal. A beam of sunlight steals through a high window and falls upon the stage, giving an impressive effect.

STAGE-MANAGER (to Assistant Stage-Manager): Put a curtain over that window; if he sees it, he'll want it in the play.

GUTHRIE (entering auditorium, at back): Too late! Saw it! Like it! Want it!

★ ★ ★ ★ ★

Guthrie writes about reading for George Bernard Shaw in 1923:

Shaw is always said to have read his own plays wonderfully. I cannot remember. I was charmed by the modest gravity of his demeanour, when he arrived and received our deferential greetings. Then I recall being a little surprised when, during the reading, he would go into fits of laughter at his own jokes.

The next morning we were to start rehearsal. I was there first, word-perfect, humbly but smugly conscious of being one of the youngest members of the company yet playing the longest part [Captain Shotover in *Heartbreak House*] — the wonder-boy. The rehearsal began. The wonder-boy, who had been free all summer and knew the words inside out, strode about, now whispering, now shouting, throwing his arms about in a way which had been so effective in Glendower, making long, thrilling pauses. Miss [Dorothy] Green, bless her, was in glasses with her handsome nose pressed to the very small print. Mr [Earle] Grey was hardly attempting to act at all, just reading, just mumbling really. I hoped he would eventually do better than that.

When we broke for lunch, Mr Fagan [the repertory company manager] beckoned me to follow him out of the room. We paced a dingy basement passage — three dustbins and a door marked 'Mr Fothergill — strictly private'.

He took my arm. It had all been a great mistake, he said; he was to blame, not I. He had never realised *quite* how inexperienced I was, not only technically, but in every way.

'After all, you *are* rather young for your age — twenty-one, is it?'

★ ★ ★ ★ ★

Guthrie was a member of the Lilian Baylis company that played Hamlet *in Elsinore. Opening night was so wet that the performance had to be taken into a hotel ballroom. Royalty and a diplomatic party had arrived from Copenhagen for the gala occasion and there was some panic as new methods of staging the performance were hurriedly discussed. Guthrie described the frustration of the players at being denied the most effective entrance to the ballroom by a dour, six-foot porter in frock-coat and brass buttons. Despite numerous pleas, he refused to open the door. Next morning, Guthrie met the fellow and asked why he had been so unaccommodating:*

'I will show you,' he said, and tiptoed down a veranda towards the double door. In the architrave was the nest of blue-tits; the little hen, nervous but gallant, fluttered about our heads. 'If this door had been used, she would have deserted her eggs; you wouldn't have wanted that.'

★ ★ ★ ★ ★

The actor Godfrey Quigley once telephoned Guthrie to make an appointment for a discussion on a new musical. Dinner at Annaghmakerrig was suggested and Guthrie added, 'Bring a pound of sausages.' Quigley thought the request a little unusual but it was Saturday and the director's home was in the country, so he assumed his host was simply saving himself a trip to Newbliss, the nearest village.

Quigley lost his way and arrived late for his eight o'clock appointment. Guthrie bore down upon him as he stepped from his car and demanded, 'Did you bring the sausages?' Quigley felt lucky that he had, and handed them over. Guthrie showed his guest into the drawing-room, left and returned in a moment, then suggested an aperitif.

The discussion began. Quigley's plan was for a musical based on the life of Percy French (*The Golden Years* had not then been launched). The moment French's name was mentioned, Guthrie's attitude changed completely. He refused point-blank to have anything to do with the project, explaining that the French sisters were friends of his. Of Percy, he ranted, 'That buffoon made a show of his family.' Quigley was taken aback at this outburst of righteousness, and moved the conversation to another subject, thinking that the pending meal could be very strained. Soon dinner was announced and they retired to the dining-room — for sausage and mash!

In Astonish Us in the Morning *(London 1977), theatre director Michael Langham told Alfred Rossi, the book's editor:*

[Guthrie] had invited us to a luxurious French restaurant on Third Avenue [New York] (since, alas, defunct). It seemed an extravagant choice for Tony [the name by which his friends knew him] whose favorite dish was bacon and eggs, but he was clearly bent on making this an evening to remember. After dinner he was going to take us to *Inherit the Wind* [by Lawrence and Lee] with Paul Muni. The meal was delectable; Tony was in great from; wine flowed. So did conversation. So did the liqueur. At last I ventured, 'It's getting on, Tony, we really ought to . . . '

'*Trois cognacs*,' he barked in a Churchillian French understandable only to the English.

We arrived about three-quarters of an hour late at the theatre. 'You have seats in the name of Guthrie.'

'Yes,' said the box office bloke, 'that'll be . . . ' Tony was outraged.

'That's for *three* acts; what's the price for *two*?'

Guthrie was kind to retired actors or those down on their luck. Annette Prevost, and her husband George Chamberlain worked with him when he was artistic director at the Old Vic. They were friends too. Annette recalled Guthrie's directing them to send a contract to a lady for a book called *The House in the Malone Road*, with an advance royalty cheque for £200. The lady wrote back thanking them, but adding that never in her life would she dream of writing a book. It was Guthrie's scheme to tender financial assistance without embarrassment.

GREAT PLAYS NEVER HAVE AND NEVER WILL BE WRITTEN
ABOUT HATE
Tyrone Guthrie

★ ★ ★ ★ ★

JOSEPH
HOLLOWAY
1861–1944

Joseph Holloway was born in Camden Street, Dublin and educated at Castleknock and Dublin School of Art, studying architecture, which he practised until around 1918. He designed the old Abbey Theatre and was a true theatre addict, rubbing shoulders with the stars and dropping names the way politicians drop clangers. He joined societies connected with the theatre, and rarely missed a first night. Holloway kept a diary and his total writings on Dublin literary and theatrical topics neared 28,000,000 words.

★ ★ ★ ★ ★

On 4 February 1932, Holloway described macLiammóir's *Hamlet* as 'almost flawless, save the too suddenly declamatory lines here and there in the "Get thee to a nunnery" scene and at the end of the Play scene, and the too theatrical declamation of "The play's the thing".' He also faulted the inaudible lines in the King's Chapel episode. However, he found macLiammóir's diction beautiful, 'laden with music and gentle pathos . . . .'

Holloway bred an Irish calf, if not exactly a bull, when he wrote: 'Orson Welles made the speech of "The Ghost" almost human as well as awesome . . . .'

★ ★ ★ ★ ★

Wednesday, June 28, 1939.

Eileen and a taxi called for me, and we drove down to the Gaiety where we saw a melodrama, *Bulldog Drummond Hits Out*, played in true Queen's Theatre style with Henry Edwards as the cool, quick-witted, brightly conversational hero of the occasion. He went through his part in a calm, unruffled manner and the best of humour in the most trying of circumstances . . . . The play was all about a hidden stolen trinket. Some of the thrills were discounted by the lack of care in details. Such as one of the characters saying, 'I saw a face at the window through the mirror ' — and no mirror was there; or the second 'Warder' entering carrying his rifle upside down; or one of the characters screaming twice before the rise of the curtain shews her strangled . . . . Jack B. Yeats and Mrs were in the parterre . . . . at the end of the play, Henry Edwards addressed the house and called attention to the Three Stooges in a stagebox . . .

'A formless thing full of empty talk' was how Holloway described Mervyn Wall's play *The Lady in the Twilight*, which opened at the Abbey Theatre on 19 May 1941. He felt that it led nowhere and seldom held the attention, with characters who entered and left in a haphazard manner or sat around 'waiting their turn to put in their say'. A young man left during the second act but not before remarking, 'It was as full of words and as empty of ideas as the literary page of *The Irish Times*.' The following day, that newspaper pronounced that the play revealed Wall as 'a dramatist of power and distinction'.

A GREAT PIECE OF ACTING OR SUPERB VOCALISM MEANS
NOTHING TO A SMOKER WHOSE PIPE, CIGAR OR CIGARETTE
HAPPENS TO WANT RELIGHTING
Joseph Holloway

★ ★ ★ ★ ★

JAMES
JOYCE
1882–1941

Dublin-born James Joyce was educated at Clongowes Wood College from the age of six. Later he attended Belvedere College and University College, Dublin. After graduating, he left for Paris and lived there until his mother's death in 1903 brought him back. The following year he met Nora Barnacle and the couple left for Zurich. They travelled further before returning to Dublin, where Joyce managed a cinema. But Zurich became his base. Dubliners *and* A Portrait of the Artist as a Young Man *preceded* Ulysses, *a work that is still discussed, revised, and argued about vehemently.* Finnegans Wake, *written in a confluence of tongues, attracts even more argument and theorising. Indeed, it may be said that a Joycean 'industry' has emerged, attracting both genuine and pseudo-academics. If it could be ascertained that the man played pitch-and-toss in a townland, claims would be made for its head-and-harp influence on the author's work!*

In 1931 Joyce eventually married Nora and nine years afterwards they returned to Zurich, where he died a year later.

★ ★ ★ ★ ★

At university, Joyce played an unscrupulous rake in a college play, 'Cupid's Confidante', by Hanna Sheehy (later Sheehy Skeffington), who also played the heroine. Stan Gébler Davies writes:

Perhaps the part was congenial to [him]. At any rate, he enjoyed hamming it up and was extravagantly praised by the critic of the *Evening Telegraph*, who compared his technique to that of Charles Matthews, the English comedian whose skill was still celebrated twenty-five years after his death. Joyce was modest about his performance. He told Stanislaus 'the virgin cheeks of my arse blushed for it'. But he kept the clipping in his wallet.

One day, Joyce asked poet and dramatist Padraic Colum for the loan of a half-sovereign. Colum elaborates:

A financial scheme was involved in its use. He had been given a pawn ticket as a contribution to a fund he was raising for himself. Now, to anyone else a pawn ticket would be a minus quantity, but to Joyce it was realizable. The ticket was for books, and six shillings was the amount they were in for. As the ticket had been contributed by a medical student, Joyce told me, the books were undoubtedly medical, and so of value. And we would take them to our friend George Webb on the Quays, and sell them, and make fifty or even a hundred per cent on the transaction.

So we handed out the money with its interest, at Terence Kelly's pawn shop, and the books came across the counter to us. Hastily we undid the wrappings. And lo and behold! the books were an unsaleable edition of the Waverley Novels of Sir Walter Scott, with one volume missing.

★ ★ ★ ★ ★

J oyce won a bronze medal at Dublin's Feis Ceoil (Ireland's premier music competition) when John McCormack took the gold in the same tenors' event. Joyce's songs were 'Come Ye Children' and 'Whom the Lord Chasteneth'. When the sight-reading test was handed to him, he looked at it, then dashed from the stage and headed for a nearby public house.

★ ★ ★ ★ ★

In My Brother's Keeper, *Stanislaus Joyce describes playing charades and indulging in amateur dramatics:*

I n one charade that I remember, while Margaret Sheehy was reciting, [James] was sitting on the floor, half reclining, half resting on one hand, looking up at her with an expression of blank imbecility on his face. Then, following the recitation, his face showed indignation, or astonishment or happiness, always at an imbecile level. At any point of irony he would go into a kink of silly giggles, the perfect reproduction of the laugh of a girl friend of ours, and recovering himself to find that the point of the irony was long past and that the tone was now pathetic, fall to weeping and blowing his nose loudly. I have seen performances far less funny than this impromptu dumbshow applauded on the stage, but except during these lighthearted evenings at the Sheehy's, he did not indulge in this vein. I find traces of it, however, in certain passages of *Ulysses*.

✹ ✹ ✹ ✹ ✹

A marked antagonism between W.B. Yeats and Joyce may have had its foundation in an alleged remark by Joyce when the pair first met: 'You and I have met too late; you are too old for me to have any effect on you.'

✹ ✹ ✹ ✹ ✹

Sandycove's Martello Tower, now the James Joyce Museum, holds an important place in Joycean lore. He, Gogarty and Oxonian Samuel Chenevix Trench (who called himself Diarmuid) were sleeping there when Trench had a nightmare in which he was being attacked by a panther. He awoke, took a gun and fired aimlessly about the room at the imagined animal, then went back to sleep. When some time later Trench shouted in his sleep, Gogarty grabbed the gun and fired at pots, pans, tea-caddy and books above Joyce's bed. Extremely annoyed, Joyce dressed and went walking to the city in the rain. The wetting was worth while, according to some commentators, for the opening chapter of *Ulysses*, based on the incident, is said to have been inspired during the walk.

✹ ✹ ✹ ✹ ✹

Gogarty and Joyce left the Martello Tower after giving their last pennies to pay the milkwoman. Without the tram-fare, they faced a long walk into the city centre. Approaching them they saw John B. Yeats, the painter and father of W.B. and Jack. Gogarty describes what happened:

He was swinging along with a stick and Joyce, whenever he wished to make a joke, assumed an attitude of great seriousness and said, 'It is your privilege to touch the elder Yeats who is now approaching.' And I said, 'Quickly! What do we want?' 'Well, we want threepence each for the tram, that's sixpence, and we want a shilling for drinks this evening in "The Ship", that's one shilling and sixpence each.' Well, you could get a pint of porter for twopence in those days, so by the time I stopped the elder Yeats I got awful timid, and I reduced the sum. I said, 'Mr Yeats?' 'Yes, sir, what do you want?' I said, 'Could you oblige us with the loan of ninepence?' 'Make it a shilling, Gogarty,' whispered Joyce. I said, 'Even a shilling?' 'Certainly not,' Yeats answered. 'First of all I haven't got such a thing and secondly, you and your companion there will spend it on drink.'

Then Joyce came forward and said, 'Might I interpose a moment? By the rules of logic, by the razor of Occam [William of. *c* 1270–1349] — who was a thirteenth-century monk, and lived in Surrey — you're not allowed to have a second explanation if the first is adequate. You have stated that you haven't got a shilling and at the same time you begin to prognosticate what would happen if you had it. It is not allowable to discuss the fate of a thing that doesn't exist. I bid you good morning, sir.' So we had to foot it to 'The Ship'.

✶ ✶ ✶ ✶ ✶

Joyce once received a solicitor's letter with a difference:

Dear Sir,

We are instructed to write to you on behalf of an admirer of your writing, who desires to be anonymous, to say that we are to forward you a cheque for £50 in the 1st of May, August, November and February next, making a total of £200, which we hope you will accept without any enquiry as to the source of the gift.

We trust that this letter will reach you, the address having been taken by our client from 'Who's Who' for 1917.

Yours faithfully
Slack Monro Saw & Co.

✶ ✶ ✶ ✶ ✶

Richard Ellmann tells of Joyce's curiosity about the incident, of his sending copies of his books to the solicitor in gratitude and getting,

103

in return, another letter saying that 'the arrangement would continue while the war lasted and until he was able to settle down again'. Ellmann continues:

When he asked what his patron liked in his work, the solicitor replied . . . 'Briefly, the qualities in your writing that most interest her are your searching piercing spirit, your scorching truth, the power and startling penetration of your "intense instant of imagination".' He knew now it was a patroness.

★ ★ ★ ★ ★

Italian painter Nino Franck told W.R. Rodgers about Joyce taking a taxi into the Bois de Boulogne:

When he spoke to the chauffeur he called him 'choufleur' — that's cauliflower, and naturally the man was astonished and a little insulted, and Joyce paid and went out laughing. When he told me that he said, 'You know, I looked in and really he had the head of a cauliflower.'

★

Maria Jolas, Joyce's first Parisian publisher of Work in Progress, *contributed too:*

He realised that I was destined to have all his proofs go through my hands, and that it might be worthwhile for me to have some understanding of what it was all about. But I remember he picked up a book — the *Book of Kells* — and he showed me one of its most intricate plates, a very beautiful plate, and after joking a bit about the quality of the figures — for instance I remember he laughed about the thirty-five-year-old [sic] Christ who looked as if he had just robbed the hen-house, who was sitting on his mother's knee — he took me down into the left-hand corner of this very intricate plate and showed me, through a magnifying-glass, the beauties of the design in the illumination, and he said to me, 'That's what I would like to feel that I am doing in my work — I would like it to be possible to pick up any page of this work and realise that this is a particular work. I want it to be as evident as this is. Nobody who is acquainted with early illuminations could possibly confuse those of the *Book of Kells* with others.'

Jolas went on to recall the excitement when the final proofs had been settled upon, and driving home eighty kilometres to a celebratory dinner. During it, Joyce telephoned from Paris. He had six further pages to add:

Well, he was accustomed to great indulgence on our part, and a great desire to help, but we did say rather painedly that the *bon à tirer* [fit to print] had been given, and he replied rather stubbornly, not the least bit excitedly, well, he thought we'd better get in touch with the printer because the six pages had to go in.

It was quite evident after a few minutes' conversation that we had lost and he had won, so we called our poor, long-suffering printer and told him to hold up the binding and by Monday morning we were back at Saint Cyr with our little Ford and the six pages had arrived. And they did get in, need-less to say.

Jolas remembered Joyce pointing out that nobody in any of his books had any money. She continued:

Unless I'm dreaming, I remember a conversation one evening in which he explained that the apostrophe was left out of [*Finnegans Wake*] in the intention of giving it another dimension, which was to the effect that Finnegans and the humble people of the world do wake.

His friend Frank Budgen offered a revealing insight:

Talking about Victorianism, there's another angle that was very Joycean, another piece of him that was very Victorian, and that was his attachment — that's the right word I think — to the underclothing of ladies of Victorian days. He regarded these articles of underclothing as being just as important to feminine allurement as the curves and volumes of the female body itself; he even went to the length of carrying a small pair, I might say, a miniature pair, of ladies' drawers, of Victorian pattern, in his pocket — tapes and all complete. And I've known him flaunt these around at the convivial table and when the laughter had died away he could go back to talking about Socratic dialectic and so on. But he waved these around just like a football fan might wave a rattle.

★ ★ ★ ★ ★

Arthur Power, painter and writer, remembered Joyce attending a studio party to meet an American journalist:

The pair sat in a corner, the journalist getting nothing out of him and afterwards remarking, 'I guess everything he has to say has gone into his book.'

★ ★ ★ ★ ★

Oliver St John Gogarty claimed that he once showed some of *Finnegans Wake* to a psychiatrist who said, 'Obviously schizophrenia.'

★ ★ ★ ★ ★

Difficulties with the courting of Nora Barnacle are recollected by Stan Gébler Davies:

Two weeks after she met him she was addressing him in a note as 'My Precious Darling', but signing herself N. Barnacle. By 8 July he was calling her 'Little Pouting Nora' and 'dear little brown head' but signing himself J.A.J. A few days later she is 'My dear little Goodie Brown Shoes' — a little too good for Joyce's taste since he has evidently attempted more liberties than he was allowed. He has slept with her glove beside him all night, and it has conducted itself very properly — like Nora. 'Please leave off that breastplate as I do not like embracing a letterbox.' He plants kisses on her neck, being allowed not much further, and seems quite soon to have gone too far — since his 'particular pouting Nora' withdraws her company for four days without explanation and Joyce is 'trying to console his hand but can't.'

★

Gébler Davies also writes:

[Frank] Budgen dredged from his memory the story of the king of a cannibal island who chose his consort by lining all the women of the tribe up against a horizontal pole, then picked the one whose posterior protruded to the greatest extent. Joyce, he recalled, said 'without the ghost of a smile' — 'I sincerely hope that when Bolshevism finally sweeps the world it will spare that enlightened potentate.'

★ ★ ★ ★ ★

A youth approached Joyce in Zürich and asked if he might kiss the hand that wrote *Ulysses*. Joyce refused, explaining that it had done lots of other things too.

★ ★ ★ ★ ★

Stan Gébler Davies recounts Joyce's resourcefulness when he reviewed Shaw's The Shewing-Up of Blanco Posnet — *using the opportunity to describe the author as having a variegated past; 'every progressive movement, whether in art or in politics, has had him for champion':*

Joyce got free tickets off the manager of the Abbey Theatre by representing himself as a reporter from the *Piccolo*, only afterwards offering the piece to Prezioso, the editor, who accepted it. Armed with this acceptance, Joyce felt free to have cards printed with the legend, James A. Joyce, *Piccolo della Sera*, Trieste. These he used as an entrée to the *Dublin Evening Telegraph*, whose editor showed him round the building, providing thereby more material for *Ulysses*, the Aeolus episode.

★ ★ ★ ★ ★

The celebrated actors William and Frank Fay produced their early plays on a tiny makeshift stage in an out-office of a grocer's shop in

Camden Street, Dublin. Joyce heard about them and came to a performance. He was so drunk that he collapsed at the entrance and patrons were forced to step over him. They complained to the Fays, who had Joyce removed unceremoniously. When he sobered up, Joyce retaliated with a twin limerick:

Oh there were two brothers, the Fays,
Who were excellent players of plays;
And needless to mention, all
Most unconventional;
Filling the world with amaze.

But I angered those brothers, the Fays,
Whose ways are conventional ways;
For I lay in my urine
While ladies so pure in
White petticoats ravished my gaze.

★ ★ ★ ★ ★

For its time, Ulysses *presented printing problems, as indicated in a letter included by André Bernard:*

We have read the chapters of Mr Joyce's novel with great interest, and we wish we could offer to print it. But the length is an insuperable difficulty to us at present. We can get no one to help us, and at our rate of progress a book of 300 pages would take at least two years to produce . . . . I have told my servants to send the MS back to you.

★

A Portrait of the Artist as a Young Man, however, was, according to one memo, 'rather discursive and the point of view is not an attractive one'. Another observes, 'It is not possible to get hold of an intelligent audience in wartime.'

★ ★ ★ ★ ★

Stanislaus Joyce explains the inspiration for an exclamation from Ulysses, *'Jay, look at the drunken minister coming out of the maternity hospital!':*

The echoes of his drinking bouts generally reached my ears at once, and I could hear, as the latest and greatest jest, how after swilling all night he sank insensibly under the table and was borne by his boon companions on their shoulders to some neighbouring park or garden to sleep on the grass there and digest his drunkenness in the open air. It seems that one of the group walked in front, intoning and carrying my brother's [round wide-brimmed soft felt] hat hoisted on his ash-plant after the manner of a processional cross. Some little ragamuffins who were still in the street at that late hour began to run and cut capers around the mock funeral, and, seeing the hat, shouted to one another:

— Yurah, come and look at the drunken Protestan' minister. Did you ever see the like? He's blind to Jaysus.

✹ ✹ ✹ ✹ ✹

Writing of the same incident, Richard Ellmann quotes Stanislaus freely:

He thought his brother was destroying himself, but James met his expostulations with sardonic balderdash. 'What's the matter with you,' he said to Stanislaus, 'is that you're afraid to live. You and people like you. This city is suffering from hemiplegia of the will. I'm not afraid to live.' Stanislaus expostulated, 'Then you don't want to be a writer?' 'I don't care if I never write another line. I want to live. I should be supported at the expense of the state because I am capable of enjoying life. As for writing, I may perhaps employ my sober moments in correcting the grammatical errors of the more illiterate among the rugged geniuses.' When Stanislaus asked him what he could find to say to 'those drunken yahoos of medical students', Joyce replied, 'At least, they don't bore me as you do.'

✹ ✹ ✹ ✹ ✹

Joyce often dubbed *Ulysses* 'The Blue Book of Eccles'. The door of No. 7 Eccles Street, Leopold and Molly Bloom's house, is on display at The Bailey tavern, called 'Burton's' in the novel. Dubliners tell how in 1967 word spread that the Eccles Street house, owned by an order of nuns, was to be demolished. The writer John Ryan owned the Bailey, so he, Patrick Kavanagh and the journalist/film-maker Leslie Mallory arrived with a handcart and asked the Sister in Charge for the door. She would have preferred to see it go with the demolition because of its association with such a 'pagan writer'. A charitable donation swayed her, however, and the trio pushed their cart and No. 7 across the city to Duke Street.

★ ★ ★ ★ ★

Broadcaster and poet Niall Sheridan told W.R. Rodgers how, when researching Joyce in Dublin, he called to a Garda station.

I . . . discovered the station sergeant who was on duty, and of course he was straight out of 'Lady Gregory', an enormous man, very comfortable looking. So I inquired about the whereabouts of this address which was connected with Mr James Joyce, the well-known writer, who was recently dead. And this man scratched his head, and said, 'Would he be from Connemara?' So I explained that he had antecedents in Connemara, but this man was a well-known writer who had died in Zurich. 'Was he a teacher?' said he. 'I knew a Joyce, a teacher, that died foreign. Would that be him?'

★ ★ ★ ★ ★

In 1992 there was a ceremonial unveiling of a plaque at Number 52 Upper Clanbrassil Street, Dublin, the birth-place, in *Ulysses*, of Leopold Bloom. At the edge of a crowd listening to the speeches, a resident of the street said to a passer-by, 'Sure they're all wrong! The Blooms never lived there at all, they lived two doors away.'

★ ★ ★ ★ ★

HISTORY IS A NIGHTMARE FROM WHICH I AM TRYING TO
AWAKE
James Joyce

★ ★ ★ ★ ★

PATRICK KAVANAGH 1904–1967

Patrick Kavanagh was born in Iniskeen, Co. Monaghan where he worked on his father's smallholding before becoming a shoemaker. At twenty-five years of age he arrived in Dublin, having just had his first collection of verse published. He led a frugal life and was often the butt of Dubliners' jokes as he attempted to eke out a living by contributing to assorted publications like Envoy *and* The Bell *and to the BBC. His best-known long poem,* The Great Hunger, *and novel,* Tarry Flynn, *appeared in the nineteen forties. Sixteen issues of* Kavanagh's Weekly *were published in collaboration with his brother Peter between April and July 1952. They carried satirical and comic comment on literature, politics and social affairs. Kavanagh lectured in University College, Dublin between 1955 and 1959 and gained recognition as a major poet in the Gaelic tradition. Hugh Oram writes of him:*

He was a most moody man; on some occasions, he would be in great form and everyone within reach in [Bewley's] café would find him tremendous fun, but at other times, he would lapse into a sulk, totally ignore all around him, push his hat to the back of his head and carry on like a one-man threshing machine.

Paddy was never seen in Bewley's without his hat and coat — these remained on for the duration. He would sit sideways at the table and in what was perhaps a throwback to his childhood days on a barren Monaghan farm, would always hold his cup by the body rather than the handle.

Despite his reputation for consuming prodigious quantities of drink in certain pubs around Grafton Street, he had quite a fondness for Bewley's Jersey milk.

In such a way do we denigrate the living that we must wait until they are safely dead and unable to retort before we praise them loudly. So it was with Paddy Kavanagh; his skills were largely

111

unrecognised in his own time, but now that he is over a decade gone from us, we can complacently add our applause without fear of contradiction. He offered pages of his verse to Joan Swan, one of the waitresses in Bewley's, but she had little realisation at the time of their worth and passed no heed.

Kavanagh's work was plain, earthy and free of gimmicks. He married and died in the same year.

★ ★ ★ ★ ★

Kavanagh once remarked that a local 'bard' in his homeplace held more status there than himself. Yet a former neighbour of his in Iniskeen was seen reading *Tarry Flynn* in a bar and jumping up shouting, 'Begod, that's me!' Kavanagh did not like theatre; he cared less for actors. But he came to the opening night of the P.J. O'Connor adaptation of *Tarry Flynn* at the Abbey Theatre. During his curtain speech he said, 'I wouldn't bring any of my friends to see this vulgar play.' After some applause he continued, 'Look, it's not worth it,' and a voice from the audience retorted, 'You're bloody well right.' This time Kavanagh applauded, and in a public house later on he declared it was only right that the punter should have the last word.

★ ★ ★ ★ ★

Luke Kelly of the 'Dubliners' folk-group made Kavanagh's ballad 'Raglan Road' more popular than it had ever been previously. Its origin is recalled by Benedict Kiely, who was present in the sub-editor's office of the *Catholic Standard* office when the song was first sung. Peter O'Curry was editor and had told Kiely, then a part-time journalist with the paper, to bring in some of his university friends. Kevin B. Nowlan, Associate Professor of Modern History at UCD, was one of them. Both men were working in the sub-editor's office when Kavanagh came in and tossed a sheet on the desk, telling them to sing the verse it contained to the air of 'The Dawning of the Day'.

'Kevin B. and myself singing would clear the Eucharistic Congress out of the Phoenix Park,' admitted Kiely. Kavanagh sang too and when O'Curry heard the commotion, he peeped in and asked, 'What in the name of Jesus is going on here?'

They told him, and he too began to sing. There followed a most inharmonious first rendering of the ballad, written for a lady friend, that was to become world-famous.

✯ ✯ ✯ ✯ ✯

In another editor's office, that of John Ryan's literary journal, Envoy *(1949–51), J.P. Donleavy met the poet:*

Kavanagh could often be found there by mornings reading snippets from submitted manuscripts to which his invariable reply was.

'Rubbish. Utter drivel and the most appalling nonsense I have ever had the disinterest to read.'

Of course Kavanagh hadn't read more than four words of a single line but would fling the offending pages back where they came from. And upon this occasion and as the door opened a manuscript of my own hit me in the face. Kavanagh had the good manners to apologize. And knowing that Kavanagh had been a farmer or at least from a farming family I took the opportunity to avail of farming if not literary advice and asked him about growing potatoes. He looked at me with the most brilliant portrayal of sceptical disgust.

'Ah God, I suppose now you've got an acre or two.'

'Four acres.'

'Four acres have you. And I suppose you've got chickens.'

'Thirteen.'

'Thirteen have you. And I suppose too you've got cabbage, their leaves sparkling of a morning with dew.'

'Six rows.'

'And you're wading twice a day through the nettles and docks to fetch a bucket of water from the nearby stream.'

'Five times a day.'

'And I suppose it's a nice little three room cottage with a hedge around it and you've got a cow to milk and a patch of strawberries ripening for June.'

'I have.'

'Phoney, phoney, phoney. Utterly phoney. The whole thing is phoney. Nothing but phoniness.'

Kavanagh shook his fist as he shouted and lurched in his

mock high dudgeon like a ship pitching in a storm. One saw the truth of his remarks knowing that this simple way of life had cost a fortune in education and existed upon a small private emolument arriving every week from an attentive mother and that I had come to this peasant land with my nice big American pot to piss in. And I laughed outright at his wisdom. But what he did not know was that I had taken my college mattress out of Trinity and placed it on a door torn off one of the cottage rooms and this stacked on bricks was my bed. And that I had found an old face of a rusted shovel in a hedgerow, cut down an ash sapling and shaped and fitted it as a handle. And with this same spade, dug a basin in the tiny nearby stream from where one fetched water. But as I left the office of *Envoy* that day. Still laughing. Kavanagh turned to talk behind my back.

'That man's no phoney. Sure if he were he couldn't laugh at what I said.'

I wasn't exactly

Guffawing

And Kavanagh left me

Feeling

Phoney enough

I can tell

You.

★ ★ ★ ★ ★

John Ryan's family owned the Monument Creameries chain of restaurants. Over one of these, in Grafton Street, was Desmond MacNamara's studio. Ulick O'Connor writes about activities there:

Among regular visitors to the studio were J.P. Donleavy, Phyllis Teale, Ernie Gebler (later to marry Edna O'Brien), Dan O'Herlihy, H.A.L. Craig, Patrick Kavanagh and Anthony Cronin . . . . Once, an aggressive young woman, enraged that the poet Kavanagh had not offered her a drink, said, 'Did you not see I had a mouth on me?'

'How could I miss it,' said Kavanagh, 'and it swinging between your two ears like a skipping-rope.'

Kavanagh once wrote a piece in the *Irish Independent* about Croagh Patrick, which he described as 'flamboyant and colourful as some warm-faithed corner of mediaeval Christendom'.

On the day it appeared, the author was attending a court case; he had sued the British and Irish Steamship Company when he was knocked from his bicycle by one of its horse-drawn carts. Many agreed that his allegations of mental anguish and grievous bodily harm may have been rather exaggerated. In any event, the Justice, who had seen the article, complimented Kavanagh on it and awarded him thirty-five pounds in damages.

☆ ☆ ☆ ☆ ☆

It was probably his dislike for The Irish Times *editor, Bertie Smyllie, that brought about Kavanagh's desertion of the Palace and Pearl bars. He opted instead for McDaid's, and Anthony Cronin recalls:*

There was at one time a somewhat elderly and habitually rather bemused barman in McDaid's whose name was John. He was very slow in movement, more than a little deaf and had the petulance of the aged, so, roar though he might, Kavanagh did not always get served as promptly as he would have liked. Because of the white hair he decided to call this barman 'Whitehead'; indeed he would often heavily pretend that he was the philosopher in person and refer when talking at him to negative prehension and such matters. This was a cause of growing annoyance to John, often expressed by mutterings as he shuffled off down the bar. One Good Friday, a day on which the pubs are of course shut in Dublin, Kavanagh apparently had the luck to meet 'the Pope' O'Mahony, who was a member of the Zoological Society, and persuaded him to take him up to the Zoo, where drink could be obtained in the members' restaurant. The following day I was in McDaid's.

'I believe Paddy Kavanagh went up to the Zoo yesterday lookin' for drink,' remarked a red-faced gurrier who was sitting at the counter.

John looked up from the pulling of a pint and said, 'It's a wonder they didn't keep him there.' Then he paused for a moment, topped off the pint and added viciously: 'I suppose they thought he might frighten the animals.'

☆ ☆ ☆ ☆ ☆

Eoin ('The Pope') O'Mahony was a barrister, lecturer and genealogist who wandered afar, calling on celebrities uninvited and being welcomed, for a while at least, because of his scintillating conversation. Cronin writes:

The unfortunate Pope was in fact the subject of a classical Irish bull which Kavanagh once made and of which, when I pointed it out to him, he was very proud. We were in the George in Great Portland Street, a BBC pub much frequented by Hibernophiles who worked for the Corporation in various capacities. The Pope was holding forth at great length to an admiring audience while Kavanagh sat and suffered. The performance lasted a long time, but eventually he departed. After he had gone there were murmurs of admiration and appreciation all round. Kavanagh broke in on them. 'That's a terrible bore,' he said. 'He must be the greatest bore on God's earth.'

'Oh come now, Paddy,' said one of the circle. 'You can't say that. Everyone knows he's a brilliant talker. After all he successfully talks for his dinner.'

'He'd eat a damn sight more if he kept his mouth shut,' replied Kavanagh.

☆ ☆ ☆ ☆ ☆

In London also, on one occasion, Kavanagh had been drinking in the home of a dentist friend but had become involved in an argument and was asked to leave. Broke and facing a long day without booze, he conceived a plan. He enlisted Anthony Cronin's aid. Cronin brought a note of apology from Kavanagh around to the dentist, who was still drinking. The plan envisaged his stealing a bottle of whiskey and hiding it inside his coat while the dentist read the letter. But Cronin was given a drink and told to sit down. The dentist stuffed the note into his pocket and never read it.

Kavanagh was furious that his ruse had failed.

⋆ ⋆ ⋆ ⋆ ⋆

In McDaid's on a Sunday morning, Cronin met Kavanagh and remarked that a distinguished jockey, Tommy Weston, was writing his memoirs in the News of the World:

'I see that,' said Kavanagh.

'He must be broke,' I said.

'Any man at all that's writing anything whatever is broke. Don't you know that by now?' was the Johnsonian answer.

⋆ ⋆ ⋆ ⋆ ⋆

There was an alleged attempt to murder Kavanagh for exposing a scandal through the columns of the *Farmers' Journal*. His drink was doped and when he dozed off he was thrown into the canal near Baggot Street. Apparently it was thought that even if he did not drown, pneumonia would kill him, because he had only one lung. However, the shock of the cold water brought him to his senses and he clambered out. Although he had lost one shoe and his glasses, he succeeded in climbing a high wall and reaching the residence of a medical friend, where he was treated for exposure. He also managed to write an account of the incident in his column. But he did not write what he truly believed saved him — the spirit of his dead father.

⋆ ⋆ ⋆ ⋆ ⋆

Dr Patrick Henchy, director of the National Library, dined with Kavanagh and was embarrassed when the poet could be overheard four tables away saying, 'I'd love to be married to an aristocratic English lady. Do you know what I'd marry her for? I'd marry her for the soup she'd make.'

⋆ ⋆ ⋆ ⋆ ⋆

Henchy, Kavanagh and Harry Craig met to play cards one day. Although Craig brought along some pleasant young ladies, Kavanagh wore his old coat, his hat thrown on the back of his head, and was constantly reaching across and taking Henchy's money. When Kavanagh whispered something to one of the girls, she seemed to be offended. Henchy's innate chivalry prompted him to challenge Kavanagh.

'What did you say to the lady?'

'I only told her she was a cute hoor!'

*****

Kavanagh regarded Brendan Behan as 'incarnate evil'. Their rivalry may have stemmed from the 1952 libel action taken by Kavanagh against *The Leader*, in the course of which Behan's name was mentioned. But an article written by Behan for *Vogue* in 1956 surely exacerbated things. Although it decried bogmen in general who spoke English that Behan could not understand, the phonetics used definitely pointed towards the accents of Kavanagh's native Monaghan: 'Hah sure Aydit [Edith Sitwell] is a naice semple wamman at the back avitt, aye shewerly . . . .'

*****

During the Leader *trial Kavanagh said of Behan: 'There was always something in [him] that to my mind was not good. I have been friendly with him hoping that I would be free from the horror of his acquaintanceship.' Ulick O'Connor elaborates on the case:*

In court the following day Kavanagh was handed a copy of his novel *Tarry Flynn*, autographed to 'my friend Brendan Behan'.

Kavanagh was nonplussed.

Actually, Behan's brother, Rory, without Brendan's knowledge, had given the book to the Defence. Brendan was furious with Rory for doing this, and told him he should never interfere between writers.

*****

Kavanagh won an appeal for a new trial. On the day the judgment was given, he was having an operation for lung cancer, so later he settled out of court. Recuperating, he went to New York. Peter Kavanagh quotes Patric (sic) Farrell:

On New Year's Day bitter and raw we called to the Farrelly's home on East 72nd Street for Patrick to take him to a salon, open house celebration, at the home of the Aerosol heiress who had an art collection of note. The party was so filled with high personages of art, literature and the social world that Patrick inquired of me if I thought it was safe to leave his overcoat with the butler who had tried to take it from him. It was precious to Patrick. Because of the bitterness of the day and Patrick's post-operative condition as he was fitting on the garment I solicitously asked if he thought such a coat would be warm enough for such a bad day. He indignantly scowled at me and asked, 'What's wrong with this coat? It is thornproof!' And this in the fashionable silk-stocking district.

★ ★ ★ ★ ★

Peter Kavanagh writes about his brother's final illness:

Pat O'Connor arrived in his car and we all set out for the Rialto Hospital along the canal bank. At the hospital we met Dr Keith Shaw. He questioned Patrick on his symptoms as Patrick sat wearing his overcoat, his hat and scarf. 'For the past six months', he began, 'I have been suffering from the delusion that I had catarrh.'

Patrick wanted us to wait for him — he'd be right with us immediately after the bronchiscope test. It wouldn't take a budge out of him. I persuaded him it would be best if we left now, and came back at noon to pick him up. Meanwhile he would rest at the hospital.

On his way back into town Pat told me that a priest friend of his had visited him a week before with the exact same story — he was suffering from a fatal disease. The priest was scared. Patrick, on the other hand, was very philosophical about it and told Marthe (Pat's wife): 'Very likely it is cancer and it will kill me, but to tell you the truth, Marthe, I don't give a shite.'

★ ★ ★ ★ ★

MY SOUL WAS AN OLD HORSE
OFFERED FOR SALE IN TWENTY FAIRS
Patrick Kavanagh

★ ★ ★ ★ ★

JOHN B.
KEANE
1928–

Striding across the stage of popular writing, John B. Keane was for years shunned by the National Theatre. However, due to enthusiastic responses from amateurs and from one professional company, Phyllis Ryan's Gemini, he became a huge success. His play The Field *(1965) was made into a film starring Richard Harris, bringing widespread recognition and a new lease of professional life. Keane's prose is full of rural fun and his collections of 'Letters', to parish priests, Dáil deputies and others in England are best-sellers.*

Keane spent part of his early adulthood working at road-sweeping, bartending and in a pharmacy. He and his wife, Mary, own a public house in Listowel, Co. Kerry, which provides the author with a considerable amount of material for his prolific output. After a day spent writing, he likes to drink a pint or two outside the counter and engage in conversation with the customers. He admits to having 'a short fuse' on certain topics and his work reflects a critical attitude towards the Roman Catholic Church's teaching on sex. Best known for his plays and books, Keane has written poetry and a musical. Impishly, he claims to have no objections to long, tedious plays: 'I always feel fresh when I wake up at the end,' he says.

★ ★ ★ ★ ★

The Listowel playwright's own favourite anecdotes include one about an author who went on stage after the first presentation of his new play.

As moderate applause rippled all around he said, 'It's not so much me as the help of God which saw this fine play through to a finish.' From the back of the auditorium came the retort: 'Take the blame yourself, you scoundrel.'

★ ★ ★ ★ ★

Keane's first play Sive *got its first performance in Listowel in 1959 and the town was buzzing with rumour that some of its earthy con-*

tent would find disfavour with the Catholic Church. Gus Smith and Des Hickey tell:

In the audience was a clergyman who had earlier intimated he would have to leave for a sick call at nine-thirty. Instead of giving the priest an aisle seat so as to make his departure less conspicuous, someone had placed him in the centre of the hall, eight rows from the stage. At nine-thirty the priest stood up and, to the annoyance of those in his row, pushed his way out of the hall. Nothing would convince some of the audience but that he had walked out in protest.

★

The Smith/Hickey biography recalls that Charles Stewart Parnell once held a monster rally in Keane's home town and addressed the attendance from a window in the Listowel Arms, then goes on to describe Keane, the prankster, injecting some fun into a general election campaign in 1951:

With his friends from Curly's [public house] he set about organising a political skit involving a fictional politician to be named Tom Doodle. By his own admission, the stunt was aimed at taking the bitterness out of local politics.

One of the first locals to notice that something was happening was Kieran O'Shea [who] noticed posters hung on telegraph poles . . . proclaiming: 'Vote No. 1 Tom Doodle. Use Your Noodle and Give the Whole Caboodle to Tom Doodle'.

The townspeople were puzzled. 'Who is Tom Doodle?' they asked. A week later new posters appeared announcing that Tom Doodle would address a big political rally in the square in Listowel. The rally was scheduled for a Holy Day, and that evening scarcely any worshippers turned up for Benediction in the local church; everybody had gone to the railway station to greet Tom Doodle.

O'Shea knew by now that John Keane was involved in the affair. At the station he saw him step down from the train with Doodle, who wore a top hat and a swallowtail coat, and was conspicuous by his luxuriant beard. Keane stood beside him as the election lorry proceeded, to cheers, through the crowd towards the local square.

'John was pokerfaced all the time,' said O'Shea. 'I couldn't tell if he was serious or not.' The story is that as the lorry was coming down Church Street an old woman looked up at Doodle and called, 'Parnell, my boy, you are back with us again!'

★ ★ ★ ★ ★

In Keane's busy pub in Listowel, during Writers' Week, a tinker was asked on three occasions in the one evening to leave the premises. Returning a fourth time, he leaned over and confided in a customer: 'You know why he won't serve me? He knows that I knows who really wrote *Sive*.' (*Sive* features two tinkers; the complainant said he was one of them and he should know!)

★ ★ ★ ★ ★

The actor Mick Lally is given as the source of the story about an actress arriving in Listowel, seeing Keane's public house and saying, 'God, they must love John B. here. They've even named a pub after him!'

★ ★ ★ ★ ★

At the height of his popularity for the 'Letters' series, I asked Keane for a list of letters he would like to have written. He replied:

1. A letter to the Queen of England requesting her to write an article on matchmaking [and this was long before any Royal nuptial difficulties!].

2. A letter to the Quebec Chamber of Commerce asking what they really think of the GAA.

3. A letter to the Shah of Iran asking him who does he really think he is.

4. A letter to Ian Paisley asking him to repent the same as any other so-called Christian.

5. A letter to Saint Paul thanking him for putting letter-writing on a respectable basis.

In his autobiography, Keane writes about a schoolfriend, Murphy, who had emigrated before him, met him by arrangement in Northampton and introduced him to his landlady:

Murphy knocked again and finally a small fat woman of middle-age, with a cigarette in her mouth and a tam on her head, opened the door.

'I'm not 'aving 'im!' she said.

'Why not?' Murphy demanded.

'I'm not 'avin' Paddies!' She was adamant.

'He's not a Paddy,' Murphy said. 'He's a Jock the same as myself.'

'Awright,' she asked quickly, 'which part you from?'

'Glasgie!' I lied, without batting an eyelid.

Finally, she said: 'You'd better come in, then.'

☆

When he entered, Keane spotted a notice that went something like this:

Guests will not use chamber pots, bedpans, urinals or commodes in bedrooms. Guests will not keep cage-birds, dogs or pets of any kind. Guests will not entertain female visitors. Guests will not spit while indoors. Guests will not bring alcoholic drinks into bedrooms. Guests will flush toilets immediately after use.

Keane translated it into pidgin English for a Polish guest who previously had thought it to be a house blessing.

★ ★ ★ ★ ★

THE LIKES OF US THAT'S IGNORANT HAS TO BE CLEVER
John B. Keane

★ ★ ★ ★ ★

BENEDICT
KIELY
1919–

He was born in County Tyrone and never lost its rich accent. A master storyteller, Benedict Kiely turns a conversation into an art form. He was educated in Omagh and at University College, Dublin, became a journalist and spent some years as literary editor of the Irish Press. *For four years from 1964 he lectured in American universities.*

Many Irish people associate Ben Kiely with the radio programme 'Sunday Miscellany'; indeed for years, the morning of the day of rest would not have held promise without him spinning a yarn over the airwaves. Kiely has written many fine short stories and novels; a play, Proxopera, *adapted from one novel, was not particularly successful. A fair and scholarly critic, he has written a study of William Carleton's work and* Modern Irish Fiction — A Critique. *He lives in Donnybrook, Dublin, which he still describes as a village, even though it bustles with commuter traffic and personnel from the nearby radio and television studios.*

★ ★ ★ ★ ★

In a Presses de l'Université d'Angers journal, Kiely writes about an incident that forms the basis of his short story 'A Great God's Angel Standing':

I became a great friend of an old priest, a Father Paul McKenna, in the 1940s. I was home convalescing out of hospital and I got friendly with old Father Paul. And he used to go out to the Tyrone and Fermanagh Mental Hospital to hear the confessions of the inmates. Now Paul was a very distinguished old man, he was very literary; he was a great man to quote Robert Burns, but always the more puritanical portions of Burns, like 'Pleasures are like poppies spread/You clutch the flower, the bloom is dead.' And one day we went into the Tyrone and Fermanagh Mental Hospital, and on the bridge as we went in we met two British soldiers. One from Devon, and one from Somerset. That was just after the Battle of Dunkirk. And these two men had married two Irish girls before they went to France, and they were walking from the barracks in Omagh — the war clouds were heavy all over the world — to meet the two girls at Six Mile Cross. So we joked with them about zider and all the sort of things you say to fellows from Somerset. Zomerset. And they walked on. Then we met the chief doctor in the mental hospital, and then we went into the hospital. I was out of the Jesuit novitiate at the time, and out of hospital, and I was wearing a black jacket. And this poor devil there, Joe Sharkey, came up and knelt down at my feet. He only saw my back. And he said, 'Father, could you hear my confession.' And I said, 'Get up, Joe Sharkey.' And he said, 'God, it's Tom Kiely's son.' Joe was put into the mental home for a very simple crime. He just chased women. He never overtook them. If they walked, he walked, if they ran, he ran. But they put him away for that.

In the same publication he gives a hint on the making of a short story:

I want to come back to another story told to me by a Sligo man, Arthur Hunter. He was a friend of Michael Mahon who told me the story about the body in the bed. Both Mahon and Hunter are now dead. But Arthur told me about a friend of his from Sligo, who was up in Dublin, and he was on a bit of a blinder. And he finds himself one morning walking up O'Connell Street. He is unshaven, he is in a dinner jacket, and rather rumpled trousers. So he's been at some function the night before, but he can't remember what it was. And he walks into the Gresham Hotel where he would be known, and he walks through the foyer, and up to the first floor, and a man comes out of a bedroom. So he tries the door as he passes, and the door opens, and he goes in. He has no money, and the banks aren't open, and he can't cash a cheque. So he gets into the man's bed, and then the idea comes to him: he orders a large brandy and soda. And they catch him on the third brandy and soda, but they're very nice about it. He's quite a respectable gentleman from Sligo. And he says he'll be back later when the banks open. But I heard that story and I said now that can't be the end of that; there must be more to it. Something happened when he was lying in that bed. So I wrote a story called 'Bloodless Byrne of a Monday' [*A Letter to Peachtree*]. Then the story about Bloodless Byrne was told to me by men who literally were sending Connemara ponies to England. And the old joke about what the man said to the horse — that's an old Dublin chestnut. But you see if the man got into that bed, would it not have been possible that the phone rang looking for the man who should have been in the bed. All of a sudden, he finds himself living another man's life under these rather curious circumstances. So a story gives you a hint, and you get a bit here and there, and try to compose the thing the best you can. After all, *Mr Joyce* began to write a short story and it got out of hand, and ended up as *Ulysses*. Even the best gentlemen get out of control at times.

✴ ✴ ✴ ✴ ✴

In The Hollins Critic, *vol. XXIX, no. 2 (April 1992), Kiely, writing about the novels of Kate O'Brien, observes that in 1992:*

No little rural Irish colleen is likely to remark [as did an O'Brien heroine] on a lady wearing lipstick, or anything or nothing else. In fact the little rural Irish *cailín* is herself liable to be wearing the oddest garments.

It seems a long time since the old parish priest in a Kerry seaside resort said from the pulpit, and in the height of the holiday season, that he saw a lot of strange women going around in trousers: and it would be much more pleasing to God if they went around without them.

✴ ✴ ✴ ✴ ✴

A MAN'S COUNTRY BEGINS . . . WITH HIS FATHER AND
MOTHER
Benedict Kiely

HUGH LEONARD
(JOHN KEYES-BYRNE)
1926–

Nicholas Keyes, Hugh Leonard's Da, worked as gardener and factotum at the home of the wealthy Jacob family near Dalkey, Co. Dublin. Jack Keyes-Byrne came under the normal pressures from his mother, Margaret, to be educated and get a steady job in the civil service. Spells in the 'nuns' at Loreto and at 'Harolds Boys' led him to a scholarship at Presentation College, Glasthule. There he met sons of snobs, whom he learned to insult with a deftly selected phrase. It was enough to nurture a talent for fine humour and deadly satire.

He did accomplish his mother's dream, and spent fourteen years in the Land Commission. He acted with its dramatic society, but a visit to the Abbey Theatre sparked the desire to become a playwright. Success came when, after having a few works staged by amateurs, he changed the name of one of them and submitted it to the Abbey over the pseudonym Hugh Leonard. The Big Birthday was produced in 1956 and an incredible out-put of radio, television and stage work followed. His plays are assured and technically perfect; they entertain immensely. Da, the most popular, won four Tony Awards and was made into a film starring Barnard Hughes. Leonard himself prefers Summer.

★ ★ ★ ★ ★

Rightly peeved at constant insinuations that, because they are enjoy-able, his plays are somehow lacking in quality, Leonard told a journalist who asked why he did not write a play that 'says some-thing':

I am saying something, if with a small 's', and it is this. If you care to come in out of the rain for a couple of hours, I shall attempt to entertain you and send you out again feeling as if you have had a good meal. Mind, I may not be successful in this intention, for I am not using the crutches of either the missionary or the Artist (capital 'A'), which, if they do not keep the play upright, at least excite our pity and indulgence.

✶ ✶ ✶ ✶ ✶

An adopted child, Leonard confessed to having thought often about his natural parents. For some unknown reason, he sometimes fancied that Denis Johnston might have been his father and told the Johnstons so. Johnston's daughter and Leonard thereafter jokingly called each other 'Bud' and 'Sis'.

✶ ✶ ✶ ✶ ✶

Hugh Leonard is a devastatingly humorous columnist and public speaker. When he opened the thirty-second All-Ireland Amateur Drama Festival at Athlone, he spoke of a certain seminar on theatre held in Salzburg. As well as lecturing there, he took part in associated activities. At one session, the importance of trust among actors was being stressed — trust in the author, in the director, in the stage-manager, in the other members of the cast, in the prompter! An exercise was carried out to assess the strength of this trust. Participants were placed along the wall of a room. One by one, each of them had to move, with eyes closed, to the other end. Here, a floor-level window was left wide open and only the clasped hands of two colleagues would keep the walker from passing right through to an eight-foot drop. Leonard described the experience something like this:

You are certain they're your friends; you know they like you. But when you're halfway across, you think of a dozen things about yourself which would give them sufficient cause to unclasp their hands.

✶ ✶ ✶ ✶ ✶

Before that Athlone event, I spoke with Leonard and complimented him on an obituary he had written on the accountant and theatre buff Russell Murphy. Leonard laughed heartily and told me what the world and its wife was to know the next day — that Russell Murphy had misappropriated a gigantic sum of Leonard's and others' money. In his published reaction to the incident, Leonard added that he intended writing a play about it and calling it 'You Can Take It With You'.

128

A gentleman from the firm of accountants called on Leonard to break the bad news that he was down a quarter of a million pounds. He was beating around the bush until Leonard said, 'Don't bother telling me how much is gone; tell me how much is left.'

*****

Leonard told of giving up his attempts at acting after playing the part of an unfrocked priest in *The Intruder* (from François Mauriac's *Asmodée*) at Dublin's Peacock Theatre. 'It was such a success that we transferred to the Little Flower Hall in Bray,' he said. There they performed to complete families and while he was soliloquising at one point, a child in the audience began to cry. Leonard continued: 'I heard a woman shout, "Shut up!" While I wondered was the order directed at me, the lady repeated, "Shut up — or I'll get him down to you!"'

*****

Leonard was adjudicating at a drama festival in which a university group performed Sartre's *The Flies*, a retelling of the *Oresteia*. In Act 2 a great stone was rolled back from a cave. There was a considerable rake on the stage and the boulder (papier mâché, but big) careered right across the apron and landed on the front row of the audience.

It was a long, wearying production and he was glad when the third act ended at a very late hour. Quickly gathering up his papers and briefcase, he strode up the centre aisle and moved briskly backstage. A surprised stage-manager saw him and exclaimed: 'Jaysus, Mr Leonard, you know this is a four-act play!'

*****

Attempts at soldiering are among Leonard's admitted failures:

Third Port of Dublin Sea Scouts: Dismissed by drumhead court-martial on a trumped-up charge of hooliganism.

Emergency Communications Corps: Dishonourable discharge when, due to an unexpected 'fixed' wheel on my bicycle, I cycled into Bulloch Harbour [Dalkey], sustaining the loss of a tin helmet and terminal rust to the vehicle and myself.

Local Defence Force: Enforced resignation when accused of causing the aborting of a major all-night exercise by mistaking two enemy commandos for a snogging couple ('Whoever', Groucho Marx observed, 'called it necking has a very poor sense of anatomy').

★ ★ ★ ★ ★

Nonetheless, while he cannot be hailed as a Patton or a Montgomery, Leonard does have military experience:

Indeed, I did see military service during the war and was killed on three occasions at the Battle of Agincourt. Mr (as he then was) Laurence Olivier was directing his film of *Henry V* in Powerscourt Demesne, and his dramatis personae was drawn from the ranks of the Local Defence Force — or 'Da's Army', as we might now term it. We were a fine body of boys, and we prayed that the third Reich would not be such a pack of lousers as to invade the country prematurely and take the bread out of our pyorrhoeal mouths.

The work of a film extra was most congenial to the Irish temperament, consisting as it did of sitting around for most of the day and doing nothing. The French infantrymen wore doublets, bits of sacking around their feet and tin helmets one could poke a sausage through; but because of war-time shortages we did not wear hose. Instead, our legs were painted blue, green or yellow; which was a mildly voluptuous experience until the paint dried and one attempted to walk.

Being on the losing side, I spent most of my time in blind retreat, and of my three deaths, the worst was by drowning in a swamp. With some five hundred others, I was directed to stagger into a mud-pit, assume a facial expression of extreme annoyance and emulate the *Titanic*. When I saw the film later, it was with feelings of having been ill done by. So many of us had been packed together that the morass itself was invisible: all one saw was a mass of bodies heaving together in what looked like communal constipation.

We lived in tents, each one of which was furnished with

twenty straw palliasses and two one-gallon cans intended to accommodate the results of nocturnal emergencies. Anyone who wished to see a man about a dog of a different breed would, of course, use the latrines, and a corporal of my acquaintance, while returning from such an expedition, had the misfortune to stray into the wrong tent.

It was occupied by a group of stalwarts from the Ringsend battalion, compared with whom the Visigoths could have been categorised as pacifists. They seized the intruder and, to chasten him for his presumptuousness, proceeded to embellish his private regions with boot polish of such indelibility that his wife — a simple soul — later accused him of infidelity with a black Protestant.

✶ ✶ ✶ ✶ ✶

In June 1978, Hugh Leonard's *Da* won Tony Awards for Best Play, Best Actor (Barnard Hughes), Best Director (Melvin Bernhardt) and Best Featured Actor (Lester Rawlins). The presentation was the last on the programme and host Jack Lemmon forgot to ask for the award to be handed back for engraving. The playwright quipped the morning after: 'I am not going to give it back now in case they forget to return it.' He got the engraving done himself.

✶ ✶ ✶ ✶ ✶

In one of Leonard's plays there is a passage which is based on an incident in the author's own life, when he was twenty years of age. He went into a cinema, sat down and to his amazement (and delight) the girl in the next seat put her arms about him and kissed him passionately. She maintained the initiative and the petting became as heavy as a critic's pen. No words were spoken until the pair left the cinema. Then the girl looked at the young Leonard and said, 'You're not Charlie.'

✶ ✶ ✶ ✶ ✶

Leonard gave the actor Cyril Cusack a signed copy of his autobiography Home Before Night *as a first-night present. It was not yet on sale and the author wrote what he hoped was a graceful dedication*

131

on the flyleaf before sending the copy backstage. He did not know that the copy's dust-jacket had been attached upside down, so the tribute was written the wrong way up and at the bottom of the last page. Leonard describes their meeting after the show:

'You don't like actors very much, do you, Jack?' [Cusack] said in that affable voice in which an eloquent and sceptical 'Mmmm' was never far away.

☆ ☆ ☆ ☆ ☆

In the civil service, Leonard encountered correspondence concerning a War of Independence veteran who was drawing a pension for an injury received when he was shot in the right ankle. He had a motor-cycle accident and his right leg had to be amputated — so he lost the pension!

☆ ☆ ☆ ☆ ☆

Few can evoke the atmosphere of early amateur theatre in Ireland like Hugh Leonard:

We called ourselves Lancos Productions because we all worked — no let me be exact and say that we were employed — in the Land Commission. One of our two yearly plays was a prestigious affair, such as *Hedda Gabler* or *All My Sons*, with which we astonished audiences at the Peacock Theatre or the Dagg Hall. The other play was chosen with an eye to touring.

For our forays to the parish halls of Kinnegad and Enfield, Summerhill and Kildalkey, we broached the works of Lennox Robinson, George Shiels and Frank Kearney. We did not offer caviare to the general; what they got was honest bacon and cabbage, with rhubarb and custard for afters; and we shared the profits with the local parish priest.

Once, I recall, we went to Ballymore Eustace, where the late Father Maurice Browne was the incumbent. Years previously, he had himself written a play; it was called *Prelude to Victory* and I had played the 'Third Black and Tan', with only one line to say: i.e. 'Which wy did the bawstid double back?' In portraying village life under the Saxon thumb, it made

132

Auschwitz seem like Butlins.

Anyway, on this evening in Ballymore Eustace, I regarded the parochial hall with some pleasure. It was packed; they hung from the rafters; they sat on radiators, on the edge of the very stage. A kitten, had it wandered in, would have suffocated. 'Not bad,' I said to Father Browne. He fetched me a look of clerical disgust. 'A wash-out!' he trumpeted. With a gesture of his arm, he embraced all of the Black Hole of Ballymore Eustace, 'Are you blind? The place is half empty!'

Sure enough, two weeks later, instead of our share of the takings, we received a box of Milk Tray [chocolates] and a note to say that the people of Ballymore Eustace were a dreadful lot who never supported anything.

Leonard had other clerical experiences:

There were priests of a very different kind in nearby Blessington, [Co. Wicklow] where we presented *The Righteous Are Bold* to such a storm of acclaim that a return performance was insisted on. What we did not know was that the local curates decided that our production would be improved no end with a few special effects.

The Righteous Are Bold is a play about diabolic possession in a remote part of Mayo — which, I suppose, means anywhere in Mayo. It is strong stuff. I, as one might expect, played the lovable, valorous old priest who exorcises the demon, and in Act Two there was a scene where I put a flea in the ear of the local doctor, an agnostic.

This role was played by a burly fellow with a military moustache. He happened to be a roaring alcoholic, and had just climbed most painfully on board the water-wagon. He was in a state of acute fragility. His face had a damp look.

'Doctor,' I said to him suavely, running a finger around my Roman collar, 'Have you ever heard of a person being possessed by the devil?'

As he opened his mouth to reply there was an apocalyptic roll of thunder and a hellish green light enveloped the stage. There were yelps of gleeful terror from the audience. The effect was not so pleasurable, however, upon the 'Doctor', who by a supreme effort of will managed not to drop dead. Even so, when the lighting reverted to normal, his face remained green, as if it had been dyed. He shook. Perspiration flowed torrentially down his brow. Then he spoke.

What he was supposed to say, scoffingly, was: 'Possessed by the Devil, Father? Pshaw, what superstitious mumbo-jumbo!' I cannot swear to the 'pshaw', but it was along those lines. What he actually said was: 'Christ, I'm in the jigs.'

After a pause, I thought it best if at least one of us adhered to the original script. Ignoring the bit about the jigs, I said my next line, which was: 'My dear Doctor, it is a foolhardy man who denies the existence of Lucifer.' At this, there was another thunderclap and the stage was again bathed in corpse-like green. The 'Doctor' shook even more violently; the image came into my head of an epileptic cycling on cobbles.

It was now clear that whenever the Devil, Lucifer or Satan was mentioned, one curate, standing in the wings, would rattle his home-made thunder-sheet, while the other would switch on the green fairy-lights that he had lovingly strung above the stage. We tottered to the end of Act Two, attaining it only by cutting every reference to the Powers of Darkness, which, in the context of *The Righteous Are Bold*, was rather like *Othello* without the handkerchief or *Antony and Cleopatra* minus the asp. Worse awaited us, however, in Act Three.

The high point of the play was, of course, the exorcism, to be performed by myself while our star actress, Róisín Ní Nualláin, lay writhing and snarling at my feet, her wrists and ankles tied. The 'Doctor', now shaking sporadically, had been persuaded to remain in the theatre and was on stage as an onlooker. The moment came, and, as I got into my act, curates got into theirs. 'EXORCISO TE!' I bellowed, while Miss Ní Nualláin screamed her head off. Then, out of the corner of my eye, I saw the double barrel of a shotgun poking from the wings.

My first reaction was disbelief. Then I wondered if there were, perhaps, drama critics in Blessington and one of them had had enough. Meanwhile, the words of the exorcism tumbled out, and today, thirty years on, I flinch from describing what happened next.

There was an explosion that was heard in Poulaphouca. And a ball of fire travelled across the stage. It is not generally regarded as possible for a supine person, bound hand and foot, to move in an upward direction, but Miss Ní Nualláin achieved that feat, reaching, at her zenith, an altitude of some forty inches.

The Righteous Are Bold ends with the death of the priest from heart failure. It was a scene that in my condition required not much acting ability; and, as for the 'Doctor', all that was required of him was that he pronounce me dead and close my eyes. By now, he was shaking so violently that he left me unable to read small print for a week.

The curtain fell to wild applause, and the parish priest came up on the stage, raffled two hundred cigarettes and made a speech. He thanked Cosmos Productions — our name, as I have said, was Lancos — and told the audience that the play was true in every detail and showed what happened to Irish girls who went to work in England.

The 'Doctor' was not present. He had gone to the nearest hostelry and, although it was after hours, persuaded the landlord to help him alight from the water-wagon. He has not been seen anywhere near that kind of vehicle ever since. As the rest of us left the parochial hall, we noticed members of our audience standing in quiet groups on the unlit village street. Later I learned that they were afraid to walk home along the country roads in the dark. It was hard to blame them.

✸ ✸ ✸ ✸ ✸

MY GRANDMOTHER MADE DYING HER LIFE'S WORK
Hugh Leonard

✸ ✸ ✸ ✸ ✸

MICHEÁL
macLIAMMÓIR
1899–1978

(See also 'Hilton Edwards' and 'The Gate Theatre'. Note: The subject used different arrangements of his pseudonym but 'macLiammóir' during his final years. I use this form, but quote other writers in their own usage.)

★ ★ ★ ★ ★

When the eleven-year-old Alfred Willmore played in Miss Lila Field's The Goldfish *in London, Noël Coward was in the cast.* The Daily Express *said: 'A little boy — Master Alfred Willmore — is "Sir Herbert Tree" — so called because he is a finished little actor and has great ambitions. But his pet name is "Bubbles", for he has the little angel face and the golden curls of the child in Millais' famous picture.'*

Alfred became Micheál macLiammóir. Until Micheál Ó hAodha's excellent biography (published in 1990), it had always been accepted that the actor was born in Blackrock, Co. Cork, and macLiammóir had allowed the myth to flourish. However, Ó hAodha traced his birth to 150 Purves Road, Willesden, London, as the son of a forage dealer's buyer.

Travelling, painting and Gaelic League activities occupied the young man's time before he joined Anew McMaster's touring company in 1927. Hilton Edwards was a member. MacLiammóir designed and acted in a production of his own Diarmuid agus Grainne *for Taibhdhearc na Gaillimhe, the Galway Irish-speaking theatre, just weeks before he and Edwards launched the Gate Theatre Company at Dublin's Peacock Theatre. Two years later they moved to Cavendish Row and began a lifetime devoted to stylish presentation of the classics.*

Affected, ever acting, courteous but sometimes domineering, macLiammóir came across as a vain man, but close acquaintances testify to his winning and warm personality. He hated vulgarity and the violence which was perpetrated in the name of the Ireland he loved so much. He prayed each night by his bedside for people who were suffering in the world, saying that if he prayed in bed he might fall asleep before his list was complete! He also kept a diary in Irish and wanted a Gaelic/European

*Ireland rather than an Anglo-American one. Among his pleasures he list-
ed watching ballet, listening to Chopin and being alone with a friend 'in
the mountains or forests when one comes close to God'. Towards the end of
his long career, his celebrated one-man show on Wilde,* The Importance
of Being Oscar, *was a* tour de force.

★ ★ ★ ★ ★

*Manuscripts written by macLiammóir in pencil on exercise-book
paper, and containing a number of spelling mistakes, tell how he
and Hilton Edwards discussed the setting up of a theatre to stage
dramatic masterpieces of all nations and periods. He writes:*

Where the miracle was to be accomplished was one of
the first questions that cropped up — how to accomplish it being to our youthful minds, aflame with enthusiasm,
a negligible affair — and I, bitten from childhood with the
nationalist bug that has attacked my particular generation in
my particular country, I shouted Dublin.

'Why Dublin?' asked my companion, between two sips of
steaming whisky punch — the scene was a pub in Tipperary
and the day was bitter — and our companion Coralie
Carmichael who was to become for many years our leading
actress looked at me with sympathetic curiosity. 'Why not
London?' he continued. 'There are more people there.'

'And more everything else,' I said. 'London has everything,
Dublin next to nothing. What's growing must be fed.'

★ ★ ★ ★ ★

When the Edwards-macLiammóir company were working on Tolstoy's *The Power of Darkness* in 1929, they
had great difficulty in finding a samovar, demanded by the
script. After a search of the city, one was found in a junk shop
— but nobody knew how to use it. So another search had to
be made for a 'Samovarian Expert'. A Russian lady was discovered who, according to macLiammóir, 'explained, in a
melancholy musical contralto and in four languages,' all
about it.

The company became proficient in its use; not alone that,
they used it to make their tea during rehearsal breaks.

A tall sixteen-year-old singer, later the RTE newsreader Charles Mitchel, was brought by his mother to audition for Henri Gheon's *The Marvellous History of St Bernard*. He took his place in an actual rehearsal, where he was to perform a brief cantor's intonation of *Dies Irae*. His mother had not mentioned that his voice still had not broken. When he sang, macLiammóir called him aside and said, 'My dear boy, I do not think the public is quite ready for a soprano monk.'

★ ★ ★ ★ ★

When Edwards and macLiammóir were getting the Gate into shape for their February 1930 opening of Goethe's *Faust* (translated by Tristan and Graham Rawson), macLiammóir suddenly was seized with enthusiasm for the Irish language. On the doors of the lavatories, in expensive gold leaf, he directed the painters to inscribe FIR and MNÁ.

Officials from Dublin Corporation inspecting the premises insisted that these directions were inadequate and instructed that MEN and LADIES should be added. Users of the King's English might wish to avail of the facilities too, they reasoned.

MacLiammóir had to give in but, mischievously, under Men he also added Hommes, Manner, Hombres, Uomini, Ferfiak and Andron.

★ ★ ★ ★ ★

While playing Oberon, King of the Fairies, in *A Midsummer Night's Dream*, macLiammóir received a letter from one Vivian Butler-Burke. It contained a cheque for £100 as a token of admiration for his performance and for opening the donor's eyes to the 'Gates of Fairyland'. There was an invitation to lunch at the Gresham Hotel too, so macLiammóir went along and met this sixty-year-old admirer, her escort (a small Indian who disappeared when lunch was over) and her dog, Connla. She told him he hadn't changed a bit.

That was strange, for they had never met. At least, that's what macLiammóir thought, but Vivian insisted — and she swore Connla agreed with her — that they had known each other last time round, when macLiammóir belonged to a different race — Persian, Chaldean or something!

When macLiammóir told her he couldn't accept the £100, she said, 'You can't accept — a mere symbol! Well, I see you *have* changed.'

The pair compromised. She would accept £100 worth of shares in the Gate Theatre.

★ ★ ★ ★ ★

Hilton Edwards found Butler-Burke tiresome. MacLiammóir accompanied her, therefore, on some of her archaeological trips and 'sentimental masquerade[s] that cloaked a half forgotten sincerity'. He tolerated her enthusiasm and 'mild paganism', consoling himself that 'only the simple can accompany the great on the eternal cavalcade'. Her part in the evolution of the Gate was 'incongruous, maddening and quite inexplicable'.

At the end of their 1934 summer season, Vivian had been missing for some time before macLiammóir met her walking her dog one morning in St Stephen's Green. She had news for him! He was a Navaho Indian! And it had been revealed to her that he was going to America! America was in the air; did he not feel it?

MacLiammóir studied her closely. He studied, and wondered. There was no possible way she could have known about the telegram in his pocket. It had arrived from Orson Welles in New York before macLiammóir had set out for his walk. It invited the company over to join him for a summer season at Woodstock, Illinois!

★ ★ ★ ★ ★

At a symposium in Benburb, Co. Tyrone in April 1970, the writer Eugene McCabe stated that Brendan Behan had spent a considerable part of his life writing political hatred out of his system. Tyrone Guthrie blamed the Churches for Sean O'Casey's 'namby-pamby' love scenes, because all Churches in Ireland promoted the idea that Irish girls are so pure and Irishmen so brutal. MacLiammóir bluntly stated that O'Casey was overrated as a dramatist. He was a fine comedian and character-creator — 'Ireland's answer to Dickens', in fact — but his love scenes would make you blush: '"Little Nora of the sweet red lips"'! In the name of Jaysus, could you imagine it? And they say this in front of the Tans or the IRA or whoever it happens to be!'

★ ★ ★ ★ ★

Micheál Ó hAodha noted macLiammóir's reservations about television, especially 'the spurious spontaneity of such shows as "This Is Your Life"'. MacLiammóir once said, 'I dislike television trying to bring theatre to the fireside. It's like bringing religious sacraments to bed with the breakfast tray.'

★ ★ ★ ★ ★

MacLiammóir often regaled friends with startling stories which indicated that he was an extremely psychic person. After rehearsing late into the night on one occasion, he returned home with Hilton Edwards, to find there had been a power failure. Edwards moved upstairs quickly but as macLiammóir slowly followed, despite the darkness, he saw a distraught man dashing past him, chased by four others. When he reached their apartment and Edwards told him he had not seen anything, macLiammóir was quite overcome.

He made enquiries, and a long time later learned that the house had been one of those raided by the IRA on Bloody Sunday morning, 21 November 1920. A number of British servicemen were shot there. MacLiammóir was convinced that he had seen the scene re-enacted.

★ ★ ★ ★ ★

MacLiammóir agreed to deliver a late-afternoon reading for a charitable organisation, so he arranged for a member of the committee to pick him up at the theatre after a matinée performance.

When the actor emerged from the stage door, the lady apologised, saying, 'You haven't even had time to remove your make-up.' MacLiammóir smiled and said he had indeed removed it, but was now in his 'street make-up'. And he was.

The actor Simon Callow was a devotee of macLiammóir's. He described meeting Micheál as 'a headlong plunge into a bubble-bath spiked with cinnamon'. He was macLiammóir's dresser for some performances of The Importance of Being Oscar *in Belfast. Very touching is his account of helping the great actor reach the stage through the difficult passages and corridors of Belfast's Grand Opera House:*

I was keeping a close watch on the clock. I had been firmly instructed that I was to announce when there was half an hour before the curtain rose, when there was a quarter of an hour, when five minutes, and finally, when it was time for us to go to the stage.

As the time approached, a change came over Micheál. The patter became a trickle and finally dried up. His make-up — which in fact only amounted to touching up his street make-up — was quickly effected; his costume consisted of nothing more than evening dress, and of course a green carnation. He sat in front of his mirror staring, haunted, at his face. He seemed barely to hear the calls. As the curtain got closer and closer, he started to tremble. Sweat trickled through his rouge. He grasped on to the table in front of him till his knuckles were white. The stage manager arrived to give him his call. He reached out for my hand. 'Lead me,' he said. 'I can't see, d'you see.' Down the pitch dark corridor we went, his finger nails digging ruts into my palms, while with his free hand he crossed himself again and again. 'Jesus Mary and Joseph. Jesus protect me. Jesus.' We reached the stage. I said: 'There are three stairs now.' 'Where? Where?' I helped him up, one, two, three. He fumbled with the black cotton drape, pushed it aside, and was on stage. In the pitch black, the light dazzled, but I heard big, solid, welcoming applause, and then Micheál's voice, rock-steady, as if he'd been on for hours: 'To drift with every passion till my soul . . . ' I slipped round to the front and watched the ebullient unrecognizable figure juggle words and emotions, drawing his audience of largely middle-aged, middle-class Belfast burghers and their wives into his charmed circle, luring them into a world of sophistication and wit that they would under any other circumstances abhor, somehow making them feel that he and they shared a secret and a wisdom. He used to claim that he was really a *seanchaí*, a storyteller, and here was the spell in action.

MacLiammóir was performing his celebrated The Importance of Being Oscar.

★ ★ ★ ★ ★

Micheál Ó hAodha tells:

MacLiammóir's triumphant one-man show was first performed to an audience of about two hundred at the Gaelic Hall of the Curragh Military Camp in County Kildare . . . . The squat concrete building was an unlikely venue for such an important preview, but here macLiammóir played and for a full two-and-a-half hours he 'harangued the troops on the subject of Oscar Wilde'.

★ ★ ★ ★ ★

During his later years macLiammóir wore a Cossack-style cap, which friends claimed was a form of protest against his brother-in-law, Anew McMaster.

McMaster was a man with sartorial taste and he once purchased a rather elegant, broad-brimmed hat which he loved to wear. When macLiammóir praised the article, McMaster was even more proud, but he would not tell macLiammóir where he had bought it. So one evening macLiammóir dropped in unexpectedly on his sister and brother-in-law. They all conversed a while, sipped a little wine and exchanged polite pleasantries. Close to midnight macLiammóir announced that it was time to leave, but that he would see himself out.

He did so, and next morning when McMaster reached for his hat, it was gone from the hall-stand.

The following week, macLiammóir had an unexpected visit from his sister and her husband. There was more small talk and once again the guests' departure was marked by an empty space on a hat-stand. Never had relations such close liaison as during that winter. MacLiammóir would call to McMasters' Sandymount home one week; McMaster would visit him the next — and each time the hat left with the caller. Although it must have been obvious to both parties what was happening, the millinery manoeuvres were not discussed. Indeed, it appears to have become a friendly game for no attempts were made to hide the attractive head-dress in either home. To his associates, though, macLiammóir claimed the hat was as much his as McMaster's. However, he finally conceded McMaster's rightful ownership and took to wearing the Russian-style cap.

✷ ✷ ✷ ✷ ✷

Simon Callow found being macLiammóir's dresser 'an experience compounded equally of pity and terror, and my first encounter with the reality of performance':

I would arrive at the theatre somewhat before he did, to iron and arrange his clothes. I was a stranger to these arts, and he showed them to me, as well as the arts of packing a suitcase and preparing his interval drink of gin and tea. He always arrived in the highest good humour, full of jest and profanity. He divested himself of his clothes to the accompaniment of a seamless patter of erotic speculation, literary quotation, character assassination ('of course when poor dear Cyril Cusack played Hamlet in a selection of costumes purloined from sundry shows of the previous season, he became the Prince of Great Denmark Street') and self-revelation. As he stood in his underpants he gazed in a melancholy manner at his groin. 'My testicles,' he said, moodily, 'have become *distended*' — the bulge did seem unusually substantial — 'as a result of a virus contracted, I fear, from a seaman. Are you a virgin?' The unexpectedness of the question made me blush. 'No,' I lied. 'Good, good. And to which are you more inclined, men or women?' 'Both,' I lied again. '*Very good,*' he said, 'although I must confess that the older I get, the less I am able to enjoy the company of women — except of course our own dear Enid who is so notorious a Sapphic as to be virtually *hors concours.*'

143

Callow again:

One late night in Belfast in 1968, I sat with Micheál Mac Liammóir in the Grand Hotel in Belfast, sipping Bushmills while he as usual sipped gin. We were talking about movies, of which he was an avid devotee, despite his cataracts. We discussed Zeffirelli's *Romeo and Juliet*. He said: 'You see, the boy just wasn't young enough. Oh, to be sure, he *looked* young, delightfully, beautifully young, but he *wasn't* young. Would you permit me — now don't be embarrassed, for God's sake — would you permit me to play the tomb scene?' And from memory — had it been forty years? thirty, at least — he spoke the lines, and as he did so, the mask that life had given him dissolved and he became the vision of youthfulness, beside which Leonard Whiting seemed elderly. Micheál believed in it; and it was so.

★ ★ ★ ★ ★

Micheál Ó hAodha's account of macLiammóir's funeral concludes:

Patrick Bedford threw a green carnation on the coffin, saying, 'Good night, sweet prince and flights of angels sing thee to thy rest'. Hilton Edwards bade farewell with the lines from *Cymbeline*:

Fear no more the heat o' the sun
  Nor the furious winter's rages;
Thou thy worldly task hast done,
  Home art gone, and ta'en thy wages:
Golden lads and girls all must,
As chimney-sweepers, come to dust.

★ ★ ★ ★ ★

THERE IS A GENIUS TO BE FOUND IN THIS COUNTRY OF
OURS, BUT NO TALENT
Micheál macLiammóir

★ ★ ★ ★ ★

ANEW McMASTER
1894–1962

A great actor-manager in the Victorian, Shakespearian tradition,
Monaghan-born Anew McMaster liked nothing better than to perform
the classics in less favoured parts of Ireland. He acted in Australia,
England and the Near East. Tall and handsome, with a dignified pres-
ence, his Lear, Othello, Richard III and Shylock are well remembered.
McMaster believed passionately in the text above all, and today's spectacu-
lar production gimmicks would be anathema to him. 'Mac' was always the
star, but a number of big names in Irish theatre and television cut their
teeth under his management or direction. The Edwards/macLiammóir
partnership began when the pair met in his touring company. He married
a sister of macLiammóir's and was set to play Othello to Micheál's Iago for
the Dublin Theatre Festival when he died.

★ ★ ★ ★ ★

McMaster collected extras as required from towns and
villages in which he played. It was the duty of the
stage-manager to rehearse these, often a mere hour before
curtain-up. For a production in a small western town, a youth
was recruited for the role of an attendant in *King Lear*. He
was told when to enter, where to stand and what to do —
which was nothing! 'Just remain there and don't move,'
directed the stage-manager.

The majestic McMaster had reached the fourth scene of
Act One and was absorbed in the title role when he turned to
the young man and commanded, 'Go you and call my fool
hither.' Loyal to his instructions, the lad did not move.

'Go you and call my fool hither,' Mac repeated, somewhat
perturbed. Still no response, for the lad had been given no
details about an exit. Summoning up his most stentorian
tones, McMaster pointed to the wings and roared once more,

'Go you and call my fool hither, I say!'

His gesture and glare at least conveyed to the extra that a speedy withdrawal was required, but the temporary Thespian was clearly heard by the audience saying, as he departed, 'Jaysus, the fool out there told me not to move.'

* * * * *

Everybody was surprised at the reaction from rural audiences to McMaster's policy of producing Shakespeare in the wake of fit-ups that offered plays like *Shall We Forgive Her?* and *The Lights of London*. Mac's *Othello*, *Hamlet* and *Lear* were received with acclaim in towns previously considered too unenlightened for anything adventurous or austere.

It was McMaster's custom to announce the following night's show at every curtain-call. How he must have relished the vindication of his brave conviction which rang out from the back of a hall in County Clare one evening! He had promised the light situation comedy *Charley's Aunt* by Brandon Thomas, and was heckled: 'This town is too backward for them highbrow plays; what about giving us *Julius Caesar*?'

* * * * *

For playing the part of a cardinal, McMaster had a magnificent costume. Six boys from the village were called in to bear its train. Approaching Mac in the wings for the first time, they knelt and kissed his ring.

* * * * *

A local lad was recruited to play a messenger to McMaster's *Macbeth* and was rehearsed by the stage-manager in his Act Five Scene Five appearance. Nervously he entered and said his introductory line, followed by:

As I did stand my watch upon the hill,
I look'd toward Birnam, and anon methought
The wood began to move.

In his typical melodramatic way, McMaster grabbed the lad by the throat and hurled him to the ground, shouting,

'Liar and slave!' Instead of uttering his next line, the terrified extra called, 'Honest to Jaysus, Mr McMaster, that's what the fellow out there told me to say!'

★ ★ ★ ★ ★

Harold Pinter's first proper stage job was a two-year tour with McMaster. Playing Bassanio to McMaster's Shylock in *The Merchant of Venice* one evening, Pinter fluffed the line, 'For thy three thousand ducats here is six.' He said, 'For thy three thousand buckets here is six.'

Soberly, with dramatic emphasis on the errant word, McMaster continued, while the cast tried to stifle titters:

If every bucket in six thousand buckets
Were in six parts, and every part a bucket,
I would not draw them; I would have my bond.

Venues did not always appreciate Shakespeare, as Pinter relates:

Joe Norton, the business manager, came in one day and said: 'Mac, all the cinemas in Limerick are on strike. What shall I do?' 'Book Limerick!' Mac said. 'At once. We'll open on Monday.' There was no theatre in the town. We opened on the Monday in a two-thousand seater cinema, with *Othello*. There was no stage and no wing space. It was St Patrick's night. The curtain was supposed to rise at nine o'clock. But the house wasn't full until eleven-thirty, so the play didn't begin until then. It was well past two in the morning before the curtain came down. Every one of the two thousand people in the audience was drunk. [Strange, since drink could not then be sold legally on St Patrick's Day.] Apart from that, they weren't accustomed to Shakespeare. For the first half of the play, up to 'I am your own for ever', we could not hear ourselves speak, could not hear the cues. The cast was alarmed. We expected the audience on stage at any moment. We kept our hands on our swords. I was playing Iago at the time. I came offstage with Mac at the interval and we gasped. 'Don't worry,' Mac said, 'don't worry.' After the interval he began to move. When we walked onto the stage for the 'Naked in bed, Iago, and not mean harm' scene (his great body hunched, his voice low with grit), they silenced. He tore into the fit. He made the play his and the place was his. By the time he had reached 'It is the very error of the moon; She comes more near the earth than she was wont, And makes men mad' (the word 'mad' suddenly cauterized, ugly, shocking), the audience was quite still. And sober. I congratulated Mac. 'Not bad, was it? Not bad. Godfrey Tearle [English actor, celebrated for his playing of Othello at the Shakespeare Memorial Theatre] never did the fit, you know.'

★ ★ ★ ★ ★

As he grew older, McMaster found it difficult to remember lines, especially in long speeches. So he wrote portions of them on various pillars incorporated in the setting. He delivered segments as he leaned against the appropriate columns, moving from one to another until the soliloquy was completed.

Because of a hurried setting-up by stage-hands for one performance, the pillars were incorrectly placed and Mac began his speech in the middle. He muttered, 'Wrong bloody pillar,' and went in search of the opening pilaster.

★ ★ ★ ★ ★

IT MAKES NO DIFFERENCE TO ME IF I'M ON BROADWAY OR IN THE SMALLEST VILLAGE IN IRELAND. THE ONLY THING THAT MATTERS IS THAT I'M PLAYING
Anew McMaster

BRINSLEY MacNAMARA 1890–1963

Of Irish writers remembered for a particular piece of work, Brinsley MacNamara stands out. His succès de scandale, The Valley of the Squinting Windows, *was burned in 1918 in his native Delvin, Co. Westmeath, where villagers believed themselves ridiculed and exposed by the book. His schoolteacher father, James Weldon, from whom the author received his education, was boycotted and professionally ruined. Weldon took action against Delvin's parish priest and named neighbours for loss of earnings and pension rights, but lost the case and could not afford to appeal. The novel brought John Weldon (Brinsley MacNamara) commercial success but other, better works gained less recognition. The autobiographical* In Clay and in Bronze *(New York 1920) is especially good.*

MacNamara acted with the Abbey and toured with the company in the United States. He became a director but resigned in 1935 when O'Casey's The Silver Tassie *was finally produced there. He was a broadcaster and a theatre critic for* The Irish Times *until its editor, R.M. Smyllie, of whose Palace Bar coterie he was a member, published a letter criticising one of his reviews. MacNamara was a prolific poet, novelist and playwright and contributed to assorted newspapers and journals. The story of the burning of his novel and other biographical details are contained in my book* The Burning of Brinsley MacNamara.

★ ★ ★ ★ ★

After acting with the Abbey Theatre from 1910 to 1912, MacNamara returned home to Delvin, where he began writing his first novel. In July 1914 he wrote to the poet Seumas O'Sullivan:

I have recently moved into an east room and find myself greatly improved by the change. Here in the village, I have made a study of this matter of light and have already cured one man of sleeplessness and another of neuropenia, by making them change their rooms and find that the most successful people are those with a west light. Among those who are with a north or north-east light are bankrupts, drunkards, lunatics, defectives and decayed people.

★ ★ ★ ★ ★

In A Letter to Peachtree *Benedict Kiely recalls Brinsley MacNamara's habit of prefacing statements with the words, 'Curious thing, you know':*

Curious thing, he says, how landscape, buildings, environment, physical surroundings can affect the character of people. Take, for instance, your average Dublin workingman. A rough type. A man with a young family, he goes out to the pub in the evening. He drinks a pint, two pints, three, four, five, six, perhaps ten pints. He's a noisy fellow. He sings. He talks loud. He argues. He may even quarrel. He staggers, singing, home to the bosom of his family, in tenement apartment or corporation house, goes to bed quietly and, soundly, sleeps it off. But down in the soft midlands of Meath and Westmeath, where I come from, things are different. The heavy heifers graze quietly and the bullocks, all beef to the ankles. The deep rivers flow quietly. Your average workingman there is a bachelor. Living most likely with his maiden aunt, and in a labourer's cottage. In the quiet, green evening he cycles six or so miles into the village of Delvin for a drink. He drinks quietly. One pint, two, three, anything up to ten or more. In the dusk he cycles quietly home and murders his maiden aunt with a hatchet.

Curious thing, environment. Curious thing.

★ ★ ★ ★ ★

Mystery surrounds the immediate source of Brinsley MacNamara's inspiration for The Valley of the Squinting Windows, *and is deepened by a letter to George Roberts, managing director of Maunsel & Co., in September 1917. Edward MacLysaght had read the manuscript and recommended its acceptance, but Roberts was wary of possible libel in the opening chapter. (It was Roberts who, five years earlier, had rejected Joyce's* Dubliners, *and destroyed the printed sheets at Maunsel's, before its eventual publication by Grant Richards in June 1914.) Brinsley's letter read:*

Ballinvalley
Delvin
Co. Westmeath
Sept 23rd 1917

Dear Mr Roberts,

The point raised in your letter, and note on passage in Chapter One of 'The Squinting Windows', is very interesting. However, here are the facts upon which this portion of the story is based.

Mr Henry Shannon and Mr Robinson, the solicitor, were as they actually existed here in Westmeath about thirty years ago — bosom companions and first cousins. Mr Robinson afterwards became Crown Solicitor for the county. When Henry Shannon got himself into the scrape with the girl, he went to his legal friend for advice. Whatever that advice may have been, the taking of her to Dublin was what he did as a result of it, as the people of the locality understood it. This amounted to 'making a prostitute of her' and it was in this light that she afterwards came to see herself, because of the scorn of those around her and because of Mr Robinson's letter. Mr Robinson's advice was merely that of a shrewd man with a perfect knowledge of the people of the Valley, and his letter the best means of frightening her from further action in the circumstances he had helped to create.

In the bit I have now in, I think I have fully indicated the essential portion of these facts and removed from this portion of the story any trace of legal error which may have existed. This alteration will not necessitate corresponding alterations in other parts of the story. I trust you will find it satisfactory.

Sincerely yours,
Brinsley MacNamara

When a copy of The Valley of the Squinting Windows *reached Delvin, Joseph Clyne, publican and butcher, regaled his bar-room customers with episodes from the new book, amid bawdy jeers and whoops of hilarity as villagers were recognised in its pages. If the similarities were not at once apparent, Clyne pointed them out. Midway through the sixth chapter he stammered to a halt:*

It was thus and thus that Rebecca Kerr ran through her mind a few immediate sketchy realizations of this village in Ireland. She had lived in others, and this one could not be so very different . . . . There now was the butcher's stall, kept filthily, where she might buy her bit of beef or mutton occasionally. She caught a glimpse of the victualler standing with his dirty wife amid the strong-smelling meat. The name above the door was that of the publichouse immediately beside it.

It was Clyne's!

✶ ✶ ✶ ✶ ✶

There have been allegations of clerical intervention during a court case brought by MacNamara's father against the parish priest and some of his flock. Philip Rooney told Benedict Kiely of going to Navan races with a clergyman friend and of imbibing in the public bar of Crinnion's Hotel. The priest began to talk too loudly about assorted matters. Philip got worried about what people might say and advised the priest to move with him into the residents' lounge in case some of his utterances got back to the bishop. The priest admonished Philip, saying, 'No bishop can touch me. I'm the man [who] drilled the witnesses in the Weldon case.'

✶ ✶ ✶ ✶ ✶

Seán Mac Réamoinn related a story about MacNamara's displeasure with broadcaster Philip Rooney's adaptation of his work. The pair avoided each other for some time. By chance they met in a bar which was otherwise empty. MacNamara growled a greeting, each then took turns at treating, but there was little conversation. Rooney, possibly embarrassed, launched into a long-winded story but, after some time, realised that its amusing punch-line was at MacNamara's expense. So he muttered some gibberish, finished his drink and left the bar. Some days later, a friend told Rooney that MacNamara had said of the meeting, 'It's so sad about Philip. The other day he was blind drunk at ten o'clock in the morning and told the most silly long story that had neither rhyme nor reason.'

★ ★ ★ ★ ★

The Burning of Brinsley MacNamara *describes how, at seventy years of age and crippled with arthritis, MacNamara returned to Delvin in the company of his son, Oliver:*

They stopped at Barry's public house (Harry Barry's mother had been identified with Mrs Wyse in *The Valley of the Squinting Windows*). After the long journey, Brinsley was barely able to stand and Oliver helped him from the car. Barry's was the bar previously owned by Joseph Clyne, who still ran the butcher's shop alongside. As the big but frail author was assisted towards the premises, Clyne stood at his shop doorway in a striped, bloody apron, a cleaver hanging from his belt, coldly staring at his old and crippled arch-enemy with no sign of recognition nor softening of features.

★ ★ ★ ★ ★

The part played by the clergy in the 1918 book-burning in Delvin was deplorable, and the facts are given in *The Burning of Brinsley MacNamara*. A lady in Delvin who had promised accommodation for the launching of the book in 1990 withdrew her offer without explanation. Later, it was alleged that she had received clerical advice that her hospitality would be imprudent!

★ ★ ★ ★ ★

THEY ACCEPTED THEIR NATIONALITY AS THEY ACCEPTED
THEIR RELIGION, JUST PASSIVELY
Brinsley MacNamara

★ ★ ★ ★ ★

GEORGE MOORE
1852–1933

Novelist George Moore, of Moore Hall, near Ballinrobe, Co. Mayo, rebelled against family traditions of wealthy landownership and racehorse training (although he once had an ambition to win the Grand National). During his education at Oscott College, Birmingham, his father, a Member of Parliament, received a report saying that George was deplorably deficient 'and it is by no means easy to see how his defects are to be supplied'. He went to Paris to paint and later began writing. He abandoned the Roman Catholic religion, predicting that the parish priest would, by degrees, disappear 'like his ancestor, the druid'. Provokingly un-English, Moore also held scorn for things Irish but seemed to relent in later writings. Both Sarah Purser and Susan Mitchell are credited with saying of the bachelor Moore, 'Some men kiss and tell; Moore tells but does not kiss.'

A character in his novel Esther Waters *(1898) was modelled on W.B. Yeats, from whom Moore learned about the occult. He spun this knowledge into the novel's plot, which was concerned with Wagnerian singers and musicians.* The Lake *(1905) was described in Ernest A. Boyd's* Ireland's Literary Renaissance *(1916) as the literary revival's 'first and only novel of distinction'. Its setting was Lough Carra, over which Moore Hall looks. On an island in the lake, Moore's remains, inurned in a food vessel, were interred under a quarter-ton of concrete.*

✶ ✶ ✶ ✶ ✶

W.B. Yeats describes Moore coming to him for advice on a matter that had been troubling him for years:

'O Yeats . . . how do you keep up your little pants that are inside your trousers.' And I said to him, 'Moore, if you look at the tops of your little pants that are inside your trousers, you will see that they have small tapes fastened to them. And if you put the ends of your braces through the small tapes before you fasten them to your trouser buttons, your little pants will stay up inside your trousers.' Moore thanked me and went away, and the next time I saw him he came up to me and said, 'O Yeats — God bless ye.'

★ ★ ★ ★ ★

Moore sent a copy of his *Life of Christ* to George Russell, with an inscription assuring him that he would like it. Russell wrote back, 'On the contrary, I like it less than any of your books. Jesus converted the world; your Jesus would not convert an Irish County Council.'

★ ★ ★ ★ ★

A great admirer of Russell's, Moore once exclaimed to Yeats, 'there must be a flaw in that perfect soul'. On a Sunday evening he attended one of AE's gatherings and returned 'full of dark whisperings'. 'Yeats,' he said, 'I have discovered the flaw — suppressed wife!' Yeats continues:

[He] set off to write a chapter for his book [*Hail and Fraewell*] to the effect that AE neglected his wife for Miss [Susan Langstaff] Mitchell, who happened to work in the same office with him.

Quite apart from the fact that the suggestion was absurd, only a person of Moore's *naïveté* would have supposed that such a publication would be allowed. AE at once took proceedings and stopped the chapter. 'You know, Yeats,' Moore complained, 'he's such an egotist!'

★ ★ ★ ★ ★

Terence de Vere White knew Richard Irvine Best, director of the National Library. In an Irish University Review *article (Autumn 1977), he recalls:*

Best liked to tell how he introduced Moore to the subjunctive mood. Joseph Hone put it down in his biography. Moore, in Dublin, had antagonised as many people as he pleased and, being a bachelor and not so gallant as he pretended, was often at a loss after dinner for something to do. He was not a reader. He got into the habit of walking over to the National Library, a five minutes' stroll from his house. 'If John Eglinton was not in his office, scripture was abandoned for that evening, and he would go on to Best for English grammar.' The conversation would turn, as so often with Moore, on literary style in the difficult art of writing:

'But you write well, Best. Why don't you write more? I wish I could write like you.' Moore's hand would then go to his waistcoat pocket for a slip bearing a sentence which he had found intractable during the day's work. On one occasion Best casually referred to the subjunctive mood as one that might be used in a certain predicament. 'But what is the subjunctive?' exclaimed Moore, with elevated eyebrows and shining eyes. 'Give me an instance.' When the usage of this moribund mood was explained to him, he cried out, 'Oh I would give *anything* to be able to use the subjunctive. If it be, if it rain; how wonderful! But I will *always* use the subjunctive mood.'

★

In his will, Best left Terence de Vere White a table:

He has told us its history. When he broke the news of his forthcoming marriage to Moore, adding that neither he nor his wife had any illusions about each other, Moore, rather sweetly — for him — said that he was sure that they had. Moore said, 'I should like to give you a present, Best. What would you like?' 'That is very kind of you,' Best replied. 'Well, what would you like?' 'Something for the house.' 'Would you like a table?' They set off together for Naylor's, that treasure house that used to be in Liffey Street, and there Moore selected a table with claw and ball feet. Best describes in minute detail the whole transaction to the conferring with Naylor about the price, and the great moment when Moore turned the table upside down and wrote 'George Moore' underneath it.

When I look at it now I think of his remark when Best assured him that some of his work would live for ever. 'What use is immortality to me when I am dead?'

After Moore's death, boatmen refused to bear his ashes across the waters to Castle Island on Lough Carra. They believed it lucky to take a corpse across water, but while being a 'lapsed Catholic' was bad enough, cremation was the ultimate offence. Friends attended to the task and when his remains were scattered, George Russell said in a funeral oration: 'If his ashes have any sentience they will feel at home here, for the colours of Carra Lake remained in his memory when many of his other affections had passed. It is possible that the artist's love of earth, rock, water and sky is an act of worship.'

ART MUST BE PAROCHIAL IN THE BEGINNING TO BECOME
COSMOPOLITAN IN THE END
George Moore

MORE
ASSORTED
ANECDOTES

My book The Ernie O'Malley Story *includes the following anecdote about the revolutionary and author:*

Before the end of 1933 Prohibition had been repealed and
Ernie O'Malley was back in New York. He travelled by a
hot, stuffy bus. Greasy from the clammy atmosphere, the
other passengers remained dourly silent when he suggested
opening a window. He endured the discomfort for a while,
but then asked a woman would she mind if he let in some air.
She did! Her child might catch cold. An angry Ernie opened
just the same. Later he said, in defence, 'Better a baby to die
than ten grown-ups.'

✯ ✯ ✯ ✯ ✯

*O'Malley spent a while in the artists' colony of Taos, New Mexico
with the children of the Irish American actor and lecturer, Peter
Golden. Peter's son, Terence, recalls:*

We drove to the Grand Canyon from Pasadena in the
fall of 1929. Mother found this less arduous than she
had anticipated . . . so we continued on to Santa Fe. There,
Mother discovered that an old friend, the Irish poetess, Ella
Young, was visiting in Taos; so we drove on up to Taos . . .
and were hooked! We were travelling in a 1925 Chevrolet
sedan with the paraphernalia typical of the day: an extra spare
tyre and rim roped onto the regular one at the back, bedrolls
piled on the roof of the car and more bedrolls tied between
the fenders and hood, an expandable rack on the running-
board crammed full of gear, a triplet of cans clamped to the

running-board — white for water, red for gas, and blue for oil — and water bags dangling from the bumpers.

In addition to 'the folks' there was I, aged about eleven or twelve, and Ernie O'Malley, who had been a commandant-general in the Irish Republican Army at the age of nineteen, or something. Ernie was volatile, fascinating, exciting, entertaining, infuriating, impetuous, brilliant . . . .

When we left the Grand Canyon via a terrifying trail called the 'Navahopi Road', Ernie gallantly offered to drive. His credentials as a chauffeur did not inspire confidence; he had a habit of putting his foot on the clutch instead of the brake. Well, Mother and Mariana [Howes, a friend of the family] were standing on the running-boards amongst all the clutter and junk, clinging desperately to the door frames. (I suppose they thought they were lookouts.) I was sitting on the front seat, next to Ernie. We were going down a tortuous pitch of rocks and ruts that made an abrupt right turn at the bottom of an unbelievably steep hill. There was a good reason for the turn. If you missed it, you dropped several hundred feet off a cliff into the canyon of the Little Colorado. Terror and tension mounted. Sure as hell, Ernie hit the clutch instead of the brake. We didn't quite make the turn.

The car vaulted a boulder. Mother and Mariana got bounced off into the rocks and cactus. I grabbed what was appropriately called in those days 'the emergency brake', and the car stopped two or three feet this side of Eternity.

★ ★ ★ ★ ★

O'Malley was fiercely anti-Treaty, yet his last illness was spent in the home of a captain in the Irish army. Harry Hogan was married to Kaye (Kathleen), O'Malley's sister, who described how all his prickliness seemed to have disappeared as he saw a certain humour in the situation. One evening, while Kaye was attending to his sore back, O'Malley had to be turned. Hogan offered to help and O'Malley said to his sister, 'Bloody good enough for a Free Stater to roll me over and rub my bottom; let him do it, Kathleen.'

A Kildare schoolteacher on holidays in Galway stood admiring the statue of the author Pádraic Ó Conaire, then occupying a prime position in Eyre Square. A holiday-maker came and knelt before the statue and began to say her beads — about a decade of the rosary. Then she blessed herself, stood up and genuflected. She noticed the schoolteacher looking at her and remarked, 'Poor Matt Talbot! A great saint and a great man to pray to.'

★ ★ ★ ★ ★

Micheál macLiammóir has a story about Ó Conaire:

It was on the first night of Daniel Corkery's new play *The Labour Leader*, and a malicious fate had thrown me into the company of Padraic Ó Conaire, already a great friend, under whose influence I had changed my Munster Irish into Connacht and adopted a battered black hat, a heavy stick, and a taste for whisky, none of which things really belonged to myself. Padraic, on this mellow moonlit night of autumn in the year that followed the Great War's armistice, was over-flowing with high spirits and the juice of the barley and was eager to see something of Corkery's play. The house was filled to capacity, and I think it was Arthur Shields or Eric Gorman who gave us chairs at the side of the stage, where for three acts we sat quietly enough, only leaving for refreshment in the intervals by the famous wicket gate — a feat for acro-bats as those who know the intimacies of the Abbey's anatomy will testify — and the last stages of the play seemed to burn with the strangest and most alcoholic beauty and significance. Padraic, sitting spellbound with one hand behind his ear like a peasant hearing a story at the side of the fire, was in a trance: what was it, I wondered, that was in his mind? He turned slowly towards me at last and said in Irish, 'Ah, what I could have done with a theme like that. What I could have done! I've wanted that framework for years to hang me thoughts on it. And this devil from Cork has the framework and he can't dress it, you see. Not royally. Not superbly. But I could. I could do it. By God, I think I could do it now,' and he tried to walk on to the stage.

A violent struggle began; I got him away from the proscenium and as far upstage into safety as I could, but there he broke from me, and I watched him creep with blood-curdling swiftness through the open fireplace and on to the set where, crouching on his hands and knees on the hearthrug, he said in a voice like pious thunder, '*Go Mbeannuighe Dia isteach annseo!*' (God bless all here!) A strangled roar broke from the audience; the curtain fell mercifully; it was the end of the play. But nothing could lure Padraic away; before any one could stop him he had joined hands with the artists, and when the curtain went up again he stood there bowing and smiling among Maureen Delany, Eileen Crowe, and the others, and when the calls for author began and Arthur Shields explained that unfortunately Mr Corkery was not present, Padraic doffed his hat, pursed up his lips, pointed to his own breast, bowed very low and winked diabolically, a highly successful and outrageous performance.

★

MacLiammóir also writes:

Padraic Ó Conaire, the finest writer of modern Irish and the greatest teller of tales I have known, stood at the street door, a small sinewy figure grasping a heavy stick, swaying silhouetted against the moonlight. He was only a little drunk.

'A Mhichíl abair leis an Sasanach,' he was saying. 'Micheál, tell the Englishman' (the Englishman was Hilton) 'to come out onto the Barna road. I have pipes and tobacco in my pocket and a bottle of whiskey under my coat. Tell the Englishman to come out, and we three will walk on the long road that goes west by the sea, and we'll give praise to the moon because she is dead and she still shining, and we'll sit on the ditch and smell the sweetness rising out of the sea, and you'll talk about Diarmuid that walked out of Tara after his love and brought her into the woods. And Hilton' (he pronounced it Hiltón) 'Hilton will tell us of Elizabeth, that red-haired bitch that was the fright of the world and the love of Lord Essex, and I'll tell you . . . I'll tell about a man called Padraic Ó Conaire that walked out of the city of Galway one night and met a shape standing on the bridge of the Claddagh. And the shape had a cloven hoof, and Padraic was afraid . . . .'

And one of his incomparable stories began and held me against my will, the door knob in my hand, but it ended up with, 'And now call him down. Call down the Englishman, and we'll go west up the road to Barna and give praise to the moon.'

★ ★ ★ ★ ★

In Shannon, Through Her Literature, *I write:*

Fine English was once a status symbol in rural Ireland. That was when Gaelic lived on as the language of the common folk even as it was considered a sign of having received an education if a word or two of the King's English dropped from tea-stained lips. Foolish young men learned phrases at the behest of sorely pressed matchmakers and there was little to beat a good prognostication of proving pluvial or the like in bidding for a fair fortune if not a fair figure. This trait lingered in men of the soil long after English — through great misfortune and greater carelessness — became the spoken language. Sons of gombeen men still used fine words to impress and so it came to pass that a young student of the forties entered a diocesan seminary and was asked to write an essay or 'composition'. The subject was Patrick Sarsfield, whose destruction of the Williamite siege train at Ballyneety, near Limerick, in 1690, was one of the few Irish successes in yet another lost war against the English.

Now this boy had broken everything on his father's farm except the crowbar and he bent that. Realising he was fit only for the priesthood, therefore, the father had instilled in the lad the importance of the 'turn of phrase'. A great glaum reached for an N-pen. He would show some of these smart townie classmates with scholarships and red boots a thing or two! He would impress the professor of English. Right! Patrick Sarsfield, paragraph one: 'The sun was slowly sinking in a crimson fresnel as the siege train shunted into Ballyneety . . . .'

162

The concept of Tom Murphy's play *The Blue Macushla* (1980) was highly imaginative: current situations and habits were placed in a 'roaring twenties' Chicago gangster-land setting. Despite a magnificent Abbey Theatre (Brian Collins) design, the first night was less than successful. The scene is the Abbey Theatre bar after the show:

First Patron: It didn't come off.

Second Patron: It soon will.

It did!

* * * * *

'In here, sir. Here you are!' The parking attendant invited the theatre critic to park outside a north-city church during Dublin Theatre Festival. An English group was presenting a play about Michael Collins and Ireland's Civil War. The critic thought better of accepting, for some attendants often deserted their cars and this was a rough area of the city.

During the play, when anti-Treaty forces were burning down the Four Courts, the critic noticed flames leaping outside the church windows and pondered on the director's novel touch. He thought the fire-engine's siren was too modern, however. After the performance, the critic noticed a charred chassis of a car in the spot offered to him earlier.

* * * * *

Comedian Cecil Sheridan had a speech impediment. A furious Louis Elliman of the Olympia Theatre was looking for him during a rehearsal, but he could not be found. Elliman sent stage staff to get him and when Sheridan was brought on he apologised and explained, 'I was g-g-g-etting my ph-ph-ph-ph-photograph taken in the s-s-s-s-street.' 'Photograph me arse,' replied Elliman testily and Sheridan retorted, 'I think h-h-h-e has s-s-s-s-some f-f-f-film left, all right.'

* * * * *

During the West End production of *Jesus Christ Superstar*, Dubliner Colm Wilkinson brought over his family to see the show, in which he starred. For the Crucifixion scene, a trapdoor opened in the stage to allow the erection of a cross. Unfortunately, Wilkinson had booked a box for the family and a three-year-old daughter saw this happening as Colm, playing Judas, cavorted around singing a rock number. The young child shouted, 'Daddy, mind the big hole in the stage!'

* * * * *

For a reopening of the Gaiety Theatre after major refurbishment, a number of stars performed before a distinguished audience. Peter O'Toole chose to deliver Jonathan Swift's long satire *A Modest Proposal for Preventing the Children of poor People in Ireland, from being a Burden to their Parents or Country; and for making them beneficial to the Publick*. Written in 1729, the piece suggested, among other things, the eating of infants to allay famine. However, a famine in Ethiopa was very much in the news and some dignitaries walked out — though it was near the interval and they may just have been bored. None of the media comment alluded to the alleged backstage remark of a celebrated comedian who was also on the bill. He said to a colleague, as O'Toole rambled on, 'Will you run out with the keys and ask him to lock up!'

* * * * *

During a run of Bernard Farrell's *I Do Not Like Thee, Dr Fell* at the Druid Lane Theatre in Galway, one member of the audience took at her word the play's Group Therapy leader Suzy Bernstein. She announces to her group at the beginning of the first act, 'The bathroom and kitchen are through there,' pointing to a door. One night, halfway through Act One, a man got up from his seat, walked across the stage and headed into the wings — he wanted to go to the bathroom!

* * * * *

In 1977 Druid was presenting its second production of the Synge classic *The Playboy of the Western World* in the tiny forty-six-seat theatre, The Fo'Castle. The main public entrance was also used as a stage entrance since it opened directly onto the stage. When Christy Mahon exits through that door to try on the new clothes given to him 'for the sports below', Shawn Keogh and the Widow Quin anxiously await his return. When they hear a rattling at the door, the Widow says, 'Let you whisht now for he's coming now again,' Christy enters cautiously through the creaking door and all eyes are on him in his new clothes. At that point, one evening, an American lady slipped in ahead of Mick Lally, who was playing Christy, and stood in shock as the entire audience burst into laughter at the 'newly attired' Christy Mahon!

✴ ✴ ✴ ✴ ✴

Gate Theatre artistic director Michael Colgan tells how, invariably, he discussed business with Cyril Cusack over lunch. At the first of these, in Cusack's favourite restaurant, Colgan hoped to persuade his guest to play at the Gate. Cusack said he would not eat much but would start with a martini. Then he changed his mind and called for a Gibson. Seizing what he thought was his opportunity, Colgan said that he too loved Ibsen and furiously thought over possible roles for Cusack. There followed Cusack's famous smile and the retort, 'My dear Michael, I wanted a Gibson but Ibsen will do' — and he went on to demolish lobster, Beaujolais and everything that was served, with just a promise that he would look again at the work of the Norwegian dramatist.

✴ ✴ ✴ ✴ ✴

Mary Lou Kohfeldt writes of Lady Gregory:

When she was twenty-six, she was nursing her brother Gerald through an attack of pleurisy at Roxborough, Co. Galway, and overheard the servants saying they had heard the banshee crying for a death. Though she had always considered tales of the banshee to be superstition, she felt a sudden dread and watched Gerald anxiously all night. As she was going out on the landing to reprove some of the servants for talking too loudly, her father's servant came up the stairs to her and said in a hushed voice, 'The Master is dead.'

The Irish Literary Theatre considered Dublin's licensed theatres too expensive and lacking in intimacy. This presented a difficulty, because it was illegal to charge for admission to an unlicensed venue. The doughty Lady Gregory approached William Hartpole Lecky, historian and liberal unionist Member of Parliament, who got the law changed.

★ ★ ★ ★ ★

From her home in Coole Park, Gort, Co. Galway, Lady Gregory supplied the early Abbey Theatre casts with home-baked cakes, which became known affectionately as 'Gort Cakes'. For the theatre's golden jubilee celebrations in 1954, Ernest Blythe provided a similar confection.

★ ★ ★ ★ ★

After the '*Playboy* Riots' (see 'The Abbey Theatre'), Lady Gregory was more or less shunned by her Coole Park neighbours. The Town Council of Gort boycotted her and urged that children should not be allowed to attend her picnics and other entertainments lest their morals be corrupted.

★ ★ ★ ★ ★

Of the writer Charles Kickham (1828–82), James Stephens remarked, 'If the thundering Jupiter would shout into Kickham's ears, [he] could not hear him.' The Tipperary author used an ear-trumpet to hear a fourteen-year prison sentence handed down to him for alleged treason-felony against England.

★ ★ ★ ★ ★

An author's note in The Life and Times of Charles J. Kickham *by J.J. Healy (1915) relates:*

In Mullinahone, Co. Tipperary a touching story is told about a favourite dog of his, his constant companion in all his rambles. The very evening of his arrest his sister, then in delicate health, returned from Dublin. She was in great excitement, having set off immediately on hearing the news. She arrived home, and was soon surrounded by a sympathetic audience, the members of the family all seeking to know every particular regarding him. His little dog 'Pan' lay at her feet, looking up into her face while she talked. No doubt she showed great emotion, and often mentioned Charley's name in tones of sorrow which were loudly echoed by her hearers. When she had told them all, they were surprised to see the faithful mute listener at her feet fall back and immediately expire.

W.B. Yeats writes of Kickham:

He was the most lovable of men. Women and children seem especially to have been attached to him. Some one asked him what did he miss most in gaol. 'Children, women, and fires,' he answered. One of the touching things in Kickham's character was an ever-present love for his native town; its mountains and its rivers are often referred to in his writings. A few months before his death, a friend found him gazing intently at the picture of a cow in a Dublin gallery. 'It is so like an old cow at Mullinahone,' he said.

★ ★ ★ ★ ★

THE
NATIONAL LIBRARY
OF IRELAND

Designed by Thomas Deane, the National Library of Ireland opened in 1890, having been founded three years earlier under the Art Museum Act. The Royal Dublin Society presented its first 30,000 volumes and also gave 23,000 books held in trust under a bequest from Rev. Jasper Joly. The Library is now widely used by native and foreign scholars. It administers the Genealogical Office and a substantial manuscript collection built up by enthusiastic directors over the years. The Irish Copyright Act demands that a copy of every Irish publication be sent to the Library. A Director and twelve trustees administer the library. The Minister for Arts, Culture and the Gaeltacht nominates four trustees, the Royal Dublin Society, eight.

★ ★ ★ ★ ★

Dr Edward MacLysaght was chairman of the Irish Manuscripts Commission. He had a stroke of luck one day:

I was on my way back to Dublin after an inspection at Dromana (Villiers-Stuart) and as I drove along a road in Co. Kilkenny I happened to notice a farm cart plodding along and carrying a rather unusual load — a pile of paper. I stopped and having passed the time of day with the driver I asked him what he had in the cart. "Tis a load of old papers the boss thrun out and told me to burn 'em or dump 'em out of sight,' he replied. Not to make a long story of it, all I need say is that I gave the odd £2 I had in my pocket and transferred the load to my station wagon. The 'waste paper' contained *inter alia* letters, some in cypher, from Charles II in exile to his supporter Sir George Lane in Ireland relating to his hopes and plans for Restoration, and that [sic] they are now in the National Library. Incidentally I may add that they came from an estate office and the agent was one of the people to whom we had sent our circular on the subject of waste paper in wartime.

The lucky chance of my being on that road in Co. Kilkenny that day saved what is among the more valuable of the smaller seventeenth-century collections in Ireland. I should add that the bulk of the contents of that cart was of no value but what we salvaged out of it most decidedly was.

✱

The difficulties of manuscript collection are highlighted by one MacLysaght incident:

It was my usual practice when collecting registers to check them carefully with the appropriate diocesan official. When I was at Carlow I was just about to do this when I got a rather urgent message to go and see the bishop himself and the result was that for the first and last time I went to Dublin with a load of [parish] registers not properly checked. Of course I should have done it properly later but somehow one very slim item got overlooked. Three months or so later, long after the microfilming was done and the registers returned, one parish priest wrote and said that his earliest register had not been returned with the others. I was terribly worried because owing to my (I can truthfully say unusual) carelessness in that one case I was in a dilemma. What I did was first to make sure that the waste paper in the basement had not been removed during the previous 3 months; then a team of three of us (Gerry Nash and I and one of the boys) started to go carefully through several tons of paper. By Friday midday, after nearly a week at it, having lost all hope, we came to the last crate: believe it or not, in it was the missing register, a flimsy booklet covered in brown paper: buidheachas le Dia.

✱ ✱ ✱ ✱ ✱

In April 1945 R.J. Hayes wrote a brief note to George Bernard Shaw:

Dear Sir:

I can think of no more appropriate place than the National

Library of Ireland for the permanent preservation for posterity of your manuscripts, correspondence, and first editions. Can you?

Yours very truly, R.J. Hayes, Director.

Shaw replied:

Dear Sir:

Your invitation as national librarian is in the nature of a command. I have only a few early MSS dating from my beginning as a novelist, too poor to afford a typewriter.

I am having them tidied up and bound; and when this is finished you shall have them . . .

Faithfully, G. Bernard Shaw.

★ ★ ★ ★ ★

Dr Patrick Henchy, director of the National Library from 1967 to 1976, tells:

There has been much discussion . . . about the literary remains of the poet, Patrick Kavanagh, and I was amazed that there was such a lack of knowledge, or even awareness, of the valuable Kavanagh collection in the Manuscripts Department of the National Library. In 1950, I negotiated with Paddy Kavanagh for the purchase of his manuscripts. He was a constant visitor to the Library and we had become good friends. When I asked him about his manuscripts, he replied that the early ones were in Monaghan, 'probably lying under the bed being eaten by the Mucker mice'. He expressed satisfaction when I told him that the Library would like to purchase them. He duly brought them along. A price was agreed, which, according to the standards of the time, was good, and Paddy was more than pleased. When asked about the manuscript of *The Great Hunger* which was not amongst the collection, he informed me that it did not exist. 'This', he said, 'I wrote on the backs of envelopes and scraps of paper, including lavatory paper.'

★

Henchy bought a copybook and got Kavanagh to write out what is called a 'fair copy'.

Kavanagh, to show his appreciation, bought a drink for me. When I thanked him he replied that I had been very good to him. Then folding his arms and looking sharply at me he added, 'Of course it may turn out that you are a cute hoor.' Many years later University College, Dublin purchased the remainder of Kavanagh's manuscripts at a high price, including, it was claimed, the original of *The Great Hunger*, but it is clear from Kavanagh that there was no original manuscript of this work in existence.

✳

Henchy recalls how Richard Hayes, author of *Ireland and Irishmen in the French Revolution* (1932), heard that there was a collection of manuscripts with a certain family in his native Mayo that contained the log of a ship of the Spanish Armada. The two men undertook the long journey from Dublin to Mayo, and Henchy talked to the woman of the house while Hayes searched through the material. He was not unduly impressed by what he saw, even less so when the lady produced a piece of wood that bore a mock inscription, 'Log of the Spanish Armada'.

✳

MacLysaght told Henchy of travelling about with Harold Macmillan, the British publisher, and the latter advising MacLysaght to have his memoirs published. When he heard MacLysaght had kept a diary, Macmillan promised to publish it. Henchy continues:

Now MacLysaght never had a secret thought in his head; he spoke out on everything. Consequently, the diary contained over-critical comments and material and Macmillan could not publish it. Not being a believer in red tape, MacLysaght, then Keeper of Manuscripts, went and had the diary typed, bound and put on the shelf as MS. No. 385.

That diary formed the basis of MacLysaght's memoirs, which he intended calling 'Master of None' but eventually was published by Colin Smythe under the title *Changing Times*.

Standing on the steps of the National Library one day were Harry Craig, charming and suave assistant editor of *The Bell*, Paddy Kavanagh and Patrick Henchy. Henchy was highly amused to hear his companions, two of Dublin's greatest characters, complain that there were no more characters to be found hanging around the Library.

★ ★ ★ ★ ★

FLANN O'BRIEN

(MYLES NA GOPALEEN
BRIAN O'NOLAN)

1911–1966

Brian O'Nolan is the real name, but is the least used. There were other pseudonyms. He wrote as Brother Barnabas in the University College, Dublin magazine Comhthrom Féinne *(Fair Play) and in assorted publications signed himself Lir O'Connor, John J. Dowe, James Knowall and Jimmy Cunning. He is said to have offered a number of provincial newspapers a syndicated column at a cut price.*

He had come to Dublin from Strabane, Co. Tyrone to study Celtic languages. After graduation in 1932, he joined the civil service, remaining there for twenty-one years. He was a master of comic fantasy and satire, and like many humorous writers, he could be intolerant, gruff or angry. Much of his humour was written in Irish and An Béal Bocht *(1973) is a classic of modern Irish humour. A stage adaptation of its translation has become extremely popular.* The Dalkey Archive *(1964) was also dramatised (by Hugh Leonard).*

At Swim-Two-Birds (1939) has been hailed by scholars as the only true successor to Ulysses, *but O'Brien is best known and loved for his 'Cruiskeen Lawn' column in* The Irish Times. *Bertie Smyllie, the paper's editor, had an impish sense of humour and enjoyed the suggestions of his eccentric and often crazy columnist. Ironically, the conceiver of practical jokes and comic cameos died on April Fool's Day. He is most often referred to as Myles, from his celebrated pseudonym.*

★ ★ ★ ★ ★

Micheál Ó hAodha tells how Myles and a boozing companion were on a pub-crawl one day. After visiting a number of establishments, they noticed with some alarm that the same sinister-looking character sat at the other end of whatever counter they leaned upon. If their stay was short, the fellow appeared; if long, the same. They travelled up the Dublin mountains to 'do the *bona fide*' (when late drinking was allowed to *bona fide* travellers of three miles or more out

173

of the city). Again, the suspicious-looking character imbibed at a distance. A sense of great fear possessed them but, fortified by alcohol, they eventually plucked up enough courage to ask the fellow who he was. He sullenly explained, 'I'm your fucking taxi-driver.'

★ ★ ★ ★ ★

Tony Gray writes about the creation of a celebrated column:

I explained the nature of [the] first column to Smyllie as best I could, and he seemed to find the idea hilarious. 'Send it out straight away for setting,' he said. It had a title — 'Cruiskeen Lawn' (the little overflowing goblet) but no byline. I asked Smyllie what we should do about this.

'What's the Irish for a badger?' he asked. I told him, and the first Myles column . . . was signed 'An Broc' . . . .

A few days later a second column arrived in the office, escorted by its creator, a small, shy, taciturn character with teeth like a rabbit and a greasy felt hat. The new column he offered us had an introduction in English like the first one and then lapsed into Irish . . . . It had the same headline but a new byline. It was now signed 'Myles na gCopaleen' [as the pseudonym originally was spelt].

'I didn't like that badger notion,' he said.

'But why Myles na gCopaleen?', Smyllie asked.

'A Cruiskeen Lawn is a jug full of porter, and Myles na gCopaleen, as you bloody well know, Smyllie, is the archetypal stage Irishman in Boucicault's *Colleen Bawn*.'

★ ★ ★ ★ ★

Myles and some close friends from university days took to writing under false names to the editor of *The Irish Times*. A Frank O'Connor play and a Patrick Kavanagh book review were among the targets for satirical barbs. Under the bogus name of Hazel Ellis, one letter satirised Hilton Edwards, Micheál macLiammóir and their Gate Theatre. But there *was* a Hazel Ellis, and in November 1938 her play *Women Without Men* had been produced at the Gate. With bristling pen she sprang to the defence of her director,

Edwards, and his partner. Still using the name Hazel Ellis, Myles wrote to the editor again, castigating the female correspondent as an obvious impostor.

★ ★ ★ ★ ★

Anthony Cronin and other associates often had the task of leaving Myles home after a night or afternoon spent drinking. In No Laughing Matter, *Cronin, calling his subject by his real name throughout and recollecting his long-standing feud with the* Gardaí, *writes:*

They were for the most part civilly received by Mrs O'Nolan; and, if Brian had sobered up on the way, they might be asked in for a bottle of stout. On a couple of occasions when John Ryan left him home, he found himself seated at the typewriter, taking dictation for a column, and was amazed at the fluency and lack of hesitation with which it was given. [One] day, however, Brian was pretty far gone in drink and had to be helped up the garden path. After he had gone inside, my friend began to turn the car to go back towards Donnybrook. Another car came up the road at some speed, there was a minor collision, and the driver of this car insisted on telephoning Donnybrook Police Station.

A bit of fuss followed while the road was measured and the condition and positions of the two cars were recorded. Suddenly Brian appeared at his hall door, wearing a coat over blue striped pyjamas and with his hat on the back of his head. He stood for a moment, surveying the scene in front of him. Then he spoke up. 'Would yez get those two motor cars out of there immediately,' he said, swaying slightly on the step. 'There's decent respectable people live here on this road that pay their rates and taxes and have a right of unimpeded passage up and down it. And they don't want any criminals or chancers around here that are an object of interest and concern to the police force.'

★ ★ ★ ★ ★

In Myles — Portraits of Brian O'Nolan, *Niall Sheridan's contribution describes how, while playing chess, Myles would:*

. . . sit glowering at the board, lips drawn back from his rabbit-like teeth, making odd hissing sounds as he drew in his breath in concentration. Suddenly, he would seize a piece and plonk it down in its new position, making every move with an air of delivering the *coup de grâce*. This combination of play-acting and moral blackmail had a paralysing effect on simpler souls and gave him a reputation quite out of proportion to his skill at the game.

★

Sheridan also recalls how, at a gathering in Grogan's public house, Myles announced that he was to embark upon producing the Great Irish Novel under the working title 'Children of Destiny'. Sections would be apportioned to his friends and, since compulsory education had resulted in the availability of a vast market of semi-illiterates, there would be a vast market for the first masterpiece of the 'Ready-Made or Reach-Me-Down School [in which there would be] continuous action, a series of thrilling climaxes . . . . In its power and scope, it would make the surge and thunder of the Odyssey seem like the belching and gurgling of a baby in swaddling clothes'. The book would follow the fortunes of an Irish family for almost a century after the Famine:

In America, a member of the family would rise through ward politics and Tammany Hall to the political heights, returning to Ireland to fight in the 1916 Rising, and dying gallantly (in full public view) — the last man to leave the burning ruins of the General Post Office. His son, graduating from politics to high finance, would become the first Irish-American Catholic President of the United States.

[The religious segment, written by Myles] revolved around a scion of the family who (surviving a breach-of-promise action by a farmer's daughter) pursued his vocation with such dedication and cunning that he eventually [became] Pope Patrick I.

While the Papal election is in progress, an immense throng (including a strong Irish contingent) fills St Peter's Square, tensely awaiting the plume of rising smoke which will indicate the result of the voting. Here [Myles] had invented a very characteristic touch — an Irish Monsignor, in charge of the smoke-signals, smuggles in two sods of turf and, as the white smoke rises above the Sistine Chapel, the unmistakable tang of the bog, wafting out over the Bernini colonnades, tells his waiting countrymen that a decision (and the right one) has been reached.

For the climax, the ageing Pope Patrick would come to Croke Park to throw in the ball at an All-Ireland Football Final between Cavan and Kildare. An action-packed match would be described in florid detail and Kildare would snatch a draw at the last minute, resulting in the Pope's getting a heart attack and dying:

in the arms of his countrymen, while the sun descends flamboyantly behind the Railway goal and 'Faith of our Fathers' thunders into the evening sky from eighty thousand Irish throats.

All this — and Heaven, too! Brian glared around him in triumph, as if challenging us to dissent. What more could any reader (or, indeed, any Pope) ask for at seven-and-sixpence a copy? . . . .

There was a short period of hectic activity, but the Great Irish Novel never materialized.

✶ ✶ ✶ ✶ ✶

Of an El Greco painting in the National Gallery of Ireland, Myles wrote that if the paint were scraped away in one corner it would reveal, first, a Wexford Irish Language procession banner and under that an 1880 cow drench advertisement.

✶ ✶ ✶ ✶ ✶

Once, it is said, Myles had an engine-less car placed outside the Palace Bar. He sat into it while drunk and a policeman tried to arrest him for being drunk in charge of a mechanically propelled vehicle — until Myles struggled to the bonnet and lifted it!

Myles proposed a system whereby he would select a library for the *nouveaux riches*. He would buy the books, make them grubby and used-looking and, for a small additional charge, would underline certain passages and make knowledgeable entries in the margins. A very special extra would be an author's note thanking the owner for help received in the compilation of the book.

★ ★ ★ ★ ★

THE WRITING CROWD, IT IS WELL KNOWN, ARE ONLY A PARCEL OF DUD CZECHS AND BOHEMIAN GULLS AND IF I AM SEEN IN THAT NOTORIOUS ULTIMATE RIGOUR IT WILL NOT BE IN THEIR COMPANY
Brian O'Nolan

★ ★ ★ ★ ★

SEAN
O'CASEY
1880–1964

Born in Dorset Street, Dublin, Sean O'Casey's given name was John Casey. Although hampered by weak eyes, he studied hard at his mother's insistence but had to do manual work for years before earning a living through writing. Involvement with the Gaelic League, a movement which fostered the Irish language, led him to use the proper form of his name in Irish: Seán Ó Cathasaigh. Under the name 'P. O Cathasaigh' he submitted a History of the Citizen Army *to Maunsel & Co. Ltd. When he reverted to using English in his published works, he included the 'O'. He was secretary of that Irish Citizen Army under James Connolly but left the organisation when it leaned towards nationalism rather than Marxism. O'Casey emigrated and, when the Abbey Theatre rejected* The Silver Tassie, *he shafted many a bitter barb across the Irish Sea. His 'Trilogy of the Troubles',* Juno and the Paycock, The Plough and the Stars *and* The Shadow of a Gunman *continue to receive new interpretations and to be highly popular in Ireland and abroad. Not so his later plays, however; none produced characters of the depth of Captain Boyle, Joxer Daly, Juno or Bessie Burgess. He lived his later years in Torquay, Devon. Between 1939 and 1944 he published his autobiography in six volumes.*

✮ ✮ ✮ ✮ ✮

A one-act play of O'Casey's called *Nannie's Night Out* is set in a huckster's shop. Mrs Pender is the proprietor and her customers include ballad-singers, a gunman, a young pickpocket and Nannie, who is a 'spunker' or methylated spirits addict. In its sole Abbey Theatre production (29 September 1924) Sara Allgood played the unlikely title role. O'Casey wanted Nannie to meet a grisly death; the Abbey wanted a different ending and so a compromise finale was prepared. These reasons have been given for the play's fall into oblivion. The truth, however, may lie in the suggestion that O'Casey wanted to scrap the one-act and reserve its characters for a later work. It was generally agreed that *Nannie's Night Out* was not great entertainment; yet in 1961 it surfaced and was hailed as a masterpiece by an American academic who produced it — in Indiana!

★ ★ ★ ★ ★

During rehearsals for the first production of *The Plough and the Stars*, members of the cast took exception to some aspects of the work. F.J. McCormick refused to use the word 'snotty'. Director Lennox Robinson had to cope with other problems, not least of which was Eileen Crowe's refusal to speak the line, ' . . . any kid, livin' or dead, that Jinnie Gogan's had since was got between th' bordhers of th' Ten Commandments'. This had a bearing on the final shape of the play itself. To this day, commentators are puzzled by the inclusion of the character 'A Woman from Rathmines' (called simply 'A Woman' in the first production). She is an upper-class lady who cannot find her way home and is scared of the rioting. Her entrance has nothing whatsoever to do with the action.

Far from being disturbed by Eileen Crowe's reluctance to play Mrs Gogan, O'Casey wrote this part especially for her. It has been seen as a gallant gesture, but there remains the possibility of O'Casey chuckling quietly to himself as he created such an insipid character for the protester. Ironically, in a production of the *Plough* many years later, Crowe played the prostitute, Rosie Redmond!

★ ★ ★ ★ ★

The *Plough and the Stars* evoked the same anger, when produced in 1926, as had Synge's *The Playboy of the Western World* nineteen years before. The entrance of two Volunteers bearing the tricolour into a pub sparked off the 'Plough Riots' at the Abbey. It was mainly women who leaped onto the stage to remonstrate with cast and audience alike. One irate man was ignored, even as he attempted to set fire to the house curtain. Nobody was really bothered about the attempted arson for they knew that a leak in the roof had made the drape soggy with dampness and there wasn't the least fear of its burning.

☆ ☆ ☆ ☆ ☆

Observing the riots during the second act of the play, O'Casey retired to the coffee-room and chatted with admirers as the drama was enacted in the auditorium. W.B. Yeats was contacted in Merrion Square. He rushed over to the Abbey, strode onto the stage screaming: 'You have disgraced yourselves again . . . the fame of O'Casey is born tonight. This is his apotheosis.' A number of the more vocal protesters were seen to leave. Denis Johnston was to suggest that they departed to find out what an apotheosis was, 'perhaps in the hope that it might turn out to be something irreligious, or better still, actionable'.

☆ ☆ ☆ ☆ ☆

Theatre academic, director and author Hugh Hunt was associated with the Abbey Theatre for forty years. He records O'Casey saying:

The high, hysterical, distorted voices of women kept squealing that Irish girls were noted over the whole world for their modesty, and that Ireland's name was holy; that the republican flag had never seen the inside of a public house; that this slander on the Irish race would mean the end of the Abbey Theatre; and that Ireland was Ireland through joy and tears . . . .

Barry Fitzgerald became a genuine Fluther Good and fought as that character would, sending an enemy, who had climbed onto the stage, flying into the stalls with a punch on the jaw . . . .

☆ ☆ ☆ ☆ ☆

Cyril Cusack writes of an O'Casey production in London, where he played alongside his stepfather, Breffni O'Rorke, and Molly and Sara Allgood:

Of so-called 'ensemble' I could tell a tale or two. Take, for instance, a production of *The Plough and the Stars* at the London Embassy Theatre, over forty years ago now: the Allgood sisters not on speaking terms; O'Rorke (according to Agate, 'a magnificent Fluther') and myself (the Young Covey) at purse-lipped loggerheads; then, finally, and to crown all 'togetherness', Miss Allgood — Sara — in the wings suddenly, belligerently addressing me:

'Do you think I'm fat?'

'Well . . . ', I began, a little defensively, 'no-o . . . '

'What then?'

'Well, I'd say . . . ' — I thought I had hit on the right word — 'I'd say . . . plump!'

Just then, by the grace of God, Bessie Burgess had to make an entrance on-stage. But Miss Allgood never spoke to me again.

★ ★ ★ ★ ★

When Sean O'Casey lived in London he was sometimes approached in bars and restaurants by aspiring writers, towards whom he was kindly tolerant. One shy Oxonian was ragged a little by Sean, so that when O'Casey asked the young man his name, he was reluctant to voice it. O'Casey persisted and the youth stammered out — Rupert. Sean asked him why he had hesitated, saying that Rupert was quite a nice name. Indeed, he pointed out that a street close by was called Rupert Street, 'a nice street too — full of prostitutes, here pass your glass and I'll fill it up'.

★ ★ ★ ★ ★

In her biography, Eileen O'Casey tells how O'Casey was not a Catholic while she was 'about the most bewildered Catholic ever'. Of their wedding, she writes:

Sean had accepted my wish for a Catholic marriage service, a wonderful thing to me, realising his opinions as I did, and all the routine a mixed marriage would involve. Soon reporters were ringing up, and photographers taking pictures of me, while Sean avoided as much of the publicity as he could. Telephone calls never stopped, invariably someone to ask where the wedding would be. Sean would say gravely anything that occurred to him. 'The Chelsea Baths at midnight,' he told one reporter, and the man, who must have been a serious type, asked him if he was certain. 'Absolutely!' Sean replied with conviction . . . .

★

Of baby Breon's birth in 1928, Eileen remembers:

Because of the baby's size, the birth proved to be more complicated than I thought. After a visit to Dr Harold Waller one afternoon, he told me that he would come round in the evening with a specialist. No, I said, it was not convenient. I was going to the theatre. Would another evening do? He was sorry but advised me to cancel the theatre. My mother, who was having tea with me that day, told me in her morbid style that I should prepare myself for the fact that the child might be mentally afflicted: my father had been unbalanced, and the child's father was an eccentric . . . . On the night of Breon's birth, Dr Waller . . . proposed that Sean should stay with a friend; they telephoned him later with the news that I was well and that he had a son. Returning in the morning to Woronzow Road, he saw a pile of letters on the hall table, one of them with a Dublin postmark; it was from the Abbey. He was excited about the baby; it was a glorious morning, and round us in St John's Wood the lilac and syringa and acacia trees were in bloom. I was glowingly happy. It was not for a week that Sean told me of the shock he had kept to himself; the letter was from W.B. Yeats, and the Abbey Theatre had rejected *The Silver Tassie*.

★ ★ ★ ★ ★

In an Abbey Theatre programme note, Hugh Hunt writes:

On 1 March 1928 Lady Gregory received a letter from Sean informing her that he had just finished typing his new play: 'I hope it may be suitable and that you will like it' he wrote.

'Personally I think it is the best work I have done.'

Unfortunately neither she nor her fellow directors of the Abbey — Yeats and Lennox Robinson — shared his opinion. They had expected another *Juno* or a *Plough and the Stars*. Sean, born and educated in the slums of Dublin, was not thought capable of employing the new continental expressionism; still less of embarking on so wide a subject as the Great War. 'You are not interested in the Great War,' Yeats wrote to him. 'You never stood in the battle fields or walked the hospitals.' Sean was not the man to take Yeats's criticism lying down. 'Was Shakespeare at Actium or Philippi?' he asked. 'Was G.B. Shaw in the boats with the French, or in the forts with the British when Joan and Dunois made the attack that relieved Orleans? And someone I think wrote a poem about Tír na nÓg who never took a header into the land of youth.'

★ ★ ★ ★ ★

O'Casey explained that both his brothers had served in the British army, that his uncle had fought in the Crimea and that he himself had spent long hours talking to the wounded Tommies in the Dublin hospitals. In spite of this, Yeats suggested that O'Casey could ask for the return of his play on the grounds that he wished to withdraw it for revision. O'Casey wrote to Lennox Robinson: 'There is going to be no damn secrecy with me about the Abbey's rejection of the play.' His response was to send all Yeats's and Robinson's letters — as well as his blistering replies — to the press. Yeats claimed breach of copyright and threatened action.

★ ★ ★ ★ ★

The Silver Tassie *was produced in London in 1929. Lady Gregory travelled over to see the play and begged O'Casey to allow her to visit him, but the Abbey's rejection rankled too much and he refused. Concerning the rejection, George Bernard Shaw writes:*

Of course the Abbey should have produced it — whether they liked it or not. But the people who knew your uncle when you were a child (so to speak) always want to correct

your exercises; and this is what disabled the usually competent W.B.Y. and Lady Gregory.

Still, it is surprising that they fired so wide, considering
their marksmanship . . . .

✶ ✶ ✶ ✶ ✶

*The rejection, according to Yeats, led to O'Casey's declining an invi-
tation to become an Academician of the Irish Academy of Letters.
He wrote to the papers:*

If Ireland gives birth to an original and creative artist, how
much will he care for the craft of his fellow craftsmen who
will not be a fellow craftsman at all? He won't care a damn.
But they will. They will — and especially in my opinion the
young members — try in various ways to dull the gleam of
his work so as to keep the polish on their own. No, an academy can only be an academy and nothing else.

*When a friend of Joseph Holloway's read the letter, he remarked,
'We don't want corner boys in the Academy.'*

✶ ✶ ✶ ✶ ✶

O'Casey noticed Holloway's regular attendance at theatrical events and asked 'who the little man like M. Brieux
in a bowler hat . . . was'. On being told, 'He is Mr Holloway,
the architect of the Abbey,' O'Casey queried, 'Why don't
they pay him his fees and not have him haunting the place?'

✶ ✶ ✶ ✶ ✶

During the centenary year of O'Casey's birth, Gabriel
Fallon recalled in the *Sunday Independent* how he was
performing in *The Shadow of a Gunman* when he first met the
playwright. After the first act of the play, Fallon, curious to
see how the audience was receiving the work, went to the
prompt side and noticed O'Casey standing in the shadows.
He wore a cap, trench-coat and boots. Seeing Fallon, he
moved towards him and signalled that he should take
O'Casey's position, which offered a better view of the action
on stage. Fallon demurred but O'Casey insisted, saying: 'The
stage is the actor's place, not the author's.'

185

Tomás Mac Anna visited O'Casey in exile and tells in The O'Casey Enigma *(ed. Ó hAodha):*

In London he was never impolite to offers of patronage, as far as I can remember, although he did not always accept it. I shall never forget his courteous evasion on the telephone to a Lady Somebody who was hoping to exhibit him at a society dinner party.

'Ah no,' I overheard him explain. 'You see, I've just started on another play and I have to get on with it or Cocky'll be mad. Yes'm Lady Low, it'll take me some time. There's a lot of work, you know, in writing a play. No, I couldn't say how long. Maybe the rest of the year. You never can tell. So goodbye Lady Low and thank you very much for asking me, and don't bother to ring till I call you back. It's all over my table here, and I haven't even got time for my own dinner. So goodbye Lady Low, and excuse me if I ring off law garoo.'

★ ★ ★ ★ ★

Gabriel Fallon's recollections of the first production of Juno and the Paycock *in 1924, in his biography of O'Casey, capture the intensity of an opening night:*

I arrived at the theatre at 4.30 p.m. and found the author there before me looking rather glum and wondering if a rehearsal would take place since so far as he could find out there was no one else in the theatre. I assured him that everything would be all right even though I privately thought otherwise. Sara Allgood, who had spent the night feasting us with song and story, had left the theatre in or around 3 a.m. a very tired woman. I tried to persuade Sean that dress-rehearsals were always like this but he was only half convinced. Although I did not know it at the time he was suffering much pain with his eyes and was attending the Royal Eye and Ear Hospital where he was a patient of the Senior Surgeon, the sensitive and perceptive Mr Joe Cummins, who took a particular interest in the dramatist and in the theatre.

Gradually the players filed in and quietly went to their dressing-rooms. Lennox Robinson arrived shortly before

5 o'clock and was followed by Yeats and Lady Gregory. Under the direction of Seaghan Barlow the stage staff were putting finishing touches to the setting. Yeats, Lady Gregory and Robinson took seats in the stalls. The author sat a few seats away from them. The curtain rose about 5.36 p.m. So far as I could see and hear while waiting for my cue in the wings the rehearsal seemed to be proceeding smoothly. As soon as I had finished my part of Bentham at the end of the second act I went down into the stalls and sat two seats behind the author. Here for the first time I had the opportunity of seeing something of the play from an objective point of view. I was stunned by the tragic quality of the third act which the magnificent playing of Sara Allgood made almost unbearable. But it was the blistering irony of the final scene which convinced me that this man sitting two seats in front of me was a dramatist of genius, one destined to be spoken of far beyond the confines of the Abbey Theatre.

The third act had been dominated by Allgood's tragic quality even though Barry Fitzgerald and F.J. McCormick were uproariously funny as Captain Boyle and Joxer. This was always so with Allgood in the part of Juno. She had the quality of pinning down preceding laughter to freezing point.

When Juno returns from the doctor with Mary, the author's simple directions are 'Mrs Boyle enters: it is apparent from the serious look on her face that something has happened. She takes off her hat and coat without a word and puts them by. She then sits down near the fire, and there is a few moments' pause.' That is all. Yet Sara Allgood's entrance in this scene will never be forgotten by those who saw it. Not a word was spoken: she did not even sigh: her movements were few and simply confined to the author's directions. She seemed to have shrunken from the Juno we saw in Acts 1 and 2 as if reduced by the catalytic effect of her inner consciousness.

We watched the act move on, the furniture removers come and go, the ominous entry of the IRA men, the dragging of Johnny to summary execution, the stilted scene between Jerry Devine and Mary Boyle, and then as with the ensnaring slow impetus of a ninth great wave, Allgood's tragic genius rose to an unforgettable climax and drowned the stage in sorrow. Here surely was the very butt and sea-mark of tragedy! But suddenly the curtain rises again: are Fitzgerald and McCormick fooling, letting off steam after the strain of rehearsal? Nothing of the kind; for we in the stalls are suddenly made to freeze in our seats as a note beyond tragedy, a blistering flannel-mouthed irony sears its maudlin way across the stage and slowly drops an exhausted curtain on a world disintegrating in 'chassis'.

I sat there stunned. So, indeed, so far as I could see, did Robinson, Yeats and Lady Gregory. Then Yeats ventured an opinion. He said that the play, particularly in its final scene, reminded him of a Dostoyevski novel. Lady Gregory turned to him and said: 'You know, Willie, you never read a novel by Dostoyevski.' And she promised to amend this deficiency by sending him a copy of *The Idiot*. I turned to O'Casey and found I could only say to him: 'Magnificent, Sean, magnificent.' Then we all quietly went home.

✯ ✯ ✯ ✯ ✯

Actor and director Brian de Salvo recalls an incident at a Royal Shakespeare Company's production of *Juno and the Paycock*. As the curtain fell, he overheard an American playgoer say to his wife: 'Well, honey, you finally got to see your Shakespeare.'

✯ ✯ ✯ ✯ ✯

TH' WHOLE WORL'S . . . IN A TERR . . . IBLE STATE O' . . .
CHASSIS!
Sean O'Casey

✯ ✯ ✯ ✯ ✯

FRANK
O'CONNOR
1903–1966

Short stories were the forte of the writer who was born Michael Francis O'Donovan in Cork and educated there. As a boy, he was forced to listen to his father bragging about his soldiering, images of which appear in much of his later work. Cork folklore is crammed with tales of this man, the most popular one being his claim that during a big review of her troops, Queen Victoria asked who the distinguished-looking man in the second rank was and was told, 'Michael O'Donovan from Cork, your Queenship, one of the finest-looking soldiers in the whole army.' Daniel Corkery taught Francis and encouraged his literary and republican bent. Both were members of a 'Twenty Club' that read papers of Tolstoy and French playwrights; later they produced three editions of a virulently nationalist newspaper. George Russell published, in the Irish Statesman, *the first piece to appear under the pseudonym Frank O'Connor, a mixture of his own middle name and his mother's maiden name (he disliked his father's family). A participant in the War of Independence and the Civil War, O'Connor later wrote a biography of Michael Collins (The Big Fellow), whom he had opposed in the Civil War.*

He was a railway clerk and a librarian in his youth, a director of the Abbey Theatre in his forties. His written works include plays and a travel book; he lectured at home and in America and translated. O'Connor's translation of Merriman's The Midnight Court *is highly regarded and his collection of short stories* Guests of the Nation *(1931) influenced many Irish writers, setting down as it does the conflict between England and Ireland. Some scholars place his work alongside that of de Maupassant and Chekhov, Yeats claiming that he did for Ireland what the latter did for Russia.*

A colleague of Russell and Yeats, O'Connor recorded the language of

189

his people with emotional energy, yet with accuracy. The man with the 'coal heaver's voice' (according to V.S. Pritchett) became a broadcaster for radio and television. Some critics describe his work as soft, stage Irish, or bordering on myth. Yet few have not read and enjoyed the simple, skilfully crafted tales of the man Richard Ellmann termed the 'Flaubert of the Bogs'. In the following anecdotes, the name Frank O'Connor is used throughout, although some relate to the period before he adopted the pseudonym.

★ ★ ★ ★ ★

During World War II, there was considerable public fear of a German invasion. O'Connor and his wife, Evelyn, lived in Woodenbridge, Co. Wicklow then and frequent visits from a Garda sergeant were noted in the village. In plain clothes, this man actually called to the couple's home, posing as a collector of folklore and folk-songs. Frank knew little about the subject but gave the man all the help he could. The sergeant also asked a man called Charles Davidson to keep an eye on the O'Connors for him and report anything suspicious. Davidson was friendly with the O'Connors but when he spotted a number of small flags in a field became convinced that Frank was marking a landing place for German parachutists. He reasoned, however, that if the Germans were thwarted, his friend would not be arrested, so he took up all the flags. Next day, a drainage engineer cursed the fool who had removed his survey markers!

★ ★ ★ ★ ★

O'Connor writes of his time as a librarian:

Some of the priests would allow no libraries at all. In Rathdrum, a town up the country from us, the parish priest initially resisted all our efforts to start a branch library. At last I decided that the time had come to visit him. [Geoffrey] Phibbs [his boss] and I called first on the curate, a splendid young fellow who was in despair with the parish priest and with Ireland. A couple of nights a week he went off to the local technical school and took off his coat to practise carpentry so as to encourage the unemployed lads of the town to learn a trade, all to no purpose.

'You'll go up to that parochial house', he said, 'and see the old man at the table with his dinner gone cold and a volume of Thomas Aquinas propped up in front of him. And between you and me and the wall,' he added, 'Thomas Aquinas was a bloody old cod.'

We found the parish priest exactly as the curate had predicted, Aquinas and all, but there seemed to be nothing of the obscurantist about the delightful old man we met. On the contrary, when we introduced ourselves, he beamed and regretted that we hadn't come to lunch. He took a particular fancy to me because I spoke Irish, and he was devoted to Irish and Irish literature. In fact, one of his dearest friends had been George Moore. Poor George. Of course he had been greatly wronged in Ireland, where people did not understand his work, but George had been a really dear and good man.

I didn't, of course, believe for an instant that he had been friendly with George Moore, but if the illusion made him more tolerant of our business it was all right with me. But when I introduced the subject I saw at once what the curate had meant. Oh, libraries. Libraries, hm! Well, libraries, of course, were wonderful things in their own place, but town libraries were a great responsibility. It was all very well for sophisticated people like ourselves to read the works of dear George, but could we really thrust them into the hands of simple Irish townspeople?

★ ★ ★ ★ ★

Because of his wartime activities, O'Connor found it difficult to get work during its aftermath. Hector Legge of the *Sunday Independent* came to his rescue by publishing a column under a byline 'Ben Mayo'. Anonymity was preserved through meetings in Fullers' Café in Grafton Street. Topics were discussed on Tuesdays and Legge picked up the copy each Friday.

About his native city, Cork, O'Connor writes:

The town was full of marvellous characters — Chekhov characters, Dostoevsky characters; as in the usual English interpretation of the Irish, you had only to record what they said and produce a masterpiece.

We recorded what they said all right, but it never mounted up to what you could call a masterpiece. We developed the defensive attitude of the provincial to the outsider, and yet were miserable if we hadn't an outsider to practise it on. O'Faolain ran a paper; I ran a dramatic society which produced *The Cherry Orchard*. We had to drop the line 'At your age you should have a mistress,' but we were one better than the company playing *Juno and the Paycock*, in which the heroine had to have tuberculosis instead of a baby.

★ ★ ★ ★ ★

When O'Connor was teaching in the United States, he was inclined to impart personal ideas rather than literary ones, as his biographer James Matthews, relates:

He called O'Casey 'Johnny Wet Eyes', for instance. The course . . . was primarily Yeats; Joyce to his mind was the negation or antithesis of Yeats. One young man argued continually with O'Connor, suggesting that he had not read O'Casey and was slandering Joyce. At the end of the term he discovered the heckler had failed the course. When he inquired of his assistant, he learned that this particular student made it a practice to fail any course in which he disliked the professor. O'Connor raised his mark to A–, noting that in a 'pragmatic society one must be prepared to compromise'.

★ ★ ★ ★ ★

Visiting James Joyce in Paris, O'Connor asked about a picture in the hallway. When Joyce said it was Cork, O'Connor testily said that he knew very well what his own city looked like; it was the picture's frame that intrigued him. 'It is cork,' said Joyce.

★ ★ ★ ★ ★

Speaking at a Trinity College debate on censorship in 1962, O'Connor remembered his librarian days when a young man called to complain about an indecent book he had drawn; it contained a dirty word. O'Connor asked where it was and was told, 'Page 164'. O'Connor read the page and noticed nothing that might have caused offence. He asked the young man to point out the 'dirty word' and he pointed to 'navel'. O'Connor commented afterwards, 'I felt sorry for him and wanted to ask him whether he couldn't find some nice girl to walk out with, but I decided it might be dangerous.'

★ ★ ★ ★ ★

W.B. Yeats once tried a new poem on an audience that included Sean O'Faolain and Frank O'Connor. Subsequently, he told F.R. Higgins: 'O'Faolain said he understood it and he didn't, and O'Connor said he didn't understand a word of it, and he understood it perfectly.'

★ ★ ★ ★ ★

O'Connor prevailed upon his father to come to Dublin for a few days. He visited five army barracks and one cemetery. O'Connor accompanied him to Glasnevin and they called into the Brian Boru bar:

'You'll have a little drink?' he asked uneasily.

He might well be uneasy, because he knew what I thought of his drinking bouts, and I might have been angry or rude, but there was something wistful about his tone which suggested to me that this might be an occasion.

'Very well, we will,' I said, and we went in and stood at the bar. Father continued to make the pace.

'What will you have?' he asked in a lordly way. 'You'd better have a bottle of stout' — meaning that with a father as broad-minded as himself I need not pretend that I did not drink, and I had the impression that if I refused the stout he would be bitterly hurt.

'Stout will be fine,' I said nervously.

'A stout and a bottle of lemonade, miss,' he said to the barmaid.

O'Connor claimed that Hugh Hunt trained the Abbey Players to say every 'st' as 'sht', whereupon the girls politely asked him how he wished them to pronounce 'sit'.

O'Connor describes an angry W.B. Yeats at an Abbey board meeting:

My recollection is that, as he usually did when he was looking for a fight, he moved me to the chair — it was his best way of preventing my flinging it at him.

THE WRITER SHOULD NEVER FORGET THAT HE IS ALSO A
READER, THOUGH A PREJUDICED ONE
Frank O'Connor

LENNOX
ROBINSON
1886–1958

Esmé Stuart Lennox Robinson was born the youngest of seven children in Douglas, Co. Cork. His father had abandoned stockbroking to become a Church of Ireland minister, so the family moved first to Kinsale, then to Ballymoney, Co. Cork. After some private tuition, Lennox attended the Grammar School at Bandon, but poor health caused many interruptions in his education. His passion for theatre was fired when, in Cork, he saw a performance of Cathleen Ni Houlihan *by an Abbey Theatre touring company, an experience which also prompted him to join the Irish Volunteers. His first published work was a poem in* The Royal Magazine *and his first play was* The Clancy Name. *W.B. Yeats made him manager and play director of the Abbey Theatre in 1910. He had little experience and so was sent to the Duke of York Theatre in London to study the techniques of Shaw, Dion Boucicault Jnr and Harley Granville-Barker. In 1914 he left the Abbey to concentrate on writing. His lively, charming plays earned him the title 'Modern Goldsmith'. They became popular at home and abroad, particularly* The Whiteheaded Boy, *but since no royalties were then paid to authors, he made little money. Robinson also organised the Carnegie Trust Libraries. He returned to manage the Abbey in 1919 and was largely responsible for promoting Sean O'Casey's work there.*

Robinson was a gloomy man who felt that artists were obliged to conceal their inner feelings. Frank O'Connor described him as 'long and mournful and disjointed, as though at some time he had suffered on the rack, and he had a high-pitched, disjointed voice that sounded like someone's reading of an old maid's letter from Regency times, with every third word isolated and emphasised'. Robinson had a healthy respect for the amateur theatre and worked hard to further its cause. ★ ★ ★ ★ ★

195

The *Irish Press* representative at the first night of Behan's *The Quare Fellow* was Lennox Robinson, who as a former director of the Abbey Theatre had rejected the play. Gabriel Fallon, later to replace Robinson at the National Theatre, asked him at the interval what he thought of the work. Robinson retorted, 'How can you possibly expect me to enjoy a play that I turned down?'

✶ ✶ ✶ ✶ ✶

Alpho O'Reilly, later head of design in Radio Telefís Éireann, was, at nineteen years of age, attending the Abbey School of Acting. Robinson conducted its workshops. He believed in casting young people as elders and men as women. They were rehearsing a Scandinavian play and O'Reilly was playing the much-loved father of a large family drowning in major problems. A 'charming and handsome dark-haired lady — full of fun — a bit of a minx' was cast as an old family servant (male). On her first entrance she 'strolled on wearing a marvellous crimson cloche hat and a big smile'. Robinson halted everything and said, 'Miss McNally, I suggest you play the part with a broken back!'

✶ ✶ ✶ ✶ ✶

Robinson features prominently in Maurice Craig's account of the reinterment of the remains of W.B. Yeats in 1948:

The journey to Sligo was uneventful. We looked in at the Great Southern Hotel and saw only Lennox Robinson sitting at the bar. We went straight on to the Imperial Hotel and there was Lennox Robinson sitting at the bar. (Lennox Robinson, it should be said, was not a man who could have been mistaken for any other man.) By now the expected time of arrival of the cortège was at hand, so we joined the crowd in front of the Town Hall . . . . On the Town Hall steps stood all the notabilities, Lennox Robinson at the back, towering conspicuously over the rest . . . .

Outnumbered and outflanked, the Gardaí could not prevent a crowd of shrieking children . . . from breaking into the square and swarming around the hearse . . . .

We decided that if we were to have any hope of getting anywhere near the [Drumcliff] graveyard on those narrow Co. Sligo by-roads we had better leave the official party to get on with their ceremonies and start at once. As a result we were able to park close by and walk to the churchyard. Standing by the grave was Lennox Robinson . . . .

The following week *Picture Post* (London) carried a full coverage of the funeral, including a photograph of me captioned 'son of Lennox Robinson'.

✦ ✦ ✦ ✦ ✦

Robinson has been quoted as saying, 'Sometimes auditions can be trying; one does not always discover genius.' His observation may have been inspired by an incident when an enthusiastic, middle-aged actress harassed him until he consented to hearing her reading.

The aspirant told him how she had longed for years to act, but had suppressed her passion out of consideration for Mrs Patrick Campbell. It would have been unfair to jeopardise that lady's brilliant career, she felt.

Robinson stifled a yawn as the lady announced that she intended thrilling him with Portia's speech from the Court of Justice in *The Merchant of Venice*. He may have been influenced by the sentiments expressed about the quality of mercy, for he suffered in silence as the lady threatened to put 'the dread and fear of kings' in him. He suffered in agony, and not a little dampness too, when she announced that she would do it better without her teeth, whereupon she removed her dentures and gave a salivary encore.

✦ ✦ ✦ ✦ ✦

Actor Sydney Morgan had a habit of turning up late for rehearsals. He did so when he was working with Robinson in 1952. Asked why, he replied, 'The King is dead.' Robinson laconically asked, 'What King?'

✦ ✦ ✦ ✦ ✦

Gus Smith records a late-night rendezvous after the Athlone Drama Festival of 1955 when a participant argued that he had delivered his lines from *At the Hawk's Well* in the manner that he had heard Yeats himself utter them. This postman-actor was losing an argument against his director and others when Robinson waded in to defend him. The adjudicator that year was Shelah Richards and she entered into the discussion, which soon became an animated debate. The squabbling ended abruptly when Richards fired a salvo at Robinson: 'The trouble with you is that you play acolyte to Yeats's god.' Only Gabriel Fallon heard Robinson whisper, 'Gabriel, she has called me Yeats's altar boy.' A hushed assembly awaited Robinson's public retort, but none came. He just stood up and strode out of the lounge.

The discussion became less heated then and splinter debates teased out the propriety or otherwise of Miss Richards' remark and Mr Robinson's reaction.

About thirty minutes later the double doors were dramatically pulled open. It was Lennox Robinson. Collarless, open-shirted, braces hanging off his shoulders, white socks dipping about his shoes, he drew himself up to his full height of six and a half feet. Slapping one hand across his chest and making flamboyant gestures with the other, he spoke a long passage of Yeats's most ritualistic verse.

It was pointedly delivered with W.B.'s intonation, with the Abbey Theatre's intonation and with the postman's intonation.

(P.S. The postman's group won the verse section of the festival.)

★ ★ ★ ★ ★

Hugh Leonard claims that 'Crowbar' Sweeney, a member of an amateur group with which he played, held the record for ad-libbing in a Robinson play. He tells the story thus:

The ad-lib occurred during a performance of *The Whiteheaded Boy* in Kilmacanogue, and was caused by the fact that the young lovers of the piece — let us call them Joe and Greta — had fallen deeply in lust with each other. This kind of thing happens every day in show business — Richard Burton and Elizabeth Taylor were a case in point — and one can only assume that Lennox Robinson's scorching dialogue and erotic imagery drove Joe and Greta into each other's arms. It also drove them into Kilmacanogue graveyard during the interval between Acts Two and Three.

The third act had begun by the time they were missed, and a search party was despatched. As the play moved inexorably towards the moment when they were supposed to enter hand in hand, uttering glad little cries, shadowy figures darted between the tombstones. Now and then, they paused in hopes of hearing the sound of heavy breathing or the sort of cry that can only be caused by unbearable ecstasy or nettles.

Meanwhile, back at the play, 'Crowbar' Sweeney was portraying the much put-upon family drudge, 'George'. He was an excellent actor, his only fault being that, instead of coming to rehearsals, he was usually off somewhere demonstrating that his nickname had not been lightly bestowed.

The point came where the eponymous hero and his beloved were due to rush onstage. Nothing happened. There was a kind of silence, and then 'Crowbar', realising that, to quote Rupert Brooke, God had matched him with His hour, embarked upon his immortal feat.

For the benefit of the untheatrical, let me explain that an ad-lib is a piece of rubbish invented and delivered, unrehearsed, by an actor. It should, but does not, carry the death penalty: which is why actors like Robert Morley are still alive.

This, however, was an emergency. And, to be honest, let me admit that 'Crowbar' did not begin auspiciously: in fact, he beamed upon the other actors and delivered a line borrowed from Oliver Hardy. It was: 'A lot of weather we've been having lately!'

This was merely his launching pad. Soon, he was in spanking form. Having disposed of the weather, he launched into a dissertation on the state of the crops, discoursed learnedly on diseases endemic to sheep, speculated on the results of the next election, then asked his fellow players if they had heard the one about the visiting American and the outdoor lavatory.

He continued in this vein for an astonishing ten minutes. Later, I learned that the audience were under the impression that all this was part of the play, and that 'George', the ant who had toiled while his grasshopper sibling had played and squandered his substance, had finally cracked and gone round the twist.

Finally, 'Crowbar' ground to a standstill. He turned to his colleagues, who had been staring at him, cavern-mouthed, and said: 'Well, somebody say something!' When this elicited only silence, he leered at the audience, waggled his ears and made his false front teeth go up and down like a portcullis. That brought the house down.

Providentially, at that moment, Joe and Greta came rushing in. Blades of grass clung to Joe's clothes and hair, giving him more than a passing resemblance to Worzel Gummidge; while in Greta's case there seemed to be a large 'RIP' engraved in reverse on her back. At any rate, the day was saved, and 'Crowbar' Sweeney went into legend.

(As a matter of fact, he went to Pocklington, a Yorkshire town as grisly as its name, and, for all I know, he may still be there, ad-libbing in his dreams.)

That evening, on the bus going home, a lady whose recent marriage had not been allowed to affect her virginity — inherited from her mother — made no secret of her disgust. It was, she said, a sin worthy of the blackest Protestant to indulge in animal behaviour on consecrated ground. To which an heroic member of our group replied, and I wish that the memory would yield up his name so that I might honour it: 'Actually, Joe and Greta did bear that in mind. That's why they were in the missionary position.'

★ ★ ★ ★ ★

Frank O'Connor writes of a night with Robinson, who had backed his appointment as librarian and had introduced him to the Abbey Theatre:

When I knew him first, Yeats had what I can only call a 'crush' on Lennox Robinson, whom he insisted on calling 'Lennix'. One of Robinson's 'functional' plays — 'a table, two chairs and a passion' as the author described it — had been slighted in England, and Yeats insisted on reviving it in Dublin, with a programme note by himself, trouncing

200

the English critics. 'Within five years Lennix will be a European figure,' Yeats assured me with a wave of his hand, and I was glad to report the confidence to Robinson. I had not counted on the depth of despondency in him, because he merely looked away and said drearily, 'He might as well have said five hundred.' One morning, before we went to bed, we strolled down the garden to look at the first streaks of dawn on Dublin Bay, and Robinson said with his usual Regency emphasis: 'One *night* I shall swim out into *that*, and swim and *swim* until I give up.' It sounded to me like the whiskey, and unfortunately for himself it was the whiskey.

LEADING NEWSPAPERS EMPLOY AS DRAMATIC CRITICS JOURNALISTS WHO ARE EXCELLENT ON A RACECOURSE OR A FOOTBALL FIELD
Lennox Robinson

GEORGE W. RUSSELL 1867–1935

George W. Russell (AE), writer, poet and painter, contributed to the organisation and administration of the early Irish National Theatre. His artistic advice was sought by the actors, who looked to him for leadership — a fact that Lady Gregory resented.

Lurgan, Co. Armagh was his birthplace but his family moved to Dublin while he was young and he was educated in Rathmines School and the Metropolitan School of Art: it was there that his lifelong friendship with W.B. Yeats began. He edited an agricultural journal, The Irish Homestead *for some eighteen years, before turning to poetry. He also contributed features on economics and politics, became a theosophist and painted. As editor of the* Irish Statesman, *he was host to economists, intellectuals and artists, as well as visiting foreigners.*

After his marriage in 1898, he lived at a number of south-city addresses. At Coulson Avenue, Rathgar, Maud Gonne and Constance and Casimir Markievicz were neighbours and his celebrated social evenings began there. They flourished, however, after his move to Rathgar Avenue and became an established part of Dublin's literary scene. Joseph Holloway described AE's voice as 'soft and musical, and its intonation reminded me of the rhythm of a kettle boiling over'. Aspiring writers and artists vied for an invitation to listen to it.

Russell moved to Bournemouth in 1932 and died there three years later.

★ ★ ★ ★ ★

Herbert Howarth explains the derivation of Russell's pseudonym:

It was originally Aeon, but a compositor could not read it, and left it AE, which Russell accepted and always used. Why Aeon? According to Eglinton, Russell had made a drawing of the apparition in the Divine Mind of the idea of

Heavenly Man. He lay awake considering what title he should give it. 'Something whispered to him "Call it the Birth of Aeon".' A fortnight later his eye caught the word 'Aeon' in a book in the National Library, and that led him to Neander's *History of the Christian Religion* with its passage on the Gnostics and the doctrine of the Aeons. In a letter to Carrie Rea he analyses the word into the elements of the primal language (which, as a self-educator, reconstructing human knowledge from the foundation, he had discovered by introspection):

A — sound for God
AE — is first divergence from A
Au — sound continuity for a time
N — change

Thus Aeon represents revolt from God, the passage of the separated soul through its successive incarnations in man homeward to God, and God's consequent amplification.

★ ★ ★ ★ ★

Russell once told John Eglinton:

'I see the great tree of English literature arising out of roast beef and watered with much rum and beer.'

★ ★ ★ ★ ★

AE's *Deirdre* was one of the earliest plays produced by the Irish Literary Society. When it was staged at St Theresa's Hall, Dublin in April 1902, the author played the part of Cathbad the Druid in an eerie, low monotone. A lady in the audience afterwards insisted that he was a sorcerer, because as he spoke, she felt wave after wave of darkness roll across the apron and engulf her. Because the stage was a mere thirty by twenty feet and since the hall was next door to a community centre where dancing, snooker and singing were taking place, one commentator deemed the lady's experience more likely to be occasioned by the sounds and the smoke coming from next door than the amount of 'smuts' that fell from the stage.

★ ★ ★ ★ ★

In 1902 Russell wrote to the painter Sarah Purser about *Deirdre*: 'The daughters of Erin have flung their aegis over us, and Yeats and I are being produced under their auspices.'

★ ★ ★ ★ ★

After the opening of the double bill which included Maud Gonne playing Cathleen in Cathleen Ni Houlihan, *Russell wrote to tell Yeats that in the* All-Ireland Review, *Standish O'Grady had said that they might succeed in 'degrading the ideals of Ireland and . . . banishing the soul from the land'. AE had responded with a vigorous letter:*

and if O'Grady does not publish it I will send it to the *Freeman, Irish Times* and *Independent* with a letter accusing O'Grady of a mean slander on his Irish contemporaries and of cowardice in refusing to insert [my] reply. He needs to be pulled up and I have done it with a vengeance . . . . I [told] him frankly he is not great enough to issue fiats to other literary men and accuse them of decadence in a muddle of confused and contradictory sentences. If he publishes it and replies I hope we will have a gorgeous row.

★ ★ ★ ★ ★

Although Yeats was his hero, Russell, himself one of the instigators of occult study in Ireland, could be impishly sarcastic about the poet's interests in that direction. When Yeats went to London, Russell vowed that it would make little difference:

[Because] I intend opening communication with him through the medium of astral light — that is — try thought transference between Grosvenor Square and Eardley Terrace. No doubt he will have imagination enough to think he is receiving messages from me and whenever I write to him about these airy conversations I will use expressions which will suit his conversations at any time, 'Your poem is splendid.' 'Your paradoxes are getting more startling every day.' 'You should not say harsh things about your friends.' These remarks will convince him more than ever of my occult powers . . . .

204

Ulick O'Connor relates:

Russell was not always an easy person to get on with. He had eccentric habits which made unusual demands on his friends, one of which was to demand that they accompany him to Kill-o'-the-Grange graveyard on Sundays and listen to him read his verses, usually against the competition of a howling wind. Once he called on a friend for the usual ramble and was surprised when he found that it was Christmas Day, a date which had no place in his esoteric calendar.

★ ★ ★ ★ ★

John B. Yeats did not approve of his son's friendship with Russell. His dislike of religion was intense and he feared that Russell would steer Willie towards a mystical rather than a scientific outlook. 'A saint maybe, but reared in Portadown,' he would remark, referring to the philistine northern industrial centre near which Russell had grown up.

★ ★ ★ ★ ★

Lady Glenavy (in Irish Literary Portraits, *ed. W.R. Rodgers) described a meeting between Russell and James Stephens:*

The door opened and there was the figure of AE with his arms out, and in a second James Stephens seemed to disappear into the beard, into the brown suit, into the other man, just enveloped in affection and warmth and conversation right away.

★ ★ ★ ★ ★

Frank O'Connor found Russell kind:

Russell would cheerfully get you a new doctor, a new wife, a new flat or a new job, and, if you were ill, he'd come along and cook for you and nurse you. I knew this because one evening when he came to my flat, and found I'd been ill for the preceding week, the tears came into his eyes and he said, 'You should have sent for me, you know. I could have cooked for you, I'm quite a good cook — I can cook chops, you know.'

Mervyn Wall wrote of William T. Cosgrave, President of the Executive Council and the government of the newly formed Irish Free State, sending a high-ranking civil servant to Russell's home to offer him a seat in the Senate:

This man arrived late at night (apparently the matter had to be hurried because lists had to be got out the following day) and AE came to the window after some time and just shouted out, 'What do you want?' This higher civil servant put the proposition to him, and he said, 'I'll have to consult the gods,' and banged down the window. Now this civil servant had to wait for about a half an hour in the street and then finally AE pulled up the window and shouted out 'No.'

* * * * *

George Moore once remarked that Russell's only fault was an inability to distinguish between turbot and halibut.

* * * * *

James Joyce brought some of his work to Russell for his opinion. Russell told him, 'Young man, I do not know if you are a mountain or a cistern. I do know you have not enough chaos in you to be a poet.'

* * * * *

Russell once defined a literary movement as 'a few people who live in the same town and hate each other'. An anonymous source altered this to read 'a few people who hate in the same town and love themselves'.

* * * * *

Dan Davin tells how an Irish correspondent to the Morning Post, *[C.H. Bretherton] created a myth about Russell that survived:*

Not long before his death, Michael Collins was asked to meet Mr George Russell, the bell-wether of the neo-Gaels. The two men were introduced, and the Mahatma of Merrion Square resumed the monologue where it had been interrupted. Collins, whose brains, such as they were, being of a strictly practical kind, listened with furrowed brow. To listen to George Russell is like watching the water gushing out of the mouth of a stone dolphin. Collins listened as long as he could, and then, whipping a pencil and notebook out of his pocket, said suddenly: 'Your point, Mr Russell?'

★ ★ ★ ★ ★

L.A.G. Strong quotes Yeats as saying that AE could handle situations impossible to any other human being but Dostoevsky's Idiot. Strong tells of an employee on Russell's newspaper, The Irish Statesman, *complaining that the persistent attentions of a young female staff member prevented his application to work:*

AE sent for her then and there, and so managed his rebuke that all three were friends and the girl was not humiliated. Heaven knows how he did it, but it was done.

★ ★ ★ ★ ★

Backed by enemies of Russell's, a songwriter brought a libel action against *The Irish Statesman* for a critical review. Russell supported his reviewer. When asked by the judge if any part of the song collection was good, he said that some parts were. 'Then,' asked the judge, 'why did your paper describe it as a bad book?' and Russell replied, 'My Lord, if you had an egg at your breakfast this morning and parts of it were bad, and parts of it good, I think you would have described it as a bad egg.'

★ ★ ★ ★ ★

Russell died in England but was buried in Dublin. Frank O'Connor told how Yeats was alleged to have said, 'I should have to tell the truth,' when refusing to give the funeral oration at the graveside. He also quoted Russell as saying that he was not in the least afraid of death but did fear the pain and humiliation that preceded it — 'the immortal soul being kicked out of the world like an old sick dog with a canister tied to his tail'. Death itself, Russell told Austin Clarke, 'would be an exciting adventure'.

A rthur Griffith, Tom Kettle and Gogarty were among those who attended Russell's funeral. Gogarty arrived earlier, in time to hear Russell's last words: 'I have realised all my ambitions. I have had an astonishing interest in life. I have had great friends. What more can a man want?'

THERE ARE CERTAIN FIGURES IN HISTORY WHICH ARE PIVOTAL, AND AROUND THEM MYRIADS HAVE WHEELED TO NEW DESTINIES. SHAKESPEARE WAS UNDOUBTEDLY PIVOTAL, MORE SO PERHAPS THAN ANY EXCEPT THE GREAT SPIRITUAL FIGURES. BUT DID HE LEAD LITERATURE INTO A BLIND ALLEY?
George Russell (AE)

★ ★ ★ ★ ★

GEORGE
BERNARD SHAW
1856–1950

The Shaws lived at 3 Upper Synge Street, Dublin. Another family of the same name lived around the corner in Harrington Street. Both houses sent their laundry to the same washerwoman and a tablecloth belonging to Harrington Street found its way to Synge Street. A girl from the former arrived to retrieve it and the result was a street tug-o'-war between the girls from each household. This cemented a good relationship, however, and both families played together; all except the little fellow who preferred to pick out a tune with one finger on the Synge Street piano. He wore a Holland tunic and was known as 'Sonny'. At the age of ten, this precocious lad had stopped saying his prayers, protesting that he was an atheist.

Shaw's father was an unsuccessful merchant, and the playwright had a deprived youth. He was educated at Wesley College but spent many hours listening to his mother's accomplished singing or looking at the paintings in the National Gallery of Ireland. At sixteen years of age he went to work; immediately, Mrs Shaw abandoned him to his drunken father and fled to London with her music teacher, George John Vandåleur Lee, and her two daughters. Four years later Shaw joined them. For nine years, he attempted to write novels. He also worked as a critic of books, art and music before turning to play-writing. Overcoming an innate shyness, he joined the Fabian Society and became a London borough councillor. Sidney Webb and Shaw worked to form a Parliamentary Labour Party from the Fabian Society.

Shaw's literary luck had still not turned and plays that have since become famous received little acclaim. Then, in New York, The Devil's Disciple *made an impact. That was in 1897. It took seven more years for London to recognise his genius. During that period he fell ill from over-work and married his voluntary nurse, Charlotte Payne-Townshend. Producers were wary of his socialist outlook, and downright perturbed when he defended Dublin's 1916 Rising and Roger Casement, among other causes. Papers on* Commonsense about the War, How to Settle the Irish Question *and* War Issues for Irishmen *did not endear him to a nation involved in a savage conflict in Europe.*

More plays followed, carrying long prefaces expressing his reasons for writing the work. He was regarded as the first disciple of Ibsen to write for the British stage. Then came books on religion, politics and socialism. Shaw cultivated his Dublin accent, yet would not return to Ireland to live: 'I would be treated as the common enemy,' he explained.

As a youth Shaw had found the intellectual stimulus for which he longed through frequent visits to the National Gallery of Ireland, and he remembered it in his will. The Gallery benefits from his plays' royalties, and since the film My Fair Lady *was based on* Pygmalion, *this sum became considerable.*

✯ ✯ ✯ ✯ ✯

John Cowell reveals something of the family life in Synge Street which was to make Shaw 'violently and arrogantly Protestant by family tradition':

As a small boy . . . Shaw once had a strange dream. He went into the garden and at the end of it opened the gate. The sky was filled with a bright light and in the centre was God. But suddenly God became King Billy sitting on his horse.

✯ ✯ ✯ ✯ ✯

Ford Madox Ford writes:

I well remember Mr Shaw relating a sad anecdote whose date must have fallen among the eighties. As Mr Shaw put it, like every poor young man when he first comes to London he possessed no presentable garments at all save a suit of dress clothes. In this state he received an invitation to a soirée from some gentleman high in the political world — I think it was Mr Haldane. This gentleman was careful to add a post-script in the kindness of his heart, begging Mr Shaw not to dress, since everyone would be in their morning clothes. Mr Shaw was accordingly put into an extraordinary state of per-turbation. He pawned or sold all the articles of clothing in his possession, including his evening suit, and with the proceeds purchased a decent suit of black, resembling, as he put it, that of a Wesleyan minister. Upon his going up the staircase of the house to which he was invited, the first person he perceived was Mr Balfour, in evening dress; the second was Mr Wyndham in evening dress; and immediately he was introduced into a dazzling hall that was one sea of white shirt fronts relieved by black swallow-tails. He was the only undressed person in the room. Then his kind host presented himself, his face beaming with philanthropy and with the thought of kindly encouragement that he had given to struggling genius! I think Mr Shaw does not 'dress' at all nowadays, and, in the dress affected, at all events by his disciples, the grey homespuns, the soft hats, the comfortable bagginess about the knees, and the air that the pockets have of always being full of apples, the last faint trickle of Pre-Raphaelite influence is to be perceived.

★ ★ ★ ★ ★

After a visit to the Alhambra Theatre in 1890, Shaw became enthusiastic about the performance of dancer Vincenti, whom he described as 'intelligent and cultivated and an admirable pantomimist'. Particularly, he extolled the 'perfection of his pirouettes and *entrechats*' and his 'amazing revolution about the centre of the stage combined with rotation on his own longitudinal axis'.

He attended a post-performance celebration, after which he decided to better Vincenti with a pre-dawn performance in Fitzroy Square, which struck him as an ideal hippodrome. In *The Star* of 21 February 1890 Shaw tells (according to James Sutherland) how he was unaware of his audience — a concealed constable who watched in awe as the Irish playwright performed; in glee as he fell a dozen times or more. Then he approached the frolicsome foot-tapper and demanded an explanation for the unseemly eurhythmics. Enthusiastically, and with great gesticulating and demonstrating, Shaw informed the policeman of Vincenti's magnificence. He anticipated a reprimand, if not an arrest, but the constable said, 'Would you mind 'olding my 'elmet while I 'ave a go? It don't look so 'ard.'

Off he went around the square, fell and tore his long

overcoat. Shaw expected him to be angry. He was; but he was determined too. 'I never was beaten yet and I won't be beaten now; it was my ruddy coat wot tripped me,' he declared.

Shaw decided it was time for a duet, so both of them hung their coats on the railing and took off again. They fell some; they bled some; they swore a little; they laughed a little; until eventually the limb of the law managed to manipulate his own limbs for a full two rounds of the square. He might have accomplished further feats had not his inspector arrived on the scene.

'Is this your idea of fixed point duty?' challenged the officer as Shaw giggled at the word 'point', surely a choreographic choice. 'I'll allow it ain't a fixed point, but I'll lay an 'alf-sovereign you can't do it,' replied the policeman with a daring brought about by an exhilarating performance.

So the inspector, his subordinate and Shaw began their routine of *entrechats*, splits and staggers. As dawn broke, Fitzroy Square provided a *mise en scène* for a remarkable display, especially when a milkman and a postman arrived. Indeed, a full *corps de ballet* might have assembled if the milkman had not fallen and broken his leg.

★ ★ ★ ★ ★

An entry for 19 November 1916 in Lady Gregory's Journals *(ed. Robinson) reads:*

Last night GBS read me a story he had written. He had been asked for one for a gift-book to be sold for the Belgian Children's Milk Fund, and had refused, saying the Society of Authors objected to these gift-books. But the lady came again to say she had got leave from the Society to print it if she gave them a percentage. He was quite taken aback and said he hadn't promised it, but in the end sat down and wrote it straight off. Then the lady brought it back in a few days to say she wouldn't put it in the gift-book, that Mrs Whitelaw Reid had offered £400 for it to put it in the *New York Tribune*. So the Belgian children will get plenty of money for that.

★ ★ ★ ★ ★

Shaw's big chance came when a play by another Irish dramatist, John Todhunter (1839–1916), was received with disfavour at London's Avenue Theatre. Its producer was Florence Farr, with whom Shaw had had an affair. She asked Shaw for a replacement, so he took himself off to the Embankment and finished a script upon which he had been working. It was then *Alps and Balkans* but is now known as *Arms and the Man*.

There were calls for the author at the curtain, followed by cheering when GBS appeared on stage. The applause subsided and during the pause preceding the author's speech, a single boo rang out from the balcony. It came from R. Goulding Bright, who later became a successful literary agent. He had wrongly assumed that Shaw's satirising of Balkan troops was, in fact, a castigation of the British army. Shaw adopted the disarming ploy of bowing to the dissenter and saying: 'I quite agree with you, sir, but what can two do against so many?'

★ ★ ★ ★ ★

The Sphinx scene from *Caesar and Cleopatra* was inspired by an engraving Shaw had seen as a boy in a shop window. It represented the Virgin Mary with her Child asleep in the lap of a large Sphinx staring over the desert 'so intensely that the smoke of Joseph's fire close by went straight up like a stick, remained in the rummage basket of [Shaw's] memory for thirty years before [he] took it out and exploited it on stage'.

★ ★ ★ ★ ★

'Caesar's nose was good; Calpurnia's bust was worthy of her.' The lines from a review of *Julius Caesar* were written by George Bernard Shaw, a man who never missed a chance to criticise the writer adored by so many. He considered Shakespeare far too flippant in his treatment of history and politics, and said it was impossible for the most judgmental critic to look 'without a revulsion of indignant contempt at this travestying of a great man as a silly braggart' while the pathetic mob of mischief-makers who destroyed Caesar 'are lauded as statesmen and patriots'.

Not a single sentence uttered by Caesar, he claimed, was 'even worthy of a Tammany boss'. He regarded Brutus as 'nothing but a familiar type of English suburban preacher: politically he would hardly impress the Thames Conservancy Board'.

★ ★ ★ ★ ★

Shaw would have agreed with Ronald Jeans's assessment of actor-managers: '[To them] the part is greater than the whole.' When he cut nearly two thousand lines from *Cymbeline*, Henry Irving provided himself with more time for melodramatic gestures and pauses. This gave Shaw another chance at his favourite pastime — Shakespeare-baiting!

The play was 'trash of the lowest melodramatic order, in parts abominably written, throughout intellectually vulgar, foolish, offensive, indecent and exasperating beyond all tolerance'. He accused Shakespeare of pilfering the themes and ideas of others and condemned 'his monstrous rhetorical fustian, his unbearable platitudes, his pretentious reduction of the subtlest problems of life to commonplaces against which a Polytechnic debating club would revolt'. Shaw considered him incapable of getting out of the depth of even the most ignorant audience, and decreed that 'with the single exception of Homer, there is no eminent writer, not even Sir Walter Scott, whom I can despise so entirely as I despise Shakespeare when I measure my mind against his'.

★ ★ ★ ★ ★

St John Ervine recalls an accident while Shaw was scrambling over rocks in the West of Ireland:

His wife hurried off to the village for a doctor, and was unfortunate enough to meet one who had recently read *The Doctor's Dilemma*, and was in no mood to put himself out for its author. Luckily for himself, however, he agreed to accompany her to the rocks; luckily, because Charlotte would have torn him limb from limb if he had not. They went by boat, because Charlotte thought it would be easier to bring GBS back by sea than by land. Lest his pain should be too

214

much for him, she bought a small bottle of brandy to stimulate him; and was almost overwhelmed by his wrath when she suggested that he might relax his rule of total abstinence for once. Yet he took a taste, though he swallowed none of it because, he said, his palate was purer than any carnivorous person's could possibly be, and he was able, therefore, to save her from being poisoned by a mixture of red ink and corrosive acid.

✱

Ervine also comments on how Shaw was sometimes frivolous:

There was an occasion when, discussing the character of God, who was then still regarded as the irascible and capricious deity of the Old Testament, he jeered at the widely spread belief that the Almighty, if dared to strike a person dead, would instantly do so. Pulling out his watch, he proposed to ask God to strike him dead within a couple of minutes; and was cynically amused to find that even the agnostics and atheists in the company pleaded with him to abandon his proposal.

✱ ✱ ✱ ✱ ✱

According to Shaw, Henry Irving achieved the distinction of performing *Hamlet* with the role of the Prince of Denmark and all other parts omitted, substituting for them 'the fascinating figure of Henry Irving, which for many years did not pall on his audience and never palled on himself'.

✱ ✱ ✱ ✱ ✱

In A Victorian in Orbit *(1961), the actor and director Sir Cedric Hardwicke writes:*

Shaw found fault at rehearsal with the last-act explosion in Barry Jackson's production of *Heartbreak House* and demanded a bigger bang. The stage manager assured him that on opening night there would be a bang to remember and accordingly warned the cast to that effect. When the cue came up, Edith Evans spoke the line, then prudently covered her face with her hands. Nothing happened. The audience was halfway out of the theatre when a sudden, thunderous crash brought the ceiling down and sent two players to the hospital. Shaw, for once, seemed satisfied.

★ ★ ★ ★ ★

Quoting from the diaries of Shaw's wife, Charlotte, Janet Dunbar tells how Shaw arranged a service for his sister's obsequies. He himself read some poems, one of which may have been ill chosen for a cremation. It was 'Fear no more the heat o' the sun'.

★ ★ ★ ★ ★

Influenced by reading a little-known work of Percy Bysshe Shelley's called *A Vindication of Natural Diet*, Shaw became a vegetarian. The habit often provoked hostility. During rehearsals for *Pygmalion*, Mrs Patrick Campbell married and spent a fortnight on her honeymoon. When she returned, she did not know her lines too well. Shaw made his annoyance apparent and the actress tried again, then asked if she had improved. Shaw replied in the negative and added that he wanted none of the lady's flamboyant creatures, nothing more than the 'simple, ordinary human creation' which he had conceived. Mrs Campbell was not used to such outbursts — nor did she approve of Shaw's temperate habits, obviously. Telling the author he was a dreadful man, she continued, 'One day you'll eat a beefsteak and then God help all women.'

★ ★ ★ ★ ★

Furious at a happy ending to *Pygmalion* devised by Sir Herbert Beerbohm Tree on one occasion, Shaw protested loudly. When Tree defended himself by saying, 'My finale makes money; you ought to be grateful,' Shaw retorted, 'Your finale is damnable; you ought to be shot.'

★ ★ ★ ★ ★

Shaw's acerbic wit met its match in Winston Churchill's. Once, when the statesman's political fortunes were at a low ebb, Shaw sent him four tickets for the opening night of one of his new plays. In a note, he told Churchill that they were for 'yourself and your friends — if you have any'. Churchill returned the tickets, regretting that he had a prior engagement on that evening. But he expressed interest in having tickets 'for the second night — if there is one'.

☆ ☆ ☆ ☆ ☆

During the late 1930s, an advertising representative with the *Irish Independent*, Billy King, wrote to Shaw when Irish customs impounded copies of his books ordered through an English newspaper. So began a protracted correspondence which included a questionnaire from King concerning the presidency of the Irish Free State. Shaw replied that he considered himself too old to accept the position. He claimed that he did not know enough about contemporary public life in Ireland to have an opinion on who would be suitable. He knew who was unsuitable, however: anyone old enough for him to know anything about and anyone with roots in the unhappy past. Having got copyright clearance from Shaw, King sold the correspondence to his editor for five pounds.

☆ ☆ ☆ ☆ ☆

Anonymous actress's cable to Shaw: Am crazy to play St Joan.
Cable from Shaw: I agree.

☆ ☆ ☆ ☆ ☆

Lord Northcliffe is alleged to have remarked to the very thin Shaw: 'The problem with you is that you look as if there is a famine in the land.' Shaw is said to have replied: 'The problem with you is that you look as if you caused it.'

☆ ☆ ☆ ☆ ☆

Interviewer: What's your idea of civilisation?

Shaw: It's a good idea; somebody ought to start it.

☆ ☆ ☆ ☆ ☆

An interesting reflection on London and Dublin audiences is provided by a family friend, Father Leonard (Irish Literary Portraits, *ed. W.R. Rodgers):*

[During his first public speech in Dublin] Shaw began by making very exaggerated statements. I thought that he was

217

using the technique that he used in England to startle and upset people; when he made these outrageous statements in Dublin, where they were used to them, they all began to laugh. He got quite annoyed and he said, 'This is no laughing matter, I'm perfectly serious.' They all laughed twice as much. I think he recognised his mistake, for from then on he spoke very seriously, and he was listened to very attentively.

★ ★ ★ ★ ★

St John Ervine recalls Shaw's fastidiousness in early life — 'he wouldn't pick a woman off the pavement'; he was then seduced by a woman fifteen years older than him on his twenty-ninth birthday, so swamping years of abstinence:

After that a great many women came into his life. He was very attractive to women — extraordinarily attractive to women and very intelligent women too. It was a staggering sight to watch Shaw at any kind of meeting — the way women cluttered round him like infatuated hens. He wasn't a monk, not by any manner of means, he was ardent right up to the end . . . . But the fact is that Charlotte, who was a very remarkable woman, a woman of highly individualised character totally different in every respect from GBS, loathed the whole thought of sex, and she would not marry anybody unless there was an agreement that the marriage should not be consummated, and Charlotte died a virgin.

★ ★ ★ ★ ★

Charlotte did not like Sean O'Casey and at a particular lunch attacked him, saying that he quarrelled with Yeats and James Agate and would never get anywhere by arguing with people. The exchanges became quite heated when O'Casey said:

'There's something in me that forces me to do it. I suppose it's the Holy Ghost.' 'What do you mean — the Holy Ghost?' she said. 'Define your terms before you use them. What do you mean?' Shaw intervened, 'He means', said Shaw, 'that *he* has got something, and *I* have got something, that you haven't got.' Mrs Shaw shut up. Shaw had great power over her.

When well into his eighties, Shaw wished to show Charlotte the Great Wall of China and decided that the best way to do that was by biplane with open cockpit. When they swooped down to the wall they almost became involved in a war; the Japanese had invaded Manchuria and the defending Chinese were engaging them in fierce battle.

★ ★ ★ ★ ★

Bertrand Russell told R.J. Minney about cycling with Shaw:

He wobbled uncertainly and dangerously and it seemed to me a folly to embark on this ride with him. I decided to keep well ahead of him to avoid a collision, but as Shaw knew the countryside and I didn't, I found I had to dismount at every fork and at all the crossroads, and wait for him to tell me which one to take.

At one fork, while I waited, Shaw came swooping down the hill towards me. I could see he was unable to stop . . . he swept calamitously down . . . . He wobbled, his machine zigzagged, and ended up crashing into my bicycle. The impact lifted him right out of his seat and shot him twenty feet ahead, where he lay spread-eagled on the roadway.

'That's the end of Shaw,' I thought. I rushed up to see what I could do, but felt it was already too late. On coming nearer I saw that he was still alive, for he had begun to stir and was attempting to rise. He limped towards his bicycle, which, miraculously, was almost undamaged, he mounted it and, without so much as a glance at me, rode off, quite determined apparently to keep ahead of me this time. My bicycle was a complete wreck. The wheels were twisted, the frame was bent. It was impossible for me to ride it. There was nothing I could do except finish the journey by train.

★

Russell walked a mile to the station and boarded a very slow train.

It was an unpleasant journey. I had brought nothing to read. But what was even more painful was to see the tall, slender, bearded figure of Shaw pedalling furiously beside the train, overtaking it at intervals, and whenever he came to my window, bellowing, yah-ing and jeering at me — not a very becoming performance by a man sixteen years your senior.

* * * * *

A kind person, Shaw provided for the family of a man who was in prison for his part in the 1916 Rising. When G.K. Chesterton died, St John Ervine reports that Shaw wrote to his wife saying, roughly:

I know that G.K. was careless about money, that he never bargained as he ought to have bargained for price . . . [so] if you are in any financial trouble as a result of his death please draw on me up to four figures [a considerable offer in 1936].

* * * * *

Not so kind to publishers, Shaw is quoted in Rotten Rejections *(ed. Bernard) as writing:*

I finished my first book seventy-six years ago. I offered it to every publisher on the English-speaking earth I ever heard of. Their refusals were unanimous: and it did not get into print until, fifty years later, publishers would publish anything that had my name on it . . . .

I object to publishers: the one service they have done me is to teach me to do without them. They combine commercial rascality with artistic touchiness and pettiness, without being either good business men or fine judges of literature. All that is necessary in the production of a book is an author and a bookseller, without the intermediate parasite.

* * * * *

Peter Hay includes a BBC interview where the actress Dame Sybil Thorndike described a reading with Shaw:

It was that first scene; I thought, 'God in heaven, you've given me something which I never dreamed that I was ever going to be asked to play.' He read the first three scenes and then he came to the Tent Scene. Just before he read that he said, 'Now the play really begins, the rest is all flapdoodle.'

But Shaw himself was a perfect St Joan; he could have played it far better than any of us.

Shaw said to me, 'Have you read all the histories?' I said, 'Every single one of them.' So he said, 'Forget them. I'll tell you what to say.' And when he read his play I knew they were all the things I passionately wanted to say. And to prove it, that's the only time, on a first night, that I haven't had one nerve. I was exalted. God was there and I didn't care a hoot for anything, except getting over what Shaw had written. Oh, what a wonderful man . . . he gave me a book, my book that I'd been rehearsing with, and he wrote in the beginning of it, 'To Saint Sybil Thorndike from Saint Bernard Shaw'.

★ ★ ★ ★ ★

Shaw, an admirer of Hitler and Mussolini, boasted that he had no trace of the commercially imported north Spanish strain that passes for aboriginal Irish:

I am a genuine typical Irishman of the Danish, Norman, Cromwellian and (of course) Scottish invasions. I am violently and arrogantly Protestant by family tradition; but let no English Government therefore count on my allegiance; I am English enough to be an inveterate Republican and Home Ruler. It is true that my grandfather was an Orangeman; but then his sister was an abbess, and his uncle, I am proud to say, was hanged as a rebel.

In other words, he was just a normal Irishman!

★ ★ ★ ★ ★

One day, Shaw's maid, Maggie, tiptoed down the stairs and into the kitchen to tell the housekeeper, Mrs Laden, that Shaw was trying on one of her frocks. Laden told R.J. Minney:

I hurried up the stairs. The door of his bedroom was slightly ajar and I could see him reflected in the mirror, wearing one of my dresses. I went in. He turned and smiled at me. 'What do you think you are doing?' I asked. 'This Chinese robe Sir Robert Ho Tung gave me is most attractive. I thought I'd try it on.' 'That's my dress,' I said. 'Sir Robert gave you a blue robe — this one is black.' I knew he was a little colour-blind. He couldn't distinguish blue from green as a rule, though he did get the colour of his wife's eyes right; they were certainly green. But black and blue!

★ ★ ★ ★ ★

Shaw's celebrated correspondence with Lord Alfred Douglas reached a stage when 'Dear Lord Alfred' and 'Dear Mr Shaw' gave way to 'Dear Childe Alfred' and 'Dear St Christopher'. Douglas wrote:

My dear St Christopher, I am going this afternoon to London to the Almroth Wright Ward, St Mary's Hospital, Paddington. Operation tomorrow, I suppose. I don't mind much though I feel slightly frightened. Please say a prayer for me! As Bernard Shaw you wouldn't do this I know but in your capacity of St Christopher you might rely on the powerful efficacity of your prayers . . .

Shaw replied:

Dear Childe Alfred, I talked the matter over with the Holy Ghost, who told me not to be a damned fool and to write at once to Almroth Wright [surgeon at St Mary's], recommending you to his special care. He replied, 'As to your man Lord Alfred, we gave him a little ward all by himself; and our best surgeons saw him and thought an operation would be inadvisable; and so he promptly went out of hospital and I never saw him.'

Shaw had written to Sir Almroth, describing Douglas as a very beautiful youth who had stood by Oscar Wilde.

★ ★ ★ ★ ★

A neighbour protested by phone about smoke from a garden fire. An ageing Shaw wrote a letter of apology:

I thought of you very sympathetically on Saturday when the west wind was smoking you out. You will have your revenge when the wind goes south and smokes me out. I

222

know of no remedy for the autumn bonfires, which have smoked for all of my 94 years and thousands of centuries before that . . . I shall be burnt up myself presently; but the fumes will get no farther than Golders Green.

✷ ✷ ✷ ✷ ✷

His vegetarianism caused Shaw to quip about his funeral arrangements. There would be no mourning coaches, just cattle, pigs, sheep, poultry and a mobile aquarium full of fish — all sporting white scarves to honour a man who died rather than eat his fellow creatures.

✷ ✷ ✷ ✷ ✷

Shaw's final illness was preceded by two falls in his garden. Mrs Laden told R.J. Minney:

[I] saw him totter and fall into a hedge . . . . I quickly drew back as I knew it would upset him if he saw me. Relieved at finding that no one was watching he picked himself up, dusted his clothes and walked on normally and rather nonchalantly, to the end of the garden.

I said nothing for some days. Then, quite casually, as though I had just thought of it, I said: 'I am a little worried, Mr Shaw. It's always possible for anyone of us to slip and fall in the garden. Would it be a good idea if I gave you this whistle I've got, to put in your pocket — then if by chance you happen to fall you could blow the whistle and I'd know where to find you and come along and help . . . .' He stared at me for a while, wondering, I suppose, if I had seen what happened earlier that week, or whether I just had Highland second-sight. Anyway he took the whistle, put it between his lips and tried it out. Then he smiled and stuffed it in his pocket.

✷

Minney also tells how Shaw demanded a plain wooden box with no furbelows for his cremation. As he was dying, someone telephoned from the BBC:

'We know that Mr Shaw listens to the Third Programme and enjoys the music. We should like to play for him something he would especially like to hear — a symphony by Beethoven or a concerto by Mozart perhaps.' Mrs Laden said it was most thoughtful and kind of them and she was sure Mr Shaw would appreciate it. 'I'll go and ask him.' Informed of it, Shaw merely stared at her. 'The man is on the phone, waiting for your answer. What will I tell him?' 'Tell him', Shaw said, 'to play "The Old Cow Died".'

In Ireland, if a person continually complains, he is said to be 'playing the tune the old cow died on'.

EVERY MAN OVER FORTY IS A SCOUNDREL
George Bernard Shaw

RICHARD BRINSLEY SHERIDAN
1751–1816

Dublin-born playwright Richard Brinsley Sheridan was most famous for The Critic, The Rivals *and* The School for Scandal.

It was love that drove Sheridan to play-writing. At twenty years of age he fell for the 'Maid of Bath', Elizabeth Linley, a lady of great beauty and musical talent. The couple eloped to France, married and returned to settle in London. But Sheridan would not allow Elizabeth to sing professionally any more.

They lived extravagantly, so he had to take his writing seriously in order to make money. His first success, The Rivals, *was ready for a Covent Garden production in 1775.*

Three years later the witty dialogue of The School for Scandal *was first heard. By that time he had purchased the Drury Lane Theatre, half from Garrick for £35,000 and the remaining half for £45,000. He quarrelled incessantly with managers of other theatres whose success he envied. Then he turned to politics and sat in Parliament for thirty-two years. A brilliant orator, he made a celebrated speech advocating the impeachment of the Governor General of India, Warren Hastings, for malpractice. Sheridan was defeated in the 1812 election, and — a second wife being as extravagant as himself — he died penniless in 1816.*

★ ★ ★ ★ ★

Much against his will, a contemporary British dramatist Richard Cumberland was persuaded by his children to bring them to see *The School for Scandal*. The man was not at all enamoured of Sheridan's success to date. They took a box, Cumberland sitting behind his flock, and an observer noticed that every time the children laughed, Richard chastised them, saying that there was nothing funny about the play. He was overheard scolding them, 'You should not laugh; there's nothing to laugh at so keep still, my little dunces.'

Long afterwards, Sheridan heard about the incident. His retort was: 'It was most ungrateful of Cumberland to have been displeased with his children for laughing at my comedy. I went the other night to see his tragedy, and I laughed at it from beginning to end.'

★ ★ ★ ★ ★

Thomas Moore gives an account of the night of 24 February 1809. The House of Commons was debating the Peninsular War when the night sky was lit up by the fire which destroyed Sheridan's Drury Lane Theatre. However, when an adjournment motion was proposed in the House, Sheridan said: 'Whatsoever might be the extent of the private calamity, I hope it will not interfere with the public business of the country.'

He took his leave of the assembly, arrived at Drury Lane and watched the theatre being razed. When a friend offered some light refreshments laced heavily with sympathy, he accepted, saying, 'A man may surely be allowed to take a glass of wine by his own fireside.'

★ ★ ★ ★ ★

Sheridan once had a Royal Command Performance of *The School for Scandal*. King George III afterwards compli-mented him on his work, while the Queen asked when they could expect a new drama from the author. Sheridan replied that he was putting the finishing touches to another comedy. Next day, the composer met actor Michael Kelly, who asked him if this was so; Sheridan assured him that it was. Kelly said, 'Not you! You will never write again; you are afraid to write.' A little peeved, Sheridan asked of whom he should be afraid and was told, 'You are afraid of the author of *The School for Scandal*.'

★ ★ ★ ★ ★

In *Reminiscences of Michael Kelly*, the author also tells how Sheridan lampooned Richard Cumberland in the character of Sir Fretful Plagiary in *The Critic*. The play worried its backers and the cast more than Cumberland, especially when opening night neared and the last scene was still unwritten. An actor named King, who played Puff, attempted to track down the author and force him to complete the work. He failed. Only two days remained and so Mr Linley, who was a joint manager of the company and Sheridan's father-in-law, decided that strategy was required.

He called a late-evening rehearsal, invited Sheridan out to dinner and steered him to the theatre afterwards. While watching the performance, Sheridan was approached by King, who asked him to come to the green-room for discussion on a point that was bothering him. The playwright complied. King ushered him into the room, stepped back and locked the door; a desk, paper, pen, ink, bottles of claret and a basket of anchovy sandwiches were laid out in the room. Managers and cast shouted through the keyhole that he would not be released from captivity until the final scene was finished. It was. As was the claret!

★ ★ ★ ★ ★

Samuel Rogers attended the Warren Hastings trial and praised Sheridan's oratory. The historian Edward Gibbon, author of *Decline and Fall of the Roman Empire*, was in the public gallery. Although newspaper reports disagree, Rogers quoted Sheridan's calling attention to the celebrity as 'the luminous author of the *Decline and Fall*'. A colleague chided Sheridan subsequently but Sheridan denied offering any praise. When his words were quoted back to him, Sheridan was shocked; 'Luminous? I meant voluminous!' he said.

★ ★ ★ ★ ★

Gordon Snell notes that The School for Scandal *proved a tricky play for a particular company:*

In its opening scene, planting gossip, Lady Sneerwell is supposed to say: 'The paragraphs, you say, are all inserted, Mr Snake?' and to get the reply, 'Yes, your ladyship.'

In one performance both actors got flustered, and the exchange went like this: 'The snakes, you say, are all inserted, Mr Paragraph?' 'Yes, your majesty . . . .'

On its opening night in Covent Garden, there was violent opposition to the fifth act of *The Rivals*. The character Sir Lucius O'Trigger was particularly disliked and Mr Lee, who played the part, was badly miscast. The *Morning Chronicle* was to say: 'What evil spirit could influence the writer and the managers to assign the part . . . to Mr Lee, or Mr Lee himself to receive it . . . .' The actor's attempt at affecting an Irish accent also drew fire from the *Chronicle*: 'This representation of Sir Lucius is indeed an affront to the common sense of the audience, and is so far from giving the manners of our brave and worthy neighbours (the Irish) that it scarce equals the picture of a respectable Hottentot, gabbing in an uncouth dialect, neither Welsh, English nor Irish . . . .'

Besides receiving bad notices, Lee received, in the face, an apple flung at him from the audience. He drew himself up to his full height, faced his antagonist and declared in this exaggerated Irish brogue: 'Be the powers, is it personal? Is it me or the matther?'

'TIS SAFEST IN MATRIMONY TO BEGIN WITH A LITTLE
AVERSION
Richard Brinsley Sheridan

ALAN
SIMPSON
1920–1980

Born in Dublin, educated in Belfast and at Trinity College Dublin, Alan Simpson became an engineer and joined the army during 'The Emergency' (World War II). For a few years after that he worked with Hilton Edwards and Micheál macLiammóir but rejoined the Corps of Engineers and became a captain. He remained involved with theatre and, with his wife, Carolyn Swift, founded the Pike Theatre in a Herbert Lane mews, near Upper Mount Street, Dublin. An asbestos-roofed yard became an auditorium, a garage the stage, the floor above it being cut away to allow 'flies'. Late-night 'Follies' became popular and Irish audiences were introduced to Beckett and Behan there. Simpson later wrote a book called Beckett, Behan and a Theatre in Dublin *and later still passed on to me a considerable amount of Dublin theatre lore. He became a sought-after theatre director, and a partnership with producer Noel Pearson led to the staging of spectacular musicals in Dublin.*

★ ★ ★ ★ ★

Simpson once told me that the only factual account of the *Rose Tattoo* affair was contained in *Beckett, Behan and a Theatre in Dublin*, and indeed there is enough theatre folklore about the case to fill countless tomes.

Tennessee Wiliams's play opened to rave notices during the first Dublin Theatre Festival in May 1957. Even Harold Hobson hinted that Herbert Lane was on its way to becoming as distinguished a thoroughfare as Abbey Street or Cavendish Row (locations of the Abbey and Gate).

Fifteen minutes before the second performance, a police inspector called to the Pike and asked to see Simpson. He was busy upstairs negotiating a proposed transfer of the production to the Gate Theatre, but reluctantly came down. Simpson was told that it had been brought to the attention of

229

the authorities that the play contained 'objectionable passages'. Reading from a prepared script, the inspector ordered that the imminent performance be cancelled. Simpson said he would have to consult his solicitor; instead, he instructed his wife to take up the curtain.

Festival director Brendan Smith had told Simpson about receiving a protest letter from a group called 'The League of Decency'. They objected to the play's inclusion in the Festival programme because it 'advocated the use of birth control by unnatural means'. Simpson was the son of a Church of Ireland clergyman, but he discussed this with a devout Roman Catholic member of the cast, who then went to Smith and cited instances when he had turned down parts because of their moral or religious shortcomings. He assured him that he had no scruples about *The Rose Tattoo*. Nor had former critic of the *Catholic Standard* Gabriel Fallon, who praised the play.

A solicitor arrived at Herbert Lane and asked to see the document which had been read to Simpson. The inspector refused but he did read it to him. There were no further developments that night but the solicitor wrote to the Deputy Commissioner of An Garda Síochána the next day requesting that the 'offensive passages' be stipulated.

Meanwhile, Simpson tried to keep the affair quiet. He even indicated some willingness to make certain cuts in order to save the Festival committee embarrassment. But Lord Longford by then had decided not to take the play to the Gate and duly placed a notice in the newspapers to that effect. That forced Simpson to submit a press release; appropriately it was drafted in the monkey-house at the Dublin Zoo, to which he had taken his daughter for her birthday.

Simpson went to his solicitor to clear the manifesto with him. While there, a note arrived from the Deputy Commissioner stating that the whole matter was 'being dealt with by the proper authorities according to law'. Squad cars were waiting at Herbert Lane that evening, their occupants ready to accost Simpson. But advance warning allowed him to reach the theatre without passing them.

When they realised that Simpson had given them the slip, the Gardaí sent for him but he refused to come to the top of the lane. So they converged on the tiny theatre and, after a minor scuffle, arrested him. At the Bridewell, he was charged with 'presenting for gain an indecent and profane performance'. Refused bail, he spent a night in a cell. Next morning his solicitor told him that if he undertook to take off the play, the matter would be dropped. Simpson declined. The courtroom was packed with cast and friends as the proceedings took place and the hearing was fixed for July. Simpson was granted bail.

There were rumours around Dublin that day that the cast had been arrested. They had indeed been threatened with prosecution but the play went ahead in the evening. Simpson's army colleagues were there to support him; Brendan Behan turned up and sang rebel songs. There was quite an open-air party in Herbert Lane that night.

Before the taking of depositions began on 4 July, the play moved to the Royal Opera House in Belfast. The police there described it as Sunday-school fare. The report of the Dublin police caused considerable argument at the July hearing in the Dublin District Court. This led to a High Court sitting and a subsequent appeal of its decision to the Supreme Court. A year dragged on before Simpson was finally acquitted. A commentator quoted Tennessee Williams: 'To be free is to have achieved your life.'

★ ★ ★ ★ ★

Carolyn Swift had her own particular memory of the Rose Tattoo *affair:*

Alan Simpson had been charged in the District Court and, despite vigorous objections from the prosecution, freed on bail after an uncomfortable night in the Bridewell. I was standing in the wings, waiting to go on in the part of Rosa in place of Kate Binchy. She, unlike the rest of the cast, had been unable to defy the warning given to each and every one of us before the show that, if we set foot on the stage, we would be rendering ourselves liable to prosecution. Sobbing, she had been led away after her father had explained that, since she was a minor, he was responsible for her actions and, himself being a judge, he couldn't very well defy the law, whatever his personal opinions.

I was seventeen years older than Kate and quite unsuitable for the role of the fifteen-year-old schoolgirl. On a practical level, I was twice her size and there was no way of getting her dress to zip up the back. But there was no one else who could have learned the part in the time available whereas I, as assistant director, had been at every rehearsal and knew her every move and inflection. So there I was, with a white cardigan covering the open zip of her white graduation dress and scared out of my wits, not of the police lining the back of the auditorium, but of making vulgar what had been innocent, sensitive and beautiful. I kept praying that I would be arrested before I reached the love scene!

Kate's dress was suffocatingly tight but, even so, I suddenly became aware of an even greater strain on it. Looking down I saw that the goat, who played an important part in the play and was also waiting for his entrance, was eating the very clothes off my back. As I heard the action on stage reaching a point only a few speeches before my cue, I began a wrestling match with the goat as I tugged my skirt back, inch by inch, out of his champing jaws.

★ ★ ★ ★ ★

Hugh Leonard was covering the District Court hearing for a British magazine. Twenty-eight years later, Leonard recalled in his Sunday Independent *column:*

In the dock, as it were, stood not only Mr Simpson, but a play, *The Rose Tattoo* by Tennessee Williams, and a detective-sergeant was attempting to sum up the plot.

He had admitted to having been to the theatre only twice in the past twenty years. Nonetheless, no one was other than taken aback when, in the course of his recital, he declared in a rich rural accent: 'And then Serafina's husband died and she had his ashes cremated . . . .' Better — or indeed, worse — was to follow, but perhaps one should first take a brief look at the *corpus delicti*, the play itself, which is, as it then was, a steamy piece of whatsa-da-matter Italian-American spaghetti opera.

Serafina is a lusty Sicilian widow who idolises the memory of her late husband. She scandalises her neighbours and the village priest by keeping his ashes (her husband's, not the priest's) in a domestic shrine, and guards her young daughter's virginity with a ferocity which would not shame, as if anything could, a Fianna Fáil deputy denouncing a dissenter.

Enter one Alvaro Mangiacavallo, a truck-driver with the body of an Adonis and the brain of a moth. He has amorous designs on Serafina, and, at one point, according to the stage directions: 'He stuffs his hands into his pants' pockets, then jerks them out again. A small cellophane-wrapped disc falls on the floor, escaping his notice, but not Serafina's.'

She rounds on him. 'You talk a sweet mouth about women. Then drop such a thing from your pocket? *Va via, vigliacco!* . . . Go to the Square Roof with it . . . Here is no *casa privata. Io, non sono puttana!*'

Thus morality triumphs and lechery is routed. The late Cornelis Jansen [Dutch Roman Catholic theologian 1585–1638] could ask for no more, but then Jansen had never been to Ireland. As recently as the late 1950s, there flourished those who believed that merely to acknowledge the existence of French letters was to induce an epidemic of animalistic tumescence as far as the eye could see or the hand could grope.

This was why Simpson had been arrested, and it cut no ice that the business of dropping the vile object was merely mimed. (Indeed, if memory serves, the spectacle lingers down the years of the Pike Theatre audience rising from their seats, almost *en masse*, to have a gawk at the thing.) This led to the funniest moment in the entire shabby and unfunny business.

We are back in the District Court, and the prosecuting garda has reached the offending scene in the course of his résumé. An interruption comes from counsel for the State. 'At this juncture in the play, was any object dropped on the stage?'

The good policeman thought hard and long and at last delivered himself. 'No,' he replied with some reluctance. 'Dere was nothing dropped.' Then, brightening, he added: 'But it was my dishtinct impression dat it was a contraceptive dat wasn't dropped.'

★ ★ ★ ★ ★

An unusual memorial to Simpson stands in Columb Barracks, Mullingar. As an army engineer, Simpson had designed an ornate brick hearth surround in the officers' mess ante-room. The trouble was, it was so high that it prevented the heat from the fire spreading to the room; so his colleagues named it 'Simpson's Folly'. Many years afterwards, Eileen Colgan, Simpson's widow, performed a one-woman show in the mess. Told the story, she requested that the site of the fireplace, now long gone, be suitably marked. It now bears a brass plate that reads, 'Site of Simpson's Folly. Alan Simpson — 1920–1980'.

★ ★ ★ ★ ★

IRELAND'S POSITION RELATIVE TO ENGLAND HAS GIVEN
US A BIT OF AN INFERIORITY COMPLEX
Alan Simpson

JONATHAN SWIFT
1667–1745

A great writer but a bit mad? An eccentric who rode a horse backways? A patriot who hated his country? A savage and realistic critic who became a lunatic? Fact, paradox and anecdote have made the Dean of St Patrick's Cathedral a part of old Dublin's history and lore. Born in the city, Swift was educated in Kilkenny and Trinity Colleges. Only by special exemption did he graduate, being a mediocre student. He spent a short period living in Surrey as secretary to Sir William Temple, the essayist diplomat who negotiated the Triple Alliance against France. Study for the Church followed and he was ordained in 1694. An Antrim curacy wearied him and he returned to Surrey in 1696, as tutor to Hester (Esther) Johnson. Affection for her ('Stella') inspired a considerable amount of his work.

Swift was awarded the degree of MA after just a month at Hart Hall, Oxford in 1692. He was appointed vicar of Laracor, Co. Meath in 1700. Gradually he made his name as a scholarly wit with people like Congreve and Addison. Tories entertained him, hoping for support in his writings. The Queen refused him a bishopric but appointed him Dean of St Patrick's, a cathedral described by Shaw as having been designed by the devil. Esther Vanhomrigh ('Vanessa') became infatuated with Swift and embarrassed him by arriving in Dublin in 1714. His last years were spent in advancing deafness and general decline.

★ ★ ★ ★ ★

Bernard Tucker explains:

It was at Moor Park that he met the child of eight, Hester Johnson, whom he nicknamed 'Stella' and who became his closest companion until her death in 1728. He also contracted the illness which remained with him for the rest of his life: Meniere's disease, that disturbance of the inner ear, which causes vertigo and deafness. The aetiology of this illness was not ascertained until 1861, so Swift, not surprisingly, did not understand that the various symptoms were all due to the same cause and he traced his giddiness to an overindulgence in apples and his deafness to a cold: 'I got my giddiness by eating a hundred golden pippins at a time in Richmond . . . having made a fine seat about twenty miles farther in Surrey, where I used to read and sleep, there I got my deafness.'

★ ★ ★ ★ ★

One of Swift's most remarkable works is *Gulliver's Travels*. Its little people lived in Lilliput. On the southern shore of Lough Ennell, Co. Westmeath, there exists such a place, for years the site of an annual Feis and Sports. Recently a Jonathan Swift Park has been established there. After the book's success, Swift wrote to Alexander Pope, informing him of early enthusiastic reviews but also of a bishop who thought the book was 'full of improbable lies, and for his part he hardly believed a word of it'.

★ ★ ★ ★ ★

A lawyer attempted to match Dean Swift's dinner-table wit by asking, 'If the devil and the clergy were opponents in court, who would win the case?' Swift replied, 'The devil, of course; all the lawyers would be on his side!'

★ ★ ★ ★ ★

Denis Johnston claimed to have received a letter from a lady in Kensington which read:

My mother-in-law is a direct descendant of Dean Swift and also of the Gullivers, his own relations, about whom he wrote, and I do not doubt that she could give you the information on this subject which is not generally known and might be of interest.

★ ★ ★ ★ ★

In Laracor, where he was parson, Swift fished for eel and trout while wearing his morning suit.

★ ★ ★ ★ ★

After the publication of Swift's fourth Drapier letter, which condemned the granting of a patent for producing a new copper coinage, the Lord Lieutenant offered a reward for information on its origin. Swift interrupted a formal Castle reception and berated the Lord Lieutenant in a loud voice, stating, 'I suppose you expect a statue of copper will be erected to you . . . .' The assembly was shocked, but the Lord Lieutenant was composed. In a dignified voice he cut 'The Dane' down to size, quoting Virgil: *'Res dura et regni novitas me talia cogunt moliri* (Hard fortune and newness of my reign force me to such measures).'

★ ★ ★ ★ ★

In her Memoirs *(1748), Laetitia Pilkington, a friend of Swift, writes of Swift and Stella:*

I doubt not but the world will expect to hear from me some of the Dean's amours as he has not quite escaped censure, on account of his gallantries; but here I am not able to oblige my reader, he being too advanced in years when I first had the honour of being known to him for amusements of that kind. I make no doubt but he has often been the object of love, and his *Cadenus and Vanessa* seem to allure us that he was the favourite of one lady; but to speak my sentiments, I really believe it was a passion he was wholly unacquainted with, and which he would have thought it beneath the dignity of his wisdom to entertain.

★ ★ ★ ★ ★

Swift blamed Archbishop Marsh for losing him promotion, among other things. He scorned Marsh's reputation for learning. Muriel McCarthy quotes Swift's Miscellaneous and autobiographical pieces, fragments and marginalia:

An old rusty iron chest in a banker's shop, strongly locked and wonderfully heavy, is full of gold; this is the general opinion, neither can it be disproved, provided the key be lost, and what is in it be wedged so close that it will not by any motion discover the metal by the clinking . . . . He is the first of the human race, that with great advantages of learning, piety and station escaped being a great man . . . . No man will be either glad or sorry at his death, except his successor.

The uncredited Anecdotes of Books and Authors *(1836) includes the following:*

One evening Gay and Pope went over to see Swift. On their going in, 'Hey-day, gentlemen,' said the Doctor, 'What's the meaning of this visit? How come you to leave all the great lords that you are so fond of, to come hither to see a poor dean? ' — 'Because we would rather see you than any of them.'

'Ay, any one that did not know you so well as I do, might believe you. But, since you are come, I must get some supper for you, I suppose?' — 'No, Doctor, we have supped already,' — 'Supped already! that's impossible: why, 'tis not eight o'clock yet!' —

'Indeed we have.' — 'That's very strange: but if you had not supped, I must have got something for you. Let me see, what should I have had? A couple of lobsters? Ay, that would have done very well — two shillings: tarts, a shilling. But you will drink a glass of wine with me, though you supped, and much before your usual time, only to spare my pocket? — 'No, we had rather talk with you than drink with you.' — 'But if you had supped with me, as in all reason you ought to have done, you must have drunk with me. A bottle of wine, two shillings. Two and two is four, and one is five: just two-and-six-pence apiece. There, Pope, there's half-a-crown for you; and there's another for you, Sir; for I won't save anything by you, I am determined.' This was all said and done with his usual serious-ness on such occasions; and, in spite of every thing they could say to the contrary, he actually obliged them to take the money.

★ ★ ★ ★ ★

Johnston quotes from John Orrery's Remarks on the Life and Writings of Dr Jonathan Swift *(1752):*

The small remains of his understanding became entirely confused, and the violence of his rage increased to mad-ness . . . from an outrageous lunatic he sunk afterwards into a quiet, speechless idiot and dragged out the remainder of his life in that helpless situation.

In a handbook of Directions to Servants *(posthumously published in 1745), Swift warned footmen:*

Take off the largest dishes and set them on with one hand, to show the ladies your vigour and strength of back; but always do it between two ladies, that if the dish happens to slip, the soup or sauce may fall on their clothes and not daub the floor.

✭ ✭ ✭ ✭ ✭

James Sutherland quotes from The Circle of Anecdote and Wit *by George Coleman Esq. (1823):*

Dean Swift, in one of his pedestrian journeys from London towards Chester, took shelter from a summer tempest under a large oak on the roadside, at no great distance from Lichfield. Presently a man, with a pregnant woman, were driven by the like impulse to avail themselves of the same covert. The dean, entering into conversation, found the parties were destined for Lichfield to be married. As the situation of the woman indicated no time should be lost, a proposition was made on his part to save them the rest of the journey by performing the ceremony on the spot. The offer was gladly accepted, and thanks being duly returned, the bridal pair, as the sky brightened, were about to return; but the bridegroom suddenly recollecting that a certificate was requisite to authenticate the marriage, requested one, which the dean wrote in these words:

Under an oak, in stormy weather,
I joined this rogue and whore together;
And none but he who rules the thunder
Can put this rogue and whore asunder.

✭ ✭ ✭ ✭ ✭

GOD DAMN THE WHIGS AND TORIES TOO
Jonathan Swift

JOHN MILLINGTON SYNGE
1871–1909

Dublin-born, J.M. Synge was the son of a successful barrister. His grand-father was a member of the Plymouth Brethren and his zealous mother instilled a puritan streak in her son. He was educated privately before going to Trinity College Dublin where he became a prizewinner in Hebrew and Irish. He also studied violin, flute and piano at the Royal Irish Academy of Music. He continued his musical education in Germany, then went to Paris to concentrate on literature. A number of visits to the Aran Islands and some sound advice from Yeats, whom he met in Paris, brought about his focus on Irish rural themes in his work. Often criticised for depicting peasants as uncouth and foul-mouthed, Synge swore that he never used more than one or two words that he had not heard from people he met in Wicklow, Mayo or on Aran. His early works for the Irish National Theatre were applauded by English critics but condemned at home. Synge was a lonely, sad person. Of modest tastes, he was content with forty pounds a year and a new suit only when he became too shabby.

The Abbey disturbances, in the presence of 500 policemen, during The Playboy of the Western World *in 1907 are well documented (see 'The Abbey Theatre'). Molly Allgood (stage-name Máire O'Neill) played Pegeen Mike and is said to have inspired Synge's tragic* Deirdre of the Sorrows, *a work that was uncompleted at his death. He was engaged to Molly when, at almost thirty-eight years of age, he died in a Mount Street nursing home.*

★ ★ ★ ★ ★

When he moved to Paris, Synge knew very little French. Stephen McKenna, journalist and translator of the works of the Greek philosopher Plotinus, often visited him. He suggested buying a French encyclopaedia but Synge would not hear of it and said, 'Don't buy it. Get the *Encyclopaedia Britannica*, where the writer won't stop in the middle of an article to tell you how fond he is of his mother.'

George Roberts, director of Maunsel & Co, which first published Synge's work, spoke of the mixed reception given to The Shadow of the Glen *when it was first performed in 1903 (*Irish Literary Portraits, *ed. W.R. Rodgers):*

There were calls for the author, but when he appeared there were a few hisses. His nervousness at facing an audience even to bow was plain to everybody, but when he heard the hisses a glimpse of defiant pleasure came over his face. I think the hisses pleased him much more than the applause.

✭ ✭ ✭ ✭ ✭

Synge's preciseness in stage direction was absolute. Roberts told of his bringing items of clothing from Aran as patterns for the costumes in Riders to the Sea, *and of other meticulous arrangements:*

Lady Gregory came to the rescue and sent up a large [spinning-wheel] from Galway. Synge himself instructed the girl how to use it. He was exceedingly anxious that the 'caoine' should be as close as possible to the peculiar chant that is used in the Islands and after much searching I found a Galway woman living in one of the Dublin suburbs who consented to show how the caoine was given.

She was very nervous about it . . . . At first she tried to begin in her little parlour, but she confessed after a few moments she could not do it properly there, so she brought the two girls up to a bedroom and at first it seemed no better, until she conceived the idea that I should act the corpse. She lighted the candles for the wake and then she got that note full of the terror of the dead.

✭ ✭ ✭ ✭ ✭

The Abbey actor, Fred O'Donovan, reminded W.R. Rodgers of Synge's reticence, then his stubbornness:

We had one of our little parties after a matinée, and when we came into the Green Room Synge was there,

241

Lady Gregory and Yeats. Lady Gregory was in one corner of the room, surrounded by her admirers, and Yeats was standing in the centre . . . holding forth very magnificently, surrounded by his worshippers, and then there was this quiet little figure, sitting behind the hat-rack in the corner, and I remember distinctly seeing beads of perspiration on his forehead. Nobody taking any notice of him, everybody around Yeats and Lady Gregory — and the man behind the hat-rack was Synge, and I could see on his face he had one great desire, and that was to escape from the room as quickly and as unobtrusively as possible.

✳

[During one of the *Playboy* disturbances, he insisted on going into the pit, where] he sat for a while calmly, but with a fixed look of hatred gathering on his face and his jaw set. I began to be afraid he was going to try to clear the pit himself and of course any physical opposition on his part would only give some of his enemies the excuse they longed for. I tried to persuade him to leave but he insisted on staying till the close of the act. We then went to the Green Room of the theatre to encourage the players. As the curtain was about to go up for the third act, Synge was again making his way to the pit. The charwoman of the theatre came to him crying, 'For the love of God, don't go near the pit again. They will kill you.' This amused him so much he could not resist her appeal and he stayed behind the scenes.

✶ ✶ ✶ ✶ ✶

Yeats told how, during the riot, Synge came to him and said, 'A young doctor has just told me that he can hardly keep himself from jumping onto a seat, and pointing out in that howling mob those whom he is treating for venereal disease.'

✶ ✶ ✶ ✶ ✶

Originally, Synge planned to open *The Playboy of the Western World* with the actual fight between Christy Mahon and his father, in a ploughed field with six large trees. Old Mahon was to have caught up with his runaway son at the church door as he was about to wed Pegeen Mike.

★ ★ ★ ★ ★

Benedict Kiely (in *A Letter to Peachtree*) praises a parody on Synge's melancholy style in *The Shadow of the Glen* rendered by the Abbey actor J.M. Kerrigan, which began, 'Was it on your feet you came this way, man of the roads?' 'No, 'twas not, but on my arse surely, woman of the house.'

★ ★ ★ ★ ★

Synge had a habit of wearing his hat in the theatre during rehearsals and this prompted a rumour that he wore a wig. The suspicion was compounded when he died and his brother refused permission to have a death-mask made.

★ ★ ★ ★ ★

In *The Shadow of the Glen*, the character Dan Burke is in bed for most of the one-act play, much of the time dead, so he has few lines to say. Despite this, a lazy actor neglected to become word-perfect, so he hit on the idea of having a personal prompter speaking through a small hole bored in the box set immediately behind Dan's pillow.

As he addressed Dan in the bed, the actor playing the tramp needed a prompt. He leaned over to the orifice for assistance. For this, he was later chastised backstage by Dan, who warned, 'You keep away from my _____' and the dignity of Irish theatre forbids completion!

★ ★ ★ ★ ★

André Bernard records that, as recently as 1962, a publisher made the following observation on Synge's Collected Works:

'Mrs Campbell's "Deirdre" grew on one until it quite captured by its sheer intensity. When the actress is moved by emotion or passion, her whole body moves in jerk-like wriggles that punctuate her every word . . . ' So wrote Joseph Holloway about Mrs Pat's performance in a revival of the Yeats play at the Abbey Theatre in 1908. The *Daily Mail* praised 'the wonderful combination of voices, Mrs Campbell's rich, subtle, stealthy, sense-enthralling, Miss Allgood's high and sad, stimulating as strong wind, and Mr

Sinclair's (as Conchobar) heavy with the seven years' frustrated passion'. Less impressed, Synge drolly commented, 'She'll turn it into the Second Mrs Conchobar.'

★ ★ ★ ★ ★

Undoubtedly they all have marked literary merit of a certain sort, but it is quite sure, it seems to me, that they would not in the slightest way appeal to the ordinary reading public in this country. For their sale you must depend on the little group of persons who are specially interested in the Irish Literary Movement or in odds and ends of pleasing literature.

★ ★ ★ ★ ★

WELL, THE HEART'S A WONDER
J.M. Synge

★ ★ ★ ★ ★

TALES OF TOURING

Doran's, Carrickford's, D'Alton's, Dobell's, Rice's and Bailey's fit-ups were once part of the Irish rural scene, and if a wood-and-canvas Palace of Varieties was not included in the touring company's paraphernalia, the local schoolhouse or hall was converted into a makeshift theatre. On his bicycle, Val Vousden arrived to perform his one-man show of Shakespeare and assorted monologues. Actors who learned their trade with Ronald Ibbs, Lord Longford, Anew McMaster or Cyril Cusack all have grim stories about grimmer theatrical digs, dressing-rooms or halls. Harry Bailey remembered sleeping in a cemetery, walking an elephant round the Irish countryside and a less traditional act when his mother-in-law put the lion's head in her mouth! (She also walked the tightrope, but nearly came to a sticky end: one night she was tight but the rope wasn't!)

Some companies came from abroad, particularly when the country was under British rule. In a farewell speech marking the end of his tour, Mr Lewis Ball of the Compton Comedy Company said at the Gaiety Theatre, Dublin, on 7 May 1898, that he had been terrified of coming. He dreaded facing the Dublin audiences because he had always heard they were 'different from any others in the Kingdom — first on account of their great critical capacity and secondly because if an actor did not succeed or did not quite equal their expectations, they had no hesitation in saying so, and especially this was the case with the gentlemen aloft'.

Towards the close of the nineteenth century, touring companies got special concessions from the Midland Great Western Railway. Handsomely upholstered coupés were allotted and players were allowed double the normal weight of baggage. Travelling took place on Sundays and through trips were arranged to avoid having to change at junctions.

★ ★ ★ ★ ★

245

The Longford Company was appearing in a village hall in the Irish midlands but at curtain-up time, only one old man sat in the back of the building. Some of the cast suggested cancelling the performance but Lord Longford insisted on going ahead.

During the first act the old man did not laugh or applaud and at the interval the cast repeated their suggestion, but again Longford refused to listen to them. At the end of the performance, he walked down to the back of the hall, proud of having given the solitary patron his evening's entertainment. He asked the old man how he had enjoyed the play. 'Ah, I don't have much interest in the play-actin',' he said, 'I'm only here to lock up the hall when youse are finished.'

★ ★ ★ ★ ★

Charles Doran's touring company fostered many young talents, including Hilton Edwards and Ralph Richardson, who was with the company when it toured Ireland in 1921 and 1923. The first visit coincided with the Truce which followed the War of Independence; the second with a somewhat similar situation at the end of the Civil War. Doran, it was claimed, changed his politics to suit his venue. A rabid republican in Cork became an upholder of Anglo-Irish ascendancy in Dublin and an Orange Carsonite in Belfast.

General Richard Mulcahy was General Officer Commanding the military forces of the Provisional Government during the Civil War. He held that appointment and was also Minister for Defence in the new Free State Government. He and his staff occupied a box at *Julius Caesar* in the Opera House, Cork to watch Richardson play Mark Antony to Doran's Brutus. (Norman Shelley and Donald Wolfit played Caesar and Casca, respectively.)

When Richardson had delivered the funeral oration for Caesar and the plebs had called, 'Revenge! About! Seek! Burn! Fire! Kill! Slay! Let not a traitor live!', it seemed like a masterful directional stroke when there was heard a clatter of marching feet as uniformed Free State soldiers tramped into the auditorium and backstage, sealing off all exits.

As Titinius spoke in Act Five:

> His soldiers fell to spoil,
> Whilst we by Antony are all enclos'd.

he did not realise that General Mulcahy's soldiers were waiting to arrest over forty members of the audience, one of them Countess Markievicz, a leading anti-Free State protagonist.

* * * * *

Richardson got one of his early enthusiastic reviews from a Dublin critic after he had appeared at the Gaiety Theatre. During his visit, he learned of the arrest of two schoolgirls outside the theatre. Their satchels were full of rifle ammunition. One member of the company had the nasty experience of seeing his landlady shot dead as she walked with him to her guest-house. When they moved to Belfast, they shared a coach with the corpses of two Belfast men, also shot in Dublin.

* * * * *

In Dungarvan, Co. Waterford a patron telephoned the booking office for the Irish Theatre Company and enquired about two seats for 'Juno and the Haycock'. At Cork Opera House they got a telephone caller asking for four tickets for the pantomime. They explained that it was an O'Casey play but the caller insisted, 'I was told it was 'Juno and the Beanstalk'. (She pronounced it 'Baynestalk'.)

* * * * *

Tony Ó Dálaigh was administrator of the Irish Theatre Company when it toured Ireland in 1974/5. In planning a tour he would circularise local drama groups and other interested parties, inviting them to a meeting. There he would enlist their aid with publicity and tap their local knowledge of halls, facilities and the like.

At one such meeting in a midland hotel, he was asked by a local Thespian why the company was bringing Molière's *The Miser* and not a Boucicault play which was also in their programme. Ó Dálaigh explained that the available theatre was not suitable for the Boucicault work, which required facilities for flying in the scenery.

'Then you should bring it to Abbeyshrule,' said the local man.

'Well, we were thinking of Mullingar,' ventured Ó Dálaigh, politely. He was ill prepared for the quite serious retort:

'But sure there's no airport in Mullingar to fly in the scenery.'

✶ ✶ ✶ ✶ ✶

The stage-manager and production manager of the Irish Theatre Company arrived in the magnificently polished and quite spotless convent assembly hall. It had a perfectly equipped stage with a parquet floor — just like the auditorium. And it was kept just as highly polished!

The sister in charge of recreation was friendly, co-operative and polite. She was firm, too, and told the visitors that the convent had some strict rules:

'There's to be no screwing and no banging on this stage.'

✶ ✶ ✶ ✶ ✶

Ireland's laughing girl, the inimitable Maureen Potter, remembers Brendan Behan's story of an early tour undertaken by the great P. J. Bourke and Company. A large basket of very assorted costumes travelled and it was a case of first come, first served for the night's epic, *The Royal Divorce*.

Talleyrand appeared to a flourish of trumpets, looking like a cross between Quasimodo and Dracula. He was greeted by howls of derisory laughter. Stepping forward, he loudly announced to the audience: 'Yez are laughing now! Wait till yez see Napoleon!'

✶ ✶ ✶ ✶ ✶

Harry O'Donovan, Jimmy O'Dea and Maureen Potter were in digs in Britain. In response to an enquiry from their landlady, Harry explained the old rules of fasting and abstinence which had to be observed during the season of Lent.

'You eejit,' hissed O'Dea, 'she'll have us fasting for the week.' But when they came for their evening meal, they were greeted with steaming plates. 'It's hash,' said the landlady, who went on to explain that she understood what Roman Catholics were obliged to eat on 'Hash Wednesday'.

Long before he became a television newsreader, Charles Mitchel toured with the Carl Clopet Company, among others. Props were often borrowed locally and he remembered a character dropping a gun on the stage one evening to a voice from the auditorium calling, 'For God's sake would you mind my gun.' His most amusing memory, however, concerned a theatrical digs where he called and was told by the landlady not to mind the racket that was going on. She explained that there was a party taking place but that everybody would be gone by the time the play was over. He was given a key and when he arrived back much later, all was indeed quiet. He awoke during the night, needing to go to the lavatory, but recalled from a previous visit that there was only a chamber-pot. He reached under the bed and felt something wooden. It was a coffin. Further investigation revealed that it contained a corpse. The earlier activity was a wake!

OSCAR
WILDE
1854–1900

The son of a celebrated Roscommon-born father, who was a surgeon and antiquary, and of a mother who, using the pseudonym 'Speranza', collected and chronicled Irish folklore, Oscar Fingal O'Flahertie Wills Wilde was a polished wit, poet and playwright. He was born in Dublin, educated at Portora Royal School, Enniskillen, Trinity College Dublin and Oxford, where he won the Newdigate Prize for poetry in 1878. The classics and humanities were his forte, so it was not surprising that he founded an aesthetic cult in London, propounding the importance of art for art's sake. Despite their rather narrow themes, his plays are still performed successfully. They have style, and Wilde's brilliant dialogue and rapier-like comment rescue them from mediocrity. His novel, The Picture of Dorian Gray *(1891), got a hostile reception; many believed that its hero was based on the author.*

Lectures, fairy stories and plays brought success and fame at home and across the Atlantic, but a homosexual liaison with Lord Alfred Douglas incurred the wrath of Alfred's father, the Marquess of Queensberry. Wilde foolishly took an action for libel against the Marquess but there were no Queensberry Rules to control the devastating cross-examination of the author by Edward Carson, a fellow student at Trinity. Prosecution automatically followed and Wilde was tried and sentenced to two years in prison. The experience led to his writing The Ballad of Reading Gaol *in 1898.*

He tried living in Paris and Italy, but was constantly persecuted. Another period spent with Alfred Douglas brought no consolation and he died of meningitis in a Paris hotel.

*In his viva voce examination for 'Divvers' (Divinity, which he
failed at his first attempt) at Oxford, Wilde was required to translate from the Greek version of the New Testament, which was one
of the set books. The passage chosen was from the story of the
Passion of Christ. In the anthology* Pass the Port *(1976), Sir John
Ackroyd goes on:*

Wilde began to translate, easily and accurately. The
examiners were satisfied, and told him that this was
enough. Wilde ignored them and continued to translate.
After another attempt the examiners at last succeeded in stop-
ping him, and told him that they were satisfied with his
translation.

'Oh, do let me go on,' said Wilde, 'I want to see how it
ends.'

★ ★ ★ ★ ★

When Wilde arrived in New York for a lecture tour,
journalists' interest in trivia rather than the content of
his proposed lectures annoyed him. They did not realise that
he was ridiculing them with observations like the trip being
deucedly stupid and the sea not being as noisy as he thought
it would be. The banal questioning irritated him so much
that when a customs inspector asked if he had anything to
declare, he replied, 'No. I have nothing to declare except my
genius.'

★

There were other celebrated quotes from American press
interviews. Asked why he wore a heavy overcoat during
the comparatively mild winter of 1882, Wilde replied, 'I carry
it to hide the hideous sofas in your hotel rooms!'

★

'Southern Americans have a melancholy tendency to date
every event of importance by the late war,' Wilde noted,
before giving an example: '"How beautiful the moon is
tonight," I once remarked to a gentleman standing near me.
"Yes," was his reply, "but you should have seen it before the
war!"'

Richard Ellmann tells of Wilde accompanying guests to a performance of Gilbert and Sullivan's Patience *in New York's Standard Theatre:*

They arrived some minutes after the curtain had risen, just as Lady Jane was about to inform Patience what love is. At first Wilde kept to the back of the box, out of sight, but self-effacement was not his way, and eventually he moved forward. When J.H. Ryley came on stage as Bunthorne, the whole audience turned and stared at Wilde. Bunthorne was made up as [James A. McNeill] Whistler in England, as Wilde in America. Wilde now smiled at one of his women companions and commented patronizingly, 'This is one of the compliments that mediocrity pays to those who are not mediocre.'

★

Ellmann also describes a lecture in Boston:

On the night of 31 January [1882], when Wilde was to speak in the Music Hall in Boston, snow fell again. The house was full . . . except for the first two rows, which remained mysteriously empty until just before the speaker was to appear. Then suddenly down the centre aisle came sixty Harvard students, dressed in the high aesthetic line with breeches, dinner jackets, Whistler locks of white hair, hats like Bunthorne's, each bearing in a stained glass attitude a sunflower. Their leader lounged, limp and listless and vacant-eyed, to a seat. There was great merriment as the stage door opened to admit the lecturer.

But Wilde was able to mock his mockers. Tipped off in advance, he had donned conventional dinner jacket and trousers, and hinted at iconoclasm only in the unusually wide cravat which reached nearly to his shoulders on either side. Arriving late, he had to climb some stairs at the back of the stage, so that the audience first caught sight of his upper torso, and then to their dismay saw that his legs were trousered in the usual manner. Wilde had also written a new opening paragraph. He began evenly, 'As a college man, I

252

greet you. I am very glad to address an audience in Boston, the only city in America which has influenced thought in Europe, and which has given Europe a new and great school of philosophy.' He then glanced as if by chance at the fantastic semicircle in front, and said with a smile, 'I see about me certain signs of an aesthetic movement. I see certain young men, who are no doubt sincere, but I can assure them that they are no more than caricatures. As I look around me, I am impelled for the first time to breathe a fervent prayer, "Save me from my disciples." But rather let me, as Wordsworth says, "Turn me from those bold, bad men."' By this time his audience was almost won. The students tried to recover their advantage by applauding heartily every time he drank from a glass of water, but this was small revenge.

★ ★ ★ ★ ★

A wealth of lore surrounds the play Lady Windermere's Fan. *André Bernard quotes one publisher's reaction to it:*

> My dear sir,
> I have read your manuscript. Oh, my dear sir!

★

For the original typescript of the work, Wilde was paid an advance of £100 by actor-manager George Alexander, who attempted to acquire the copyright with his offer of £1,000. Wilde pretended to consider the bid but then replied, 'My dear Alex, I have so much confidence in your excellent judgment that I cannot but refuse your most generous offer.'

★

During rehearsals, the famous Wildean emblem, the green carnation, was introduced. Wilde instructed the actor playing Mr Cecil Graham to wear one. When asked why, Wilde replied that green was a nice colour.

'But they don't exist,' came the protest.

'They will,' said Wilde, 'Nature always copies art and it is our duty to teach nature how to behave.'

In the course of an interview during the play's first run, Wilde was asked if he had a particular leading man in mind when he wrote the play. He answered, 'I never write for anyone in particular. I write [plays] to amuse myself. Later, if anyone wants to act in them, I sometimes allow them to do so.'

✶

After an early performance, he was asked by a friend how the play had gone. He replied, 'Oh, the play was a great success, but the audience was a total failure.'

✶ ✶ ✶ ✶ ✶

Hesketh Pearson tells how The Importance of Being Earnest *was written as a four-act play. George Alexander was insisting to Wilde that it should be staged in three. They argued for an hour, finishing on the following note:*

'Do you realise, Alex, what you are asking me to sacrifice?'

'You will be able to use it in another play.'

'It may not fit another play.'

'What does that matter? You are clever enough to think of a hundred things just as good.'

'Of course I am . . . a thousand if need be . . . but that is not the point. This scene that you feel is superfluous cost me terrible exhausting labour and heart-rending nerve-racking strain. You may not believe me but I assure you on my honour that it must have taken fully fifteen minutes to write.'

✶ ✶ ✶ ✶ ✶

A Woman of No Importance received a standing ovation after its first performance at the Theatre Royal, Haymarket, London in April 1893 before a distinguished audience. But when someone called 'Author', there were some hisses and boos. Wilde stood before the curtain and said, 'Ladies and gentlemen. I regret to inform you that Mr Oscar Wilde is not in the house.'

✶

Later, fans were hugging and kissing Wilde but a dissident proffered a decaying head of cabbage, saying, 'It stank.' Wilde took the cabbage, thanked the donor politely and said, 'Every time I smell it, I shall be reminded of you.'

★ ★ ★ ★ ★

Sir Henry Irving acted in one of Wilde's plays. After its opening night, Wilde commented: 'Irving's legs are distinctly precious; but his left leg is a positive poem.'

★ ★ ★ ★ ★

The actor-manager Herbert Beerbohm Tree did not escape Wilde's narcissistic teasings. Oscar informed him that when playing the part of Lord Illingworth in *A Woman of No Importance*, he would have to forget that he ever played Hamlet or Falstaff or, for that matter, that he ever acted at all. When Tree asked why, he was told arrogantly, 'The witty aristocrat whom you wish to assume in my play is quite unlike anyone who has ever been on a stage before . . . . He is like no one who has existed before.' Tree ventured that the character must have been supernatural and Wilde concurred, adding, 'Certainly he is not natural. He is a figure of art. Indeed, if you can bear the truth . . . he is myself.'

★ ★ ★ ★ ★

Despite the treatment meted out to Tree, he was one of Wilde's most avid supporters. After a successful opening night, both men congratulated each other. Wilde told Tree that he regarded him as the best critic of his plays.

'But I have never criticised your plays.'

'That's why!'

★ ★ ★ ★ ★

A trifle tipsy, the young André Gide once criticised *Salomé* while Wilde listened carefully. After the outburst, Gide glared, expecting a dressing-down. Wilde contemptuously remarked, 'I put all my genius into my life; I only put my talent into my writing.'

★ ★ ★ ★ ★

Afriend commented on the cut and thrust in a newspaper article written by George Bernard Shaw, observing to Wilde that Shaw seemed to be harsh on all his acquaintances and consequently would make many enemies. Wilde replied, 'He is not yet prominent enough to have enemies, and none of his friends likes him.'

Wilde once advised a youth to ignore advice about starting at the bottom. He told him to begin at the top and sit there. The lad asked how he could do this, when he wished to become an army officer by training at Sandhurst Academy. Wilde was horrified and told the youth that he must go to Oxford. Still the lad protested, until Wilde suggested with some uncertainty, 'If you take a degree at Oxford, they will make you a colonel immediately.' After a pause, he added, 'At least in a West Indian regiment!'

George Moore disliked Wilde intensely and conveyed as much to his colleagues. When Wilde was told this, he asked if Moore was 'the fellow who wrote excellent English until he discovered grammar'.

Wilde's volume of poems, *In Memoriam*, was first published as a limited edition. Wilde quipped, 'I had intended printing just three copies; one for myself, one for the British Museum and one for Heaven. I had some doubt about the British Museum.'

Mark Nicholls notes Wilde's attitude to sport:

His Hellenistic fervour did not stretch to prowess in Athenian-like sports, nor did he like English national games. But he was able to give a good account of himself in more than one college brawl. He was later to say, 'I do not play cricket because it requires me to assume indecent postures!' Of the energetic game of football, he chirruped, 'I feel that football is all very well as a game for rough girls, but it is hardly suitable for delicate boys!'

★ ★ ★ ★ ★

Ellmann tells of Wilde arriving an hour late for a luncheon-party at the home of his brother-in-law, Otho Holland Lloyd, and his wife in Paris:

He asked for the shutters to be closed and candles lighted, having his mother's dislike of sunlight for social occasions. The table cloth had also to be changed because the flowers on it, before he banished them too, were mauve, a colour he superstitiously feared.

★

Ellmann also relates incidents at Reading prison:

One day the prison chaplain, Reverend M.T. Friend, was visiting Wilde, and the prisoner spoke sorrowfully of the 'thickly muffled glass' in the cell window which allowed him no view of the sky. The chaplain, to comfort him, said, 'Oh my friend, let me entreat you to desist from such thoughts and not let your mind dwell on the clouds, but on Him who is above the clouds, Him who — ' 'Get out, you damned fool!' Wilde shouted, and pushed him through the door.

★

A warder killed a spider by stepping on it.

'It brings bad luck to kill a spider,' [Wilde] said, 'I shall hear worse news than I have yet heard.' He said later that he had heard the cry of the Banshee, and that he had had a vision of his mother. She was dressed for out-of-doors, and he asked her to take off her hat and cloak and sit down. She shook her head sadly and vanished. The next day, 19 February 1896, he was summoned to talk to his wife in a private room . . . . Notified by Willie of Lady Wilde's death, she had travelled from Italy to tell her husband the news that she knew would be excruciatingly painful to him. 'I knew it already,' he said and told her of his vision.

On his deathbed, Wilde, by a hand sign, agreed to the last rites of the Catholic Church.

During the winter of 1900, when Wilde was enduring his last illness in Paris, Edward Carson was at the zenith of his legal career. Rain threatened but Carson insisted on going for a walk. As he began to cross a street, a horse-carriage sped past, splashing his clothes with mud and almost overbalancing him. He staggered back and bumped into a man, knocking him down. Mark Nicholls completes the tale:

Carson turned, stooping apologetically to assist the unfortunate victim. For a fleeting second, their eyes met. Carson stared into the haggard, pained features of Oscar Wilde . . . the man he had ruined. 'I beg your pardon,' said Carson quietly. The bedraggled figure of Oscar Wilde, ignoring the lawyer's profuse apology, raised himself and walked on into the Parisian twilight.

Even in silence he was devastating.

ALL WOMEN BECOME LIKE THEIR MOTHERS. THAT IS
THEIR TRAGEDY. NO MAN DOES. THAT'S HIS
Oscar Wilde

WILLIAM
BUTLER YEATS
1865–1939

Dublin-born W.B. Yeats was moved to London as an infant and received his first schooling in Hammersmith. He spent holidays with his wealthy Sligo grandparents, the Pollexfens, and in 1880 the family moved back to Dublin. He continued his education in Harcourt High School and at the Metropolitan School of Art, where he joined a group of mystics that included George Russell. He also studied at the Royal Hibernian Academy. At twenty-one years of age, he abandoned art for poetry and, influenced by Standish J. O'Grady and the Fenian John O'Leary (of the 'noble head'), he concentrated on Irish themes. Back in London again with his family by 1887, he joined Madame Blavatsky's theosophists, the Order of the Golden Dawn and the Rhymers' Club, and helped to establish the Irish Literary Society.

Later, again with O'Leary in Dublin, he founded the National Literary Society to publish Irish folklore and mythology. The Wanderings of Oisín *appeared in 1889, the year he met Maud Gonne. Smitten by her beauty, he proposed two years later but was rejected, not before she prompted him to join the Irish Republican Brotherhood. He wrote poems to and about her. The heroine of a play,* The Countess Cathleen, *was moulded in her image and she played the title role in the* première *of* Cathleen Ni Houlihan. *With Lady Gregory he planned the Irish Literary Theatre. Together with the Fay brothers, and money from Annie Horniman, a tea-millionairess, they established themselves in the Mechanics' Institute in Dublin's Abbey Street. This led to the formation of the celebrated Abbey Players, making Dublin an important literary city.*

When Maud Gonne's husband (Major John MacBride) was executed after the 1916 Rising, Yeats proposed once more and was again refused. He then fell in love with her daughter, Iseult, but she would not marry him either. Eventually he married another theosophist, George Hyde-Lees, and settled down in Thoor Ballylee (Castle), Co. Galway. In 1923 he was awarded the Nobel Prize for literature, the first Irish person to receive it.

Of awkward stature, Yeats was called 'Willie the Spook' by Dublin urchins, a nickname inspired by his interest in the occult. His attempts at rejuvenation by means of hormonal injections earned him the title of 'Gland Old Man'.

When the young Yeats was studying at the Metropolitan School of Art in Kildare Street, Dublin, he was also rehearsing for the leading role in an amateur production of *Hamlet*. Wishing to give an individual interpretation, he decided that a lame Prince of Denmark would be unique. So he practised limping and was often seen studying his own reflected progress and mouthing soliloquies in Dublin shop windows. He developed a chest ailment from walking in his shirt — which he imagined to be a doublet —on cold afternoons. The poet Katharine Tynan offered him a box of chlorodyne lozenges, all of which he gobbled down at once. They put him to sleep for well over a day.

André Bernard records the following assessment of Poems *(1895):*

I am relieved to find the critics shrink from saying that Mr Yeats will ever be a popular author. I should really at last despair of mankind, if he could be . . . absolutely empty and void. [The work] does not please the ear, nor kindle the imagination, nor hint a thought for one's reflection . . . . Do what I will, I can see no sense in the thing: it is to me sheer nonsense. I do not say it is obscure, or uncouth or barbaric or affected — tho' it be all these evil things; I say it is to me absolute nullity . . . . I would not read a page of it again for worlds.

The early Abbey Players developed a style of acting to suit the writings of Synge, Gregory and Yeats. Yet it was more the old Senecan convention of university plays routed by Shakespeare and the Globe Theatre; the dialogue was everything and to it all was sacrificed. Thus nobody spoke as he moved, and when one actor was speaking, no other member of the cast stirred. Yeats described the delivery of words as 'Homer's way'. It took an American lady to ask him the obvious question: 'How do you know that this was Homer's method?' Yeats replied: 'The ability of the man justifies the assumption.'

✷ ✷ ✷ ✷ ✷

In Orders and Desecrations, *Denis Johnston recalls:*

. . . in the movies [Yeats] discovered Mae West. Hence the letter he wrote to Shelah Richards — the shortest, I think, of all his letters. I still have it:

> Riversdale
> 1st January 1934
>
> Dear Shelah,
>   Fatten.
>   Yours sincerely,
>   W.B. Yeats

Having seen him shortly afterwards in the Abbey vestibule with his 'dress unadjusted', we did our best to get her to reply: 'Dear W.B., Button.' But I never heard whether she did or not.

✷ ✷ ✷ ✷ ✷

The title of the Yeats play *The Words upon the Window-pane* reflects three literary people. The author himself received inspiration for the name in the Dublin home of Oliver St John Gogarty's father, Henry. The house, 'Fairfield', was at the time a rural retreat in what is now Glasnevin. According to tradition, Jonathan Swift, during a visit, was so impressed by the comeliness of a kitchen-maid that he etched a verse in her praise on a particular window of the house.

✷ ✷ ✷ ✷ ✷

Yeats suffered a bout of homesickness while walking in London's The Strand one day. Looking into a store window he saw a miniature fountain, and its 'dropping slow' inspired 'The Lake Isle of Innisfree'.

★ ★ ★ ★ ★

It was claimed that Yeats responded to 'Celtic voices' when he appointed Lennox Robinson as manager of the Abbey Theatre. They had instructed him that the head-shape of a young man in the auditorium fitted him for office. Robinson's head matched the description.

★ ★ ★ ★ ★

Rehearsing for *Deirdre*, Yeats suffered with Mrs Pat Campbell. First of all, she was far too tall for the Naoise of J.M. Kerrigan. Joseph Holloway called into a rehearsal where 'Yeats kept busily walking up and down in front of the stage, and his gesticulation occasionally sent Mrs Campbell off in a laugh until she finally had to tell him to sit down'. Yeats paced the aisle again while Mrs Pat remonstrated with him across the footlights. Possibly peeved at his ignoring the insults she hurled at him, she asked what he was thinking. He said, 'I'm thinking of the master of a wayside Indian railway station who sent a message to his company's headquarters saying: 'TIGRESS ON THE LINE. WIRE INSTRUCTIONS.'

★ ★ ★ ★ ★

The 'Limey' was the person who operated the old form of stage lighting, called 'limelight'. An intense white illumination achieved by heating cylinders of lime in oxyhydrogen flames, it gave rise to the expression 'in the limelight'. Yeats experimented at length to get a particular effect for his production of *Deirdre*. From the auditorium he studied various effects which resulted from his instructions to the 'Limey'. 'Up,' 'Down,' 'More shade upstage,' 'More on the right.' Then an excited 'Stop! Hold it; that's exactly what I require!'

The trouble was, the materials in the cylinders had caught fire!

Micheál macLiammóir, Hilton Edwards and Coralie Carmichael were playing in Paul Raynal's tragedy *The Unknown Warrior* at the Peacock when Lady Gregory brought Yeats along to see them. The actors could see the poet in the auditorium and his presence prompted them to project themselves in a magnificent manner. The next day macLiammóir received an invitation from Lady Gregory to join Yeats and herself for lunch. MacLiammóir was pleased and told her he had been waiting fourteen years to meet Yeats. Rehearsals kept him a little late for the appointment. When he arrived, Lady Gregory and W.B. were waiting. The poet rose slowly from his chair and adopted a stately pose. He addressed macLiammóir: 'You told Lady Gregory that you had wanted to meet me for fourteen years; you are exactly fourteen minutes late!'

✺ ✺ ✺ ✺ ✺

The writer L.A.G. Strong once asked Yeats what it was about George Moore's writing that forced a reader to read page after page of his work with delight, and was told, 'As I have never even read a paragraph of George Moore with delight, I am afraid I can't give you the answer.'

✺

Strong gives an example of the status Yeats enjoyed when he lived at Oxford from 1919 to 1921:

A girl undergraduate arrived one day at [his] house in a great state of agitation. She had taken a book away from the Bodleian Library, a gross breach of the rules. Overcome with horror, she sought the fountainhead of wisdom, and presented herself sobbing to the astonished poet. He gave her his complete attention, and, satisfied on the facts, sent for Mrs Yeats, who comforted the girl with tea and aspirin. Yeats then took the book back to the Bodleian, and handed it to a stupefied official with a long and flamboyant explanation which, if it conveyed anything to him at all, suggested that the book arrived at [his] Broad Street house in the form of spiritualistic apport. Yeats then departed, leaving the official to eye the book and restore it, rather gingerly, to its place on the shelves.

⋆

As demonstrated in his defence of Synge at the Playboy *disturbances, Yeats could deal with hecklers. Strong tells of another incident, this time at a lecture:*

One evening, when he was talking to a small group, he was interrupted several times by a bore, one of those pedantic souls who try to check lively and fantastic talk with heavy-footed comment. Yeats waited until the bore had roused the feeling of the room against him; he even appeared to lead him on; and when the bore, encouraged, presently put forward some theory or other, Yeats said, 'That is impossible. It would be like making love to a bald woman.'

The bore stopped short in surprise. Then, contentiously rising to the bait, he replied that he did not see why it was impossible to make love to a bald woman.

'In that case,' Yeats retorted, 'all further conversation between us is impossible'; and swept on unchecked. The rest of the room, who might well have failed to see the connection between illustration and subject, were swept along with him, leaving the bore in forced association with his phantom.

★ ★ ★ ★ ★

Frank O'Connor hailed Yeats in a Dublin street one day and asked him how he was feeling. 'Not well at all,' answered Yeats, 'I can only write prose today.'

★ ★ ★ ★ ★

W.R. Rodgers' BBC broadcast conversation with contemporaries of Yeats indicated a lack of warmth and a peculiar innocence in the man. Lennox Robinson told of the poet's connection with the BBC:

He gave certainly three recitals for the BBC, every time they loved him more and more, and they gave him more and more money, and in the end they wanted to give him the best battery, the best whatever they could do to his home in Rathfarnham [Co. Dublin], and they said, 'Have you got elec-

264

tric light in the home?' He had to wire back to his wife to find whether they had electric light in the home — he hadn't.

✶

The Irish Times *editor, Bertie Smyllie, recalled getting the news of Yeats's Nobel Prize win, worth 'between seven and eight thousand pounds', and telephoning him excitedly:*

I said, 'Mr Yeats, I've got very good news for you, a very great honour has been conferred upon you,' and I was rather enthusiastic and gushing at the time, and I said, 'This is a great honour not only for you but for your country,' and I could tell that he was getting slightly impatient to know what it was all about, so I said, 'You've been awarded the Nobel Prize, a very great honour to you and a very great honour to Ireland,' and to my amazement the only question he asked was, 'How much, Smyllie, how much is it?'

✶

Smyllie remembered being approached by Yeats to get him member-ship of a golf club and introducing him to the game:

I handed W.B. his bag, and he said, 'Smyllie, this is my quiver' — he always insisted on calling his golf bag his quiver. However, we started off, we played several times, and he'd make a wild swipe at the ball, let the club fall on the ground, and walk off with his hands behind his back in the characteristic Yeatsian fashion, leaving myself and Duncan [a friend] to pick up the quiver and the club and to look for the ball, which was very important — for the ball was very rarely to be found. He used to drive the ball into a clump of furze bushes or into a ditch or anywhere, about, say, ten yards from the tee, and we lost several balls this way. But a rather charac-teristic thing about this was that the next game we went out to play, W.B. noticed we had been losing all these balls and we had been providing him with new ones — not new ones, actually, we knew too much about it for that — but old ones. The next day he came out, and every time he hit the ball and lost it, he used produce a half-crown from his pocket, and hand the half-crown either to myself or Duncan in compensation for the ball that had been lost.

✻

Smyllie also told Rodgers:

I never believed that W.B. knew anything much about philosophy, though he talked a great deal about it, but he invented a philosophy of his own, which was rather amusing. One very interesting and amusing thing occurred, when he was expounding this highly esoteric theory of his one night up in the Arts Club. And among those present was a little man called Cruise O'Brien, a very brilliant journalist, and one of the very few people who could be rude with impunity to W.B. W.B. gave him, as he very often gave me, a fool's pardon. This night, at any rate, he was expounding this philosophy of his which was connected in some queer way with the phases of the moon; he was telling us about the twenty-eight phases of the moon and he had equated every phase against some historical figure. He said, 'Number one — the highest phase — is perfect beauty.' With a respectful silence for a few seconds we all listened, and then he said, 'Number two was Helen of Troy — the nearest approximation to perfect beauty.' And he went right round the twenty-eight, or rather twenty-seven, phases and finally he came to the last, and then he said that the lowest form of all is Thomas Carlyle and all Scotsmen. This shook us all a little bit and Cruise O'Brien spoke up at once, 'W.B.,' he said — he'd a very mincing voice, Cruise — 'have you ever read a word of Carlyle? You say Carlyle is the lowest form. Oh come! Have you ever read a word of Carlyle?' 'Carlyle, Cruise, was a dolt,' said W.B.

'But I insist, W.B., did you ever read one single word of Carlyle?' 'Carlyle, I tell you, was a dolt.' 'Yes, but you haven't read him.' 'No, I have not read him; my wife, George, has read him and she tells me he's a dolt.' That was the end of the philosophical treatise for the night.

Anne Yeats, his daughter, remembered W.B. being good at croquet, concentrating while he played:

I don't think he played to win, but I think he liked winning the game like anybody else. I remember somebody came to tea and cheated to let him win, and he never played with her again.

⋆ ⋆ ⋆ ⋆ ⋆

Maurice Craig was at the first performance of Purgatory, *when Yeats made what Craig believes was his last public appearance:*

After the curtain he came out, very slowly, from the steps on the right, up on to the stage, and made a short speech in which he spoke of his symbolical intention in the play. Then he moved slowly off to the left and disappeared from sight. I heard afterwards that Larry Morrow, a notably irreverent wit of the time, had been heard to say, from his seat in the stalls, 'Symbolical Bill the Playwright'.

⋆ ⋆ ⋆ ⋆ ⋆

Frank O'Connor writes of Yeats's last months:

The best example of his deviousness I remember was in the last year of his life, at a time when I felt that at last he and I were on the point of an understanding. By this time, like the two kings in *The Herne's Egg*, we had fought so long and so hard that there didn't seem to be much left to us except to become close friends. Paul Vincent Carroll had written a play which offended some members of the Board, and, instead of sending it along to Yeats and me in the ordinary way, they had returned the play to the author with an exceedingly insulting letter. When the Secretary showed me the letter I grew furiously angry. Quite apart from the fact that Carroll was a distinguished playwright who had earned a good deal of money for the theatre, I felt that no writer should be treated with such discourtesy, so I wrote to Carroll, asking him to submit the play again to Yeats and myself. He did so, and Yeats and I did not meet again until the Board meeting at which our two reports were read out. Yeats said, 'All the characters in this play are corrugated iron', but he went on in his noble way to praise Carroll's work and volunteered to contribute fifty pounds from his own pocket (a lot of money for an old man who made manuscript copies of *Innisfree* for American booksellers at five pounds a time) towards its production by Edwards and Mac Liammóir at the Gate or any other theatre that wanted to produce it. My report read, 'All the characters in this play are cardboard', and Yeats started and stared incredulously at me. Then, as my negative report went on, he began to chuckle grimly, and when it concluded he said, 'O'Connor, I owe you an apology. I thought you'd asked the play back because Carroll was a friend of yours. It had not occurred to me that you had asked it back because you thought he had been unfairly treated. It serves me right! I've lost my fifty pounds.' How could anyone not love the sort of man who said a thing like that?

★

O'Connor also tells:

Meanwhile the final quarrel in the theatre was being staged between Yeats and F.R. Higgins on the one hand and [Hugh] Hunt and myself on the other. 'Why do you support Hunt?' Yeats asked me bluntly one night. For want of anything better to say I replied, 'Because we must have a competent man in the theatre.' Yeats drew himself together like an old grandfather clock preparing to strike, and, as he always did whenever he wanted to say something crushing without being personal, told a story. 'My mad brother' (sometimes it was 'my father' and sometimes 'an old aunt of mine') 'once said to me: "What does an artist have to do with competence?"'

★ ★ ★ ★ ★

I HAVE SPREAD MY DREAMS UNDER YOUR FEET
W.B. Yeats

★ ★ ★ ★ ★

BIBLIOGRAPHY

JOURNALS, NEWSPAPERS, UNPUBLISHED SOURCES, ETC.

★ ★ ★ ★ ★

Evening Herald, The Irish Times, Irish Independent, Sunday Independent, Sunday Press, The Sunday Tribune (Deirdre Purcell interviews), *Kavanagh's Weekly, Irish University Review, Australian Encyclopaedia* (vol. 8). *Prompts* — Bulletin of Irish Theatre Archive, *Old Limerick Journal* (Summer 1982). Private correspondence with Eamonn Andrews, Hilton Edwards, John Finegan, Terence Golden, James N. Healy, John B. Keane, Eamon Kelly, Hugh Leonard, Bryan MacMahon, Micheál Ó hAodha, Alpho O'Reilly, Maureen Potter, Phyllis Ryan, Carolyn Swift, Niall Toibin. Documents from Irish Theatre Archive (Elgy Gillespie interviews). Theatre programmes. Interviews with Harold Clarke, Sean Dowling, Eithne Golden-Sax, Patrick Henchy, Kaye Hogan, Benedict Kiely, Hugh Leonard, Seán Mac Réamoinn, Peadar O'Donnell, Nellie and Oliver Weldon. Joseph Holloway Journals, National Library. Abbey Theatre 75th Birthday Brochure. *Abbey Theatre Productions 1966–1976 — Commemorative Record. Gate Theatre Golden Jubilee Exhibition Catalogue* (ed. Richard Pine). Theatre cuttings, National Library Ir. 399.92.

BOOKS

★ ★ ★ ★ ★

Aldington, Richard, *Life for Life's Sake* (New York 1941).

Bair, Deirdre, *Samuel Beckett* (London 1978).
Bander, Peter, *The Prophecies of St Malachy and St Columbkille* (Gerrards Cross 1978).

Barrington, Sir Jonah, *Personal Sketches of His Own Time*, vols 1–3 (London 1830–3).

Behan, Brendan, *Brendan Behan's New York* (London 1964).

Bernard, André, *Rotten Rejections* (London 1991).

Bourgeois, Maurice, *John M. Synge and the Irish Theatre* (London 1913).

Boylan, Henry, *A Dictionary of Irish Biography* (Dublin 1988).

Boylan, Patricia, *All Cultivated People* (Gerrards Cross 1988).

Boyne, Patricia, *John O'Donovan: A Biography* (Kilkenny 1987).

Bradley, Bruce, *James Joyce's Schooldays* (Dublin 1982).

Brady, Anne & Brian Cleeve, *A Biographical Dictionary of Irish Writers* (Mullingar 1985).

Brandreth, Gyles, *Great Theatrical Disasters* (London 1982).

Brown, Stephen J., *Ireland in Fiction* (Shannon 1968).

Cahill, Susan & Thomas, *A Literary Guide to Ireland* (Dublin 1973).

Callow, Simon, *Being an Actor* (London 1985).

Campbell, Mary, *Lady Morgan* (London 1988).

Chambers, Anne, *La Sheridan — Adorable Diva* (Dublin 1989).

Clark, William Smith, *The Early Irish Stage* (Oxford 1955).

—— *The Irish Stage in the Country Towns* (London 1965).

Clarke, Austin, *Twice Round the Black Church* (Dublin 1990).

Clarke, Kathleen, *Revolutionary Women* (Dublin 1991).

Colborne, Maurice, *The Real Bernard Shaw* (London 1949).

Colum, Mary & Padraic, *Our Friend James Joyce* (London 1959).

Costello, Peter, *James Joyce* (Dublin 1980).

Courtney, Sr Marie T., *Edward Martyn and the Irish Theatre* (New York 1952).

Cowell, John, *Where They Lived in Dublin* (Dublin 1980).

——*No Profit but the Name* (Dublin 1988).

Craig, Maurice, *The Elephant and the Polish Question* (Dublin 1990).

Cronin, Anthony, *Dead as Doornails* (Dublin 1976).

——*No Laughing Matter — The Life and Times of Flann O'Brien* (London 1989).

Cross, Eric, *The Tailor and Ansty* (Dublin & Cork, 1985).

Davin, Dan, *Closing Times* (Oxford 1975).
de Burca, Seamas, *The Queen's Royal Theatre, Dublin* (Dublin 1983).
Delaney, Frank, *James Joyce's Odyssey* (London 1981).
Denson, Alan (ed.), *Letters from AE* (New York 1961).
de Valors, Ninette, *Come Dance with Me* (Dublin 1993).
Donleavy, J.P., *J.P. Donleavy's Ireland* (London 1986).
Dorn, Karen, *Players and Painted Stage* (Brighton 1984).
Duggan, G.C., *The Stage Irishman* (New York & London, 1937).
Dunbar, Janet, *Mrs G.B.S., A Biographical Portrait of Charlotte Shaw* (London 1963).
Dunne, John J., *Haunted Ireland* (Belfast 1977).

Edgeworth, Maria & Richard Lovell, *The Black Book of Edgeworthstown and Other Edgeworth Memories 1587–1817*, ed. Butler and Butler (London 1925).
Ellmann, Richard, *James Joyce* (New York 1959).
——*Oscar Wilde* (London 1987).
Ervine, St John, *Bernard Shaw — His Life, Work and Friends* (London 1956).

Fallis, Richard, *The Irish Renaissance* (Dublin 1978).
Fallon, Gabriel, *Sean O'Casey, The Man I Knew* (London 1965).
Fennell, Desmond, *Bloomsway* (Co. Dublin 1990).
Fitz-Simon, Christopher, *The Arts in Ireland* (Dublin 1982).
——*The Irish Theatre* (London 1983).
Ford, Ford Madox, *Ancient Lights* (London 1911).
French, Percy, *Poems, Prose and Parodies* (Dublin 1925).

Gébler Davies, Stan, *James Joyce: A Portrait of the Artist* (London 1975).
Gogarty, Oliver St J., *Tumbling in the Hay* (London 1939).
——*It Isn't This Time of Year at All* (London 1954).

Gogarty, Oliver St J., *As I Was Going Down Sackville Street* (London 1954).

Goldsmith, Oliver, *The Vicar of Wakefield* (Dublin, undated).

Gray, Tony, *Mr Smyllie, Sir* (Dublin 1991).

Grant, John, *A Book of Numbers* (London 1984).

Guthrie, Tyrone, *A Life in the Theatre* (London 1987).

Hall, J.B., *Random Records of a Reporter* (London & Dublin, undated).

Harmon, Maurice, *Sean O'Faolain* (Dublin 1984).

Hay, Peter, *Theatrical Anecdotes* (New York 1987)

Hayley, Barbara & Christopher Murray, *Ireland and France — A Bountiful Friendship* (Gerrards Cross 1992).

Henchy, Patrick, *The National Library of Ireland 1941–1976* (Dublin 1986).

Hickey, D.J. & J.E. Doherty, *A Dictionary of Irish History Since 1800* (Dublin 1980).

Hickey, Des & Gus Smith, *A Paler Shade of Green* (London 1972).

——*Seven Days to Disaster* (London 1981).

Hogan, Robert (ed.), *Towards a National Theatre* (Dublin 1970).

Hogan, Robert & Michael J. O'Neill (eds), *Joseph Holloway's Irish Theatre*, vol. 2 (California 1969).

——(eds), *Joseph Holloway's Irish Theatre*, vol. 3 (California 1970).

Howarth, Herbert, *The Irish Writers* (London 1958).

Hudson, Jack, *James Young* (Belfast 1975).

Hunt, Hugh, *The Abbey* (Dublin 1979).

——*Sean O'Casey* (Dublin 1980).

Hyde, Mary (ed.), *Bernard Shaw & Alfred Douglas, A Correspondence* (Oxford 1982).

Johnston, Denis, *In Search of Swift* (Dublin 1959).

——*Orders and Desecrations* (Dublin 1992).

Joyce, Stanislaus, *My Brother's Keeper* (London 1958).

Kavanagh, Peter, *The Irish Theatre* (Tralee 1946).

Kavanagh, Peter, *Patrick Kavanagh — Sacred Keeper* (Curragh 1979).

Keane, John B., *Self Portrait* (Dublin & Cork, 1964).

Kelly, Michael, *Reminiscences of Michael Kelly* (London 1826).

Kenny, Herbert A., *Literary Dublin* (Dublin 1974).

Kiely, Benedict, *A Letter to Peachtree* (London 1988).

Kilroy, Thomas, *Sean O'Casey, A Collection of Critical Essays* (New Jersey 1975).

Kohfeldt, Mary Lou, *Lady Gregory — The Woman Behind the Irish Renaissance* (London 1985).

La Tourette, Stockwell, *Dublin Theatres and Theatre Customs* (New York & London, 1968).

Laurence, Dan H. & Nicholas Grene (eds), *Shaw, Lady Gregory and the Abbey* (Gerrards Cross 1993).

Leonard, Hugh, *Da/A Life/Time Was* (London 1981)..

Lyons, J.B., *Oliver St John Gogarty — The Man of Many Tales* (Dublin 1980).

Mc Cann, Sean (ed.), *The World of Brendan Behan* (New York 1966).

Mc Cann, Sean, *Just Wit* (Dublin 1968).

McCarthy, Muriel, *All Graduates and Gentlemen* (Dublin 1980).

McDermott, Hubert (ed.), *Virtue Rewarded* (Gerrards Cross 1992).

MacGill, Patrick, *Children of the Dead End* (Kerry 1982).

——*The Great Push* (Kerry 1984).

MacLiammóir, Micheál, *All for Hecuba* (Dublin 1947).

——*Theatre in Ireland* (Dublin 1950).

——*Enter a Goldfish* (London 1977).

MacLysaght, Edward, *Changing Times* (Gerrards Cross 1978).

MacMahon, Bryan, *Here's Ireland* (Dublin 1971).

——*The Master* (Dublin 1992).

MacManus, Francis (ed.), *Adventures of an Irish Bookman, A Selection from the Writings of M.J. MacManus* (Dublin 1952).

MacManus, M.J., *A Jackdaw in Dublin* (Dublin & Cork, undated).

Mahon, Sean, *Great Irish Writing* (Dublin 1978).

Martin, Augustine, *W.B. Yeats* (Dublin 1983).

Matheson, Steve, *Maurice Walsh, Storyteller* (Dingle 1985).

Matthews, James, *Voices, A Life of Frank O'Connor* (Dublin 1983).

Mikhail, E.H. (ed.), *Lady Gregory — Interviews & Recollections* (London 1977).

——(ed.), *The Art of Brendan Behan* (London 1979).

Minney, R.J., *The Bogus Image of Bernard Shaw* (London 1969).

Molloy, J. Fitzgerald, *The Romance of the Irish Stage* (London 1897).

Moore, Des, *Off Beat Ireland* (Dublin, undated).

Moore, F. Frankfort, *The Life of Oliver Goldsmith* (London 1910).

Moore, Thomas, *Memoirs of the Life of the Right Honourable Richard Brinsley Sheridan* (London 1825).

Muir, Frank, *The Frank Muir Book* (London 1978).

Murphy, D.J. (ed.), *Lady Gregory's Journals, Books 1–29* (Gerrards Cross 1978).

Nicholls, Mark, *The Importance of Being Oscar* (London 1981).

Nightingale, Benedict, *50 Modern British Plays* (London 1982).

Norris, David, *Joyce's Dublin* (Dublin 1982).

O'Brien, Kate, *Presentation Parlour* (London 1963).

O'Casey, Eileen (ed. J.C. Trewin), *Sean* (Dublin 1971).

O'Casey, Sean, *Drums Under the Windows* (Suffolk 1945).

Ó Conluain, Proinsias (ed.), *Islands and Authors* (Dublin & Cork 1983).

O'Connor, Frank, *My Father's Son* (Dublin 1968).

——*Leinster, Connaught, Munster* (London, undated).

O'Connor, Garry, *Ralph Richardson* (London 1982).

O'Connor, Ulick, *Brendan Behan* (London 1972).

——*Celtic Dawn* (London 1974).

——*Oliver St John Gogarty* (London 1981).

O'Donovan, John, *G.B. Shaw* (Dublin 1983).

O'Dowda, Brendan, *The World of Percy French* (Belfast 1982).

O'Dulaing, Donncha, *Voices of Ireland* (Dublin 1984).

O'Faolain, Sean, *An Irish Journey* (Herts. 1941).

O'Farrell, Padraic, *The Mercier Book of Irish Records* (Dublin & Cork 1978).

——*Shannon, Through Her Literature* (Dublin & Cork 1983).

——*The Ernie O'Malley Story* (Dublin & Cork 1983).

——*The Burning of Brinsley MacNamara* (Dublin 1990).

Ó hAodha, Micheál, *Theatre in Ireland* (Oxford 1974).

——*Pictures at the Abbey* (Mountrath 1983).

——*The Importance of Being Micheál* (Dingle 1990).

——(ed.), *The O'Casey Enigma* (Dublin & Cork, 1980).

O'Keefe, Timothy (ed.), *Myles; Portraits of Brian O'Nolan* (London 1973).

O'Neill, Michael J., *Lennox Robinson* (New York 1964).

O Nolan, Kevin (ed.), *The Best of Myles — A Selection from 'Cruiskeen Lawn', Myles na Gopaleen (Flann O'Brien)* (London 1968).

Oram, Hugh, *The Newspaper Book* (Dublin 1983).

——*Bewley's* (Dublin, undated).

Pearson, Hesketh, *Bernard Shaw* (London 1942).

——*The Life of Oscar Wilde* (London 1946).

Peters, Margot, *Mrs Pat* (London 1984).

Pile, Stephen, *The Book of Heroic Failures* (London 1979).

Pilkington, Laetitia, *Memoirs* (Dublin 1748).

Pine, Richard, *Oscar Wilde* (Dublin 1983).

Pinter, Harold, *Mac* (Ipswich 1968).

Robinson, Lennox, *The Irish Theatre* (London 1939).

——*Lady Gregory's Journals 1919–1930* (London 1946).

Rodgers, W.R. (ed.), *Irish Literary Portraits* (London 1972).

Rogers, Samuel, *Reminiscences and Table Talk of Samuel Rogers* (collected by G.H. Powell) (London 1903).

Rossi, Alfred (ed.), *Astonish Us in the Morning* (London 1977).

Shakespeare, William, *Complete Works* (London 1951).

Shea, Patrick, *Voices and the Sound of Drums* (Belfast 1921).

Simpson, Alan, *Beckett, Behan and a Theatre in Dublin* (London 1962).

Sinden, Donald (ed.), *Theatrical Anecdotes* (London 1987).

Smith, Gus, *Festival Glory in Athlone* (Dublin 1977).

Smith, Gus & Des Hickey (eds), *John B. The Real Keane* (Dublin & Cork 1992).

Smythe, Colin, *A Guide to Coole Park* (Gerrards Cross 1983).

Snell, Gordon, *The Book of Theatre Quotes* (London 1982).

Stanford, W.B. & R.B. McDowell, *Mahaffy, A Biography of an Anglo-Irishman* (London 1971).

Stokes, Dr W., *Life and Labours of George Petrie* (London 1968).

Strong, L.A.G., *Green Memory* (London 1961).

Sutherland, James (ed.), *The Oxford Book of Literary Anecdotes* (London 1975).

Swift, Jonathan, *Volume II of the Author's Works* (ed. George Faulkner) (Dublin 1763).

Tucker, Bernard, *Jonathan Swift* (Dublin 1983).

Tully, Jasper, *Proudly the Note* (Tralee 1945).

Ward, Margaret, *Unmanageable Revolutionaries* (Dingle 1983).

Watters, Eugene & Matthew Murtagh, *Infinite Variety* (Dublin 1975).

Yeats, W.B., *Representative Irish Tales* (Gerrards Cross 1979).

Yeats, W.B. (ed.), *The Celtic Twilight* (Gerrards Cross 1983).

★ ★ ★ ★ ★